Assessment and Placement of Minority Students

Assessment and Placement of Minority Students

Ronald J. Samuda
Queen's University

Shiu L. Kong
University of Toronto

Jim Cummins
Ontario Institute for Studies in Education

Juan Pascual-Leone
York University

John Lewis
McGill University

C.J. Hogrefe

Toronto • Lewiston, NY • Göttingen • Zurich

Intercultural Social Sciences Publications
Kingston/Toronto

Library of Congress Cataloguing-in-Publication Data

Assessment and placement of minority students
Ronald J. Samuda... [et al.].
p.   cm.
Bibliography: p.
Includes indexes.
ISBN 0-88937-024-9
1. Minorities--Education. 2. Students-- Rating of.   I. Samuda,
Ronald J.
LC3715.A85 1989
371.97--dc19

87-28871
CIP

Canadian Cataloguing in Publication Data

Main entry under title:
Assessment and placement of minority students

Bibliography: p.
Includes index.
ISBN 0-88937-024-9 (C.J. Hogrefe). - ISBN 0-921113-01-3
(Intercultural Social Sciences Publications)

1. Minorities - Education. 2. Students - Rating of.
3. Educational tests and measurements. I. Samuda,
Ronald J.

LC3719.A77 1989   371.97   C87-095210-2

Copyright © 1991 by C.J. Hogrefe and ISSP—2nd Printing

12 Bruce Park Ave.
Toronto, Ontario M4P 2S3

P.O. Box 51
Lewiston, NY 14092

Printed in Canada

ISBN 0-88937-024-9
ISBN 0-921113-01-3

Dedicated to Reuven Feuerstein

PREFACE

There was a time, back in the late fifties, while Shiu Kong and I were doing graduate work at the University of Ottawa, when we teachers and social scientists took for granted the immutability of the IQ. Indeed, the concept of the hereditary nature of human intelligence was taught in the faculties of education and psychology as if it had been ordained by some divine source. As educators, we were required to study the precepts of such eminent writers as Lewis Terman, Arthur Otis, David Wechsler, Raymond Cattell, and Charles Spearman. We dared not question the truth of the reality propounded by such illustrious scholars whose works were shrouded in the scientific façade of statistical jargon.

In the fifties, we took for granted, also, the cultural orientation of the WASP mainstream. The school was, in fact, a reflection of the middle class societal norms and teachers were frequently the purveyors of information couched in terms of a collective mindset that almost totally disregarded any kind of minority sociocultural perspective. Academic success depended largely on the individual student's capacity to process information and to function within the limits of the standard curricular programs offered in the elementary and secondary schools. Although many educators and social scientists harboured some doubts about the rightness of the status quo, they continued to function along those same ethnocentric lines that they had learned throughout their professional training.

My most significant change resulted from an incident that occurred in 1958 in the city of Ottawa. It was in that year that my own nephew was sent from Kingston, Jamaica, to live with my family in Ottawa. Since he had had a rather sporadic history of school attendance in Jamaica, Karl's academic level was definitely below par. He had spent almost two years running around with children in the ghettoes of Kinston learning the skills of the streetwise but very little about reading and arithmetic. Upon his arrival in the city of Ottawa, it was no surprise to us that Karl had to struggle through grade nine at Lisgar Collegiate Institute. It would have been a miracle if it had been otherwise. It was no surprise to us that he received low scores on almost all academic subjects while excelling in trade-related training. What did surprise and anger us was the letter we received from one school administrator stating that, on the basis of tests of mental aptitude, he was recommending that the student should be placed in a terminal occupational program ending in grade ten and leading to very limited carreer opportunities with little hope of educational or vocational advancement.

I happened to be employed at that time as a teacher/counsellor at the Technical High School and, knowing the consequences of such a placement decision, I strongly objected to it. As a result, Karl proceeded to struggle through the middle grades in high school and eventually to graduate and enter the University of Ottawa where he subsequently completed a Bachelor of Commerce degree. He then returned home to Jamaica where he established his own business before entering politics. He later became a member of parliament and presently serves as a minister of state in the government. Ironically, Karl's success as a politician is probably due, in large part, to his experiences as a teenager when he learned at first hand the realities of life on the other side of the tracks in the poorer sections of Kingston, Jamaica.

That story contains the key elements involved in the issues and problems associated with the assessment and placement of minority students. It points out the inadequate training of teachers and counsellors in the system, the paucity of curricular programs geared for dealing with the individual needs of culturally different students, and the lack of validity in measuring potential by means of standardized norm-referenced tests geared to a WASP majority perspective. But, more importantly, it demonstrates the harmful consequences that can result from the interpretation of test scores to label, place, and program students who come from culturally different backgrounds.

The second incident to spur my own interest in the assessment and placement of minorities occurred while I was teaching at Stanford University in 1969 and 1970. By a fluke of circumstances, I became associated with the Bay Area Association of Black Psychologists who had decided to confront the state's educational establishment and the existing testing procedures (particularly the issues of minority assessment and its consequences) through strategies of litigation. As an associate professor at San Francisco State University, I became involved in the issues at the very eye of the storm and got to know well such anti-testing protagonists as Reginald Jones, Robert Williams, Asa Hilliard and Harold Dent who were largely responsible for initiating the now famous case of Larry P. versus Wilson Riles. Long years of court trial and expert testimony resulted from the retesting of six black children who had been placed in classes for the mentally retarded mainly on the basis of Stanford Binet IQ scores. However, when retested by qualified psychologists, it was shown that all of the six children were functioning within the normal range and that the test results had been used to label and place them wrongly in a program of minimal educational opportunity. In short, they had been systematically robbed of their civil rights.

Throughout the years I spent at the Educational Testing Service at Princeton as director of the Institute for the Assessment of Minorities, then as professional associate to the President, Bill Turnbull, I continued to confer with and learn from my black American colleagues. Later, at Columbia University in 1972, I became even more centrally involved as secretary of the first National Conference on the Assessment of Minorities in Education and Employment at Hampton Institute, Virginia. The testing debate led to heated press reportage and court battles, with significant political consequences in the years that followed. My first book on the subject, *Psychological Testing of American Minorities*, was published by Harper & Row just before I left Columbia in 1975 to take up an appointment as professor and chairman of the counsellor education program at Queen's University at Kingston, Ontario.

Upon my return to Canada, I found the difficulties of assessing and placing minority students no less trying. Cities like Toronto, Vancouver, Miami and San Francisco share the same dilemma. Indeed, expanded immigration throughout the industrial countries of the world (excepting Japan) has created similar adjustment problems in Sydney and Melbourne, Australia, as well as in such unlikely cities as Cologne, Stockholm, Birmingham and London. The conditions of the 'eighties have intensified the need to find solutions to these pressing problems, especially if we aim at any reasonable degree of social justice and educational equity.

In the major cities of Canada and the United States, several attempts are being made to right the balance and there is welcome evidence of the increasing recognition of the need to change the attitudes of teachers and to provide resources for pre-service and in-service professional development. These endeavours could lead to the establishment of a fairer system. We know now that the old truisms no longer hold; new methods are being tried; but the importance of the re-education of teachers is not yet universally recognized.

About the beginning of 1986, I persuaded Professor Shiu Kong (my old Ottawa University classmate from 30 years ago), to join me in a project to write on the assessment of minorities and to address teacher education needs. While still partly through the early first draft stages, one fortuitous event occurred which helped to bolster our efforts enormously: on March 21, 1986, the Ontario Minister of Education Sean Conway sponsored a conference on Race and Ethnocultural Relations in Toronto. As part of the provincial government's policy, Premier Peterson pledged to develop a race relations manifesto for Ontario school boards. The central topic of that policy relates to the assessment and streaming of minorities.

The response of Premier Peterson's government is significant in that, for the first time in Canada, a concerted effort is being made to revamp the system so as to arrive at some reasonable degree of educational equity. No doubt the efforts of the government have been spurred by the growing number of parents and educators who have questioned the over-representation of minority students in vocational or basic level programs. The essential concern focuses on "the use of inappropriate testing materials, assessment practices, placement strategies and restrictive learning opportunities in some jurisdictions" (Consultative Committee on Assessment and Program Placement of Minority Students for Educational Equity, 1987).

As part of the design for changing the system and developing more appropriate principles and strategies, a consultative committee was appointed in November 1986 consisting of representatives from school boards, universities, various agencies, and the program officers of the Ministry of Education. That committee held a series of meetings between November, 1986, and May, 1987. The first task was to identify the current literature and to view the topics of assessment and placement from a variety of perspectives. To a large extent, this book represents an amalgam and elaboration of the presentations made by Professors Juan Pascual-Leone, Jim Cummins, and myself. Each of us approached the topics from our own particular perspective and expertise, enhanced by the interaction with fellow members of the consultative committee.

The fact is that no one person holds the truth when it comes to the streaming and assessment of minority students. Change can occur most effectively from the combined efforts of several scholars in the field, enhanced by the experience of program officers at the provincial or state levels, school board administrators, counsellors, teacher practitioners, and representatives of community agencies. We have been blessed by having all these elements. What we have endeavoured to accomplish is a balanced overview of the issues and problems associated with the appraisal of ethnic, cultural and linguistic minorities in a culturally diverse society. We have dealt with the issues of group and individual differences as well as the consequences of institutionalized racism still dominant in the system of assessment and curriculum programs. We have used our research to pinpoint the need for change in teacher education and in the application of psychometrics. And, finally, we have indicated the advances being made to introduce innovative approaches to assessment leading to more equitable methods of dealing with the educational needs of minority students. In short, this book is intended to lay out the basics, and to update readers on what is new in the area of minority assessment.

We feel that we have provided a much needed resource for teacher education, especially as it pertains to specific teacher re-training (at the pre-service and inservice levels) in the assessment and placement of minority students. But the book should also be most valuable for all scholars of social science and particularly for school psychologists, counsellors and social workers who must almost inevitably contend with the assessment and placement issues in the course of their normal professional activities.

We are delighted to be working cooperatively with the publishing firm of C.J. Hogrefe whose experience and contacts in Canada, the United States, Europe, and Australia will vastly facilitate the distribution of a book that has emanated from the pooled efforts of five authors, each of whom has brought a new perspective to bear on what has been a universal dilemma. We feel that this volume is timely in helping to underscore the efforts of the Multiculturalism Directorate of the Canadian Department of the Secretary of State while at the same time having special relevance for the drive of the Ontario government to cope more fairly with ethnic minority students. But we hope the book will have broader appeal in all provinces as well as in the various educational jurisdictions in the United States and indeed in all countries where there exists the dilemma of assessing and placing minority students in educational programs that will more appropriately match their needs.

We wish specifically to acknowledge the encouragement (especially of program officer Marjorie Ward) and financial support of the Multiculturalism Directorate of the Canadian Federal Department of the Secretary of State. The subsidy from that source was vital in helping to pay for expenditures associated with manuscript production, printing and administration.

ABOUT THE AUTHORS

Ronald J. Samuda was born in Jamaica and educated in England and Canada. His graduate studies comprised a Ph.D. (Ottawa University) and postdoctoral fellowship from Stanford University in Counselling Psychology. His teaching career includes appointments at Stanford University, San Francisco State University, Richmond College of the City University of New York; ETS, Princeton; Teachers' College, Columbia University, and Queen's University where he was appointed professor and chairman of the counsellor education program in 1975. He has produced seven books and numerous chapters and articles in the area of intercultural counselling and assessment. He is presently Professor Emeritus of Queens' University, a fellow of the Canadian Psychological Association, and North American delegate for the International Association of Cross-Cultural Psychology.

Shiu L. Kong was born in Hong Kong, where he completed his B.A. before emigrating to Canada in 1958. He graduated with a Ph.D. from the School of Psychology and Education of Ottawa University in 1961. He is a member of the Order of Canada, Doctor of Laws (honoris causa) from Kyung Hee University, Seoul, a fellow of the Institute of International Peace, and a holder of the Ontario Bicentennial Medal. He is presently Professor of Educational Psychology at the University of Toronto and President of the Ontario Advisory Council on Multiculturalism and Citizenship. He has written and lectured extensively on international education and is regarded as one of the foremost authorities in the areas of comparative education and the application of psychology in solving problems of education in the context of a multicultural society.

Juan Pascual-Leone was born in Spain, where he took his B.A. and M.D. at Valencia followed by studies leading to the degrees of M.A. and Ph.D. in psychology at the University of Geneva. He subsequently emigrated to Canada where he presently holds the position of full professor in the department of psychology at York University. His principal contribution to the field of assessment has been in initiating the neo-Piagetian movement in developmental psychology. His logical methods of task analysis and constructive epistomology have demonstrated the redundancy of traditional standardized IQ tests that measure the middle class socialization of the child's mind in contrast to capacity testing, which measures content-free general purpose brain resources that grow in power up to adolescence.

Jim Cummins was born in Ireland, where he took his B.A. with first class honours at the National University of Ireland before becoming a research associate at St. Patrick's College in Dublin. In 1974, he undertook graduate studies at the University of Alberta where he received his Ph.D. In 1976, he was appointed research associate at the Centre for the Study of Mental Retardation at the University of Alberta. In 1978, he moved to the Ontario Institute for Studies in Education, and in 1983 was promoted to the rank of associate professor with the Modern Languages Centre in the Department of Curriculum. In 1984 he became the director of the National Heritage Language Resource Unit in the Modern Languages Centre. He has published extensively in the area of bilingualism, assessment, and heritage language theory, research and practice.

John Lewis was born in England and emigrated to Canada as a child. He attended high school in the Guelph area and graduated as a student of classics before attending Queen's University where he completed an honours degree in psychology. He then undertook his master of education in counselling at Queen's while teaching in the Corrections Service of Canada. He subsequently completed the course requirements for his doctoral degree in counselling and guidance at Syracuse University's school of education. In 1986, he was appointed assistant professor in the counselling program at Brandon University. He presently holds the position of Assistant Professor in Educational Psychology and Counselling with McGill University's School of Graduate Studies and Research in Education. He has written several papers and chapters in the area of intercultural counselling.

Table of Contents

125914

Chapter 1

INTRODUCTION

The standard procedures for student assessment and placement used in North American schools can create injustice for minority students, resulting in racist treatment and personal damage. It is important that teachers, guidance counsellors and administrators examine the sources of bias, avoid any misuse of tests and placement procedures, and explore methods for better accommodating the special needs of individuals.

Traditionally, our schools are geared to the standards, norms, and values of a white Anglo-Saxon perspective. Today, even though North American society has become racially and culturally pluralistic, the same standards are used to assess and educate new generations. Imbedded in the system is a structural bias that cuts across the curriculum, goals, measures of achievement, teaching methods, teacher education and selection, standards of acceptable behaviour, and even the idea of what constitutes a worthwhile and successful human being.

Within a homogenous educational and social system, standardized tests do indeed discriminate between students who are gifted, students who are average, and students who are below average. They predict reasonably well the level of achievement and the rate of learning. Scores obtained on tests of intellectual potential do correlate well with grades in regular school subjects. However, for an individual from a radically different cultural or social background, particularly one with a different linguistic and perceptual orientation, being judged according to the standards and expectations of our public school system can be detrimental and inhibitive. The use of standardized tests can become discriminatory when results are viewed uncritically and are used to assess and place children from varied backgrounds into a school system originally designed for a fairly homogeneous group. Particularly for those students whose backgrounds provide little preparation for the school curriculum and standards of conduct, taking tests loaded with academic content may not reveal true ability or intelligence. Insisting on the continued use of conventional testing methods will only perpetuate this structural bias.

One could argue that since ours is a society in which people are continually being rated for their achievements, children might as well get used to being tested while still in school. Using this logic, if tests are seen as unavoidable and inevitable, the guidance teacher does indeed have the responsibility of selecting and administering standardized tests for student assessment. If the teacher has no basis for disputing the correlation between IQ test scores and academic grades, he or she can then feel justified in placing students on the basis of these scores. Many teachers find this particular practice inadequate, even inappropriate; but they continue to do the same thing year after year on the assumption that test results can be relied upon, at least to some extent. They draw comfort from the belief that as long as they are adhering to the technical requirements of the test, nothing can go wrong. We may call this kind of attitude and practice a *technical bias*.

Since the time of Galton, mental abilities such as intelligence have been regarded as innate and stable. Standardized tests of mental ability have shown that, as a group, people from higher socioeconomic classes have higher scores than people from lower classes. One explanation for this phenomenon has been in terms of genetic differences. This explanation has also been put forth regarding the difference in test scores between whites and some other races. One of the pioneers of IQ tests himself, Lewis Terman, suggested that differences in IQ were related to racial differences and as such were permanent in nature. He explained his observations of the test performances of a Mexican-American child and an Indian child in this way:

> Their dullness seems to be racial or at least inherent in the family stocks from which they come. There will be enormous significant racial differences which cannot be wiped out by any scheme of mental culture. Children of this group should be segregated in special classes...There is no possibility at present of convincing society that they should not be allowed to reproduce (quoted in Kamin, 1976, p. 318).

In contrast, environmentalists contend that it is not the genes but the family and culture of minority children that fail them; that a host of factors that are not conducive to the attitudes, skills and knowledge essential for school performance conspire against their success. Such factors cover nutritional, environmental, psychological, sociocultural and linguistic areas. Though by no means exhaustive, this list supports the view that the difference in test scores between mainstream and non-mainstream students is the result of cultural deprivation. The primary objective of educators who subscribe to this view, therefore, is to identify, arrest, repair, and prevent the effects of such deprivation.

Whereas the two preceding positions attemps to explain differences in test scores in terms of heredity and environment, respectively, a third approach is that non-mainstream students should be viewed not as genetically or culturally *deficient* but simply as culturally *different*. These theorists suggest that models of deficiency are based primarily on middle-class notions of what constitutes 'right' and 'good', and, consequently, minority behaviour is seen largely from a negative or pathological perspective (Mercer, 1971). Equality has been confused with sameness, with the all too often result that a minority individual is viewed as a 'sick white' person (Baratz and Baratz, 1970).

Implications

Concerned counsellors, teachers, and administrators need to become aware of the fact that many factors can invalidate the scores obtained by non-mainstream students on standardized tests of ability and achievement. For such students, these tests may not represent true measures of intellectual potential or ability. When used without proper sensitivity and discrimination, they can become the means by which non-mainstream children are placed in special classes for slow learners or the mentally retarded, with the likelihood of suffering stigmatizing effects. Unwittingly, a school could become the means of a self-fulfilling prophecy, where the intellectual inferiority of minorities is 'scientifically demonstrated'.

Teachers who care about their students would be appalled and deeply disturbed if it were suggested that they were administering a racist policy. However, even the best standardardized tests are not impartial. The Stanford-Binet and the WISC, for example, originally did not include non-white children in their standardized samples. Although more recent group tests such as the Otis-Lennon and the Lorge-Thorndike were standardized on much larger and more representative samples of the school population, their producers have tended to ignore the heavy concentration and over-representation of minorities in the lower socioeconomic levels.

Recent studies reveal that schools in the United States and Canada increasingly are making use of tests normed on samples of ethnic minority students. There is also welcome evidence of the growing use of dynamic testing methods, especially resulting from the pioneering efforts of Professor Reginald Jones of the University of California at Berkeley who has recently published a casebook of non-discriminatory assessment of minority group children. In Canada, the Ontario Ministry of Education is also undertaking an intensive search for better methods of improving race relations, and Premier David Peterson has vowed to make the streaming and placement of minorities a central issue for policy study.

This book addresses some of the important considerations surrounding the use of tests and assessment procedures when applied to students who are culturally, linguistically and/or socioeconomically different from mainstream North Americans. In chapter two, key issues are placed in a global and historical context. Chapter three indicates the urgency for change of the issues and concepts related to assessment and placement, and how these issues and concepts are related to a multicultural vision of North America. Chapter four is an examination of reliability and validity in testing revealing the fallacies and weaknesses inherent in norm-referenced tests used to measure the ability of individuals who differ in significant ways from the mainstream. Chapter five extends this examination further by looking at the age-old debate of nature versus nurture. Without an understanding of these two fundamental concepts, teachers cannot grasp the real significance of the assessment issue. Chapter six is concerned with aspects of individual differences. Chapter seven is mainly concerned with a comparison of policies and programs in the United States and Canada and delineates the ways in which assessment procedures tend to bolster institutionalized racism existing within school systems. Chapter eight reports the findings, implications and consequences of a study on student placement that was conducted in Ontario schools. Chapter nine surveys the alternatives and innovations in test procedures that are presently being explored. The tenth chapter goes further in exploring the concept of capacity testing as opposed to knowledge-based assessment, and provides examples of mental capacity tests as culturally fair alternatives to the traditional knowledge-based IQ tests. The essential goal of the book is to critically review the issues of assessing and placing minority students; to introduce to educators better procedures to minimize bias; to present more valid and reliable ways of training teachers to deal sensitively with minorities; and to develop suitable assessment techniques and curriculum so that *all* students will benefit.

Chapter 2

Multiculturalism:
Perspectives and Challenges

Ronald J. Samuda

Multiculturalism, as a demographic phenomenon, has existed since the beginning of written history. In the ancient empires of Persia, India, China, Rome, Greece and Turkey, people of different races, languages, ethnicities, and cultures could be found co-existing with the more dominant social group. Alexander the Great recognized the importance of respecting the customs, language and way of life of the nations he conquered. Napoleon's initial successes were partially due to his recognition of the ethnic and linguistic differences of the alien peoples he co-opted as soldiers in his army. In more recent times, the colonial administrators of the British Empire succeeded largely because, despite strong feelings of nationalism, they accepted the differences of their colonial subjects and sought to govern within the peculiarities of the local ethos.

What, then, is new about the concept of multiculturalism in the present day? What events have led to its recognition as an aspect of society and as a government policy in several countries around the world? How does North American multiculturalism compare with that of other countries? What are the implications of multiculturalism for education?

Some Comparative Immigration Trends

Perhaps the most potent factor in the emergence of modern multiculturalism has been the sudden surge in migration that occurred shortly after the Second World War. The devastation of the war had created an unprecedented demand for workers to fill the factories of the developed countries, and many European nations began competing with one another for foreign workers to fulfil goals for industrial expansion. In the prosperous years of the late 1950s and early 1960s, the competition in Europe for outside workers intensified even more. A similar economic drive was occurring in the United States, Canada, and Australia, which were trying to enhance their own industrial development through expanded immigration policies.

Britain and France permitted settled migration of nationals from colonies and ex-colonial territories. However, the major model that developed in European countries such as West Germany was the 'guest worker' program. Foreigners from countries such as Turkey were allowed to live in Germany as long as they worked, but were not allowed to become citizens. In 1983, nearly five million aliens representing 7.6 percent of the population were found to be residing in West Germany (Minsel and Herff, 1985). In contrast, the U.S., Canada, and Australia opened up their immigration policies so that people from many different countries could apply for citizenship status. Whereas immigration was once restricted to white, mostly European peoples, since 1965 people from virtually every country have been allowed to enter, resulting in increasingly diverse populations in all three countries. Britain's recent immigration policy has been similar.

Before 1965, immigration to the United States was based on preferential policies for western Europeans. Such policies were supported by questionable theories of psychological superiority and eugenics advanced by such theorists as Carl Brigham, Henry Goddard, and Robert Yerkes. It was genetic interpretations of the results of U.S. Army Alpha and Beta tests, administered to two million soldiers during World War I, that provided the United States government with 'scientific' evidence to deny entry to people who differed markedly from northwestern Europeans (Kamin, 1976). As late as 1952, the preferential quota concept was supported by the McCarran-Walter Act, which enforced quotas on the basis of 'assimilability' and gave preferential treatment to immigrants from countries with historical and cultural ties to the United States (Keeley and Elwell, 1981).

Beginning in 1965, policies in the United States moved progressively towards a more generous and regulated approach. For example, in 1969, 383,000 immigrants were allowed in, and the number increased yearly until in 1978 it reached 600,000 and included refugees from Cuba, Haiti, Indo-China and the Soviet Union (Kritz, 1981). It may be that such a massive and rapid influx of ethnically and culturally different citizens will stimulate American leaders to rethink the concept of the 'melting pot' and begin making moves towards a philosophy of multiculturalism.

Like the United States, Canada and Australia historically have depended on immigration for their economic and industrial development. Despite obvious differences in the development of these two Commonwealth countries, there are also some remarkable similarities: both traditionally have given preferential treatment to immigrants from the British Isles; and before 1960 both had restrictive immigration policies that in effect barred the entry of non-Europeans. The result of such policies was that up until the end of the Second World War their populations consisted mostly of people of Anglo-Saxon origin. Of the rest, most immigrants came from northwestern Europe and tended to become so well assimilated that in time their only distinguishing features were their names. In Canada these are called Euro-Canadians, and they have tended to become English-speaking and non-distinguishable from mainstream society.

In recent times Canada and Australia have made dramatic changes in their immigration laws which, beginning in the 1960s, have led to massive increases and diversification of their populations. In contrast to its earlier preferential British policy, Australia permitted the entry of two million 'migrants' after the war, 60 percent of whom were non-British. By 1966 there was a considerable influx of Italians, Greeks, and other southern Europeans; and by 1970, assisted passages were extended to Turks, Arabs, and other peoples of the Middle East (Fabinyi, 1971). By 1971, the combined proportion of foreign-born and native-born inhabitants of foreign parentage in Australia was about 40 percent, exceeding the comparable Canadian figure of 33 percent (Zubrzycki, 1981).

Australia has done a creditable job in coping with immigrants of non-British origin, and its many programs and policies designed to assist their socialization have been well documented (Taft and Cahill, 1981). For instance, integrative services have progressively been enlarged to include special teacher-training programs and classes for migrant students in both elementary and secondary schools (Bhatnagar, 1984). Australian society has been enriched by the presence of different ethnic groups, and while there are still vestiges of British elitism, attitudes towards migrants have become more tolerant and accepting (Taft, 1977).

Canadian immigration policies in the past were not free from the influence of racist attitudes. In promulgating an early twentieth-century 'progressive' policy, Clifford Sifton referred to biological factors as a major criterion for the admission or rejection of certain ethnic groups. In addition, the government claimed 'climatic unsuitability' of the harsh Canadian winter as a reason for refusing peoples of the southern climates, especially blacks (Hughes and Kallen, 1974). In a similiar vein, the prairie provinces were seen as geographically and climatically appropriate for the introduction of people from the Ukraine. In the words of Sifton, the Ukrainian immigrant was a "stalwart peasant, born on the soil, whose forefathers have been farmers for ten generations, with a stout wife and a half a dozen children, [and] is a very desirable settler" (Lysenko, 1947). The result was that between 1897 and 1914, 200,000 Ukrainians settled in Manitoba, Saskatchewan and Alberta. In fact, by 1914 Manitoba contained 43 percent of the Ukrainian population in Canada. The result of this heavy settlement has been the creation of a powerful and vocal group of Ukrainian descendants in the prairie provinces, especially Manitoba. This group has demanded economic and political parity, as well as the right to have their children educated in bilingual programs and in courses in Ukrainian culture.

Canadian Multiculturalism

Canada's multicultural society is unique. Unlike the United States or Australia, this country has not one but two mainstream charter groups, each with its own language and distinct religious, ethnic and cultural characteristics. For that matter, it can be claimed that the Canadian population has always been ethnically and linguistically heterogenous (Berry, Kalin and Taylor, 1977). When the French arrived in Canada in the sixteenth and seventeenth centuries, they found 300,000 native Canadians comprising more than 50 societies and at least a dozen different linguistic groups. Among the French themselves, there were the Acadians who occupied the Atlantic region and the Quebecois in lower Canada, each group with its own distinct dialect and customs. Later, as a result of French-Indian intermarriage, the Métis ethnic group was formed. After the British defeated the French in 1763, English, Irish, Scottish, and Welsh peoples began to arrive. They were soon followed by immigrants from northwestern Europe, especially Germany and Holland. By the mid-twentieth century Canada was a de facto multicultural society.

The movement towards official recognition of multiculturalism as a philosophy and government policy arose from two major factors. The change in immigration policy in the early 1960s was of paramount importance, since it resulted in waves of immigrants from southern Europe, the Middle East, Asia, and the Caribbean. However, it was mainly the French-English conflict that spurred the change. As Professor Jean Burnet states, 'the germs of nationalism had been incubating in Quebec for a long time' (Burnet, 1984). Essentially, French Canadians felt that they were being discriminated against and treated like the 'niggers' of Canada by the anglophone majority. It is probably no accident that the separatist movement in Quebec coincided with the civil rights movement of black Americans in the United States and with Prime Minister John Diefenbaker's call for a Canadian Bill of Rights.

Prime Minister Lester Pearson's response to the threat of Quebec dismemberment was to establish a Royal Commission on Bilingualism and Biculturalism in 1963. The Official Languages Act of 1969 established French as one of the two official languages of Canada and extended special language rights to francophones outside as well as within Quebec. The issue of language was of particular importance to the emergence of multiculturalism. The Commission's deliberations and the concepts of bilingualism and biculturalism prompted the more powerful ethnic minorities - the Ukrainians in particular - to demand that their language and culture also be formally recognized in what had become not a *bi*cultural but a *multicultural* and *multiethnic* society. It was the urging of ethnic minority groups, led by the Ukrainians, that prompted the government to change its policy from 'biculturalism' to 'multiculturalism'. When the federal policy was announced on October 8, 1971, Prime Minister Pierre Trudeau made it clear that "although there are two official languages, there is no official culture; nor does any ethnic group take precedence over any other. A policy of multiculturalism within a bilingual framework commends itself to the government as the suitable means of assuring the cultural freedom of Canadians" (House of Commons, 1971). What cultural freedom meant was that every ethnic group had the right to preserve and develop its own culture, values, and lifestyle within the Canadian context. In 1972, a Minister of State for Multiculturalism was appointed to administer the new policies.

The liberalized Canadian immigration policy of the 1960s resulted in the highest annual immigration rate of the post-war period. By 1977, nearly 300,000 immigrants had arrived from India and Pakistan; more than 100,000 from Jamaica and Trinidad; more than 50,000 from Africa; and unprecedented numbers from Hong Kong, the Philippines, and southern and central Europe (Portugal, Italy, Greece, Yugoslavia, etc.). Despite these developments, the political clout of the so-called 'third force' group of immigrants (non-British and non-French) remains limited. In sheer numbers, Canada's population still comprises 45 percent who originally came from Britain and 29 percent of French origin (Burnet, 1984). There is no doubt that white Anglo-Saxon Canadians and to a lesser degree French Canadians still make up the mainstream of Canadian society.

Given this situation, the viability of multiculturalism as a philosophy and a way of life depends on the continuing efforts of all Canadians, whether they belong to mainstream or minority groups. The challenges are many. They include:

1. The equitable and creative maintenance of ethnic identity and cultural diversity as a means of enriching the Canadian identity.
2. The settling of new Canadians in a manner that will enable them to feel that they belong and will have opportunities to contribute to society.
3. The uplifting of underprivileged minorities who are presently dominated by the more established and prosperous mainstream groups.
4. The dispelling of the lingering belief that only those who belong to the mainstream of society are 'true Canadians'.

Social and Educational Challenges

What does multiculturalism mean in Canada, and how does it affect people's lives? To begin, the concept of multiculturalism represents a radical shift in policy on the part of the Canadian federal government. It has been accepted to date by four provinces: Ontario, Manitoba, Saskatchewan and Alberta, and represents a recognition of the cultural diversity of Canadian society and an equality in status for the various ethnocultural groups. It means that although there are two official *languages*, there is no official *culture*. It represents a sharing of different cultures and a greater choice of lifestyles. It signifies a concern for and protection of the civil and human rights of people of different racial, ethnic and cultural origins, and provides equal access to social and political institutions. It connotes freedom of choice in religion and other cultural traits. Finally, multiculturalism in Canada means the abandonment of the Anglo-based statutes and policies for all, which until recently informed government practice in intercultural relations.

However, even after a decade and a half of policy implementation, there is still a long way to go before Canadians of all races and cultures can enjoy the true spirit of multiculturalism. Many forces and attitudes combined still inhibit the process of transforming the idea into a social goal. The reality of a pluralistic society has not yet gained an appropriate place in the school curriculum at any level of education, and it is still possible for new teachers to graduate without having had any instruction about multiculturalism and its educational implications. Similarly, the tens of thousands of practicing teachers across the country may be given only the occasional sensitization seminar on multicultural issues on 'professional development' days. Although multiculturalism has caught the attention of some government representatives, the general tendency still is to regard it as a policy only for immigrants and 'ethnics'.

'Equality of status' is another policy that exists in theory more than in reality. The powerful sector of English Canadians still assumes dominance everywhere except in Quebec. French Canadians have been loath to regard themselves as an ethnic group and, in their own striving for equality, have aggressively pursued bilingualism at the expense of neglecting or dismissing multiculturalism (Rudnyckyj, 1980). As a result, it is up to the dominating sector, aided by active members in different ethnic communities, to make an effort to be conscious of and uphold the policy of multiculturalism in an ever-diversifying society.

With regard to civil and human rights, historically there have been many instances in which legislatures and courts have not protected the basic rights of non-mainstream individuals in such areas as schooling, property, voting, private business and public service

(Mcleod, 1979). Over the years, the federal government and some provincial governments have established commissions to monitor activities related to human rights. However, infringements with respect to ethnic groups do occur, and the law is often inadequate to deal with them. In the final analysis, the maintenance of human rights depends on an educated and informed public. If the dominant groups persist in giving multiculturalism only token recognition (Breton, Reitz and Valentine, 1980), and its ethnic minorities continue to exhibit certain fixed patterns (Kalbach, 1979), then the policy will remain nothing more than symbolic.

The key to improved socioeconomic status and social mobility for ethnic groups is education. A 'vertical mosaic' (Porter, 1965) appears to exist in Canadian society, with Anglo- and Euro-Canadians occupying the top political and economic spheres; Ukrainians, Italians, and other European minorities occupying a middle level; French Canadians occupying somewhere in between; and visible minorities, such as blacks, Asians, and native peoples located at the bottom. Without education, the 'vertical mosaic' will persist. In the present attempt to establish multicultural education in schools, the most serious problems lie in the testing, assessment, placement and counselling of ethnic minority children. There are also problems in the lack of knowledge about culturally different students on the part of teachers, which makes them unable to provide suitable assistance and guidance. Although the use of IQ tests has been abandoned in some Ontario school boards (Samuda and Crawford, 1980), the teacher remains the arbiter in placement decisions. Classroom teachers and counsellors therefore need training in dealing with ethnic minorities and new Canadians. Ethnocentric teacher training methods and insufficient emphasis on appropriate curricula and counselling represent the failure of the educational system to adapt to the changing school population. Because education is placed under provincial jurisdiction, the implementation of a national multicultural policy in schools is exceedingly difficult. The federal structure further complicates matters by placing issues of multiculturalism and immigration in separate ministries.

Visible minorities have recently petitioned the federal government for a fair share in the economic and political sectors of Canadian society. A parliamentary committee has mandated research and structural changes to open up new opportunities, and the school system shares responsibility with the government in molding the social and economic structure to make these opportunities available.

As yet, however, the school is mostly a middle-class institution, guided by mainly Anglo-Saxon values.

In spite of its untidy and uneven state of existence, multiculturalism is an idea that promises to correct the anomalies in Canadian society. It represents the hope that, sooner or later, a social and political system will be developed where unconscious or covert prejudice and narrow attitudes will be replaced by a complete acceptance of cultural and ethnic diversity, and the belief that such differences are interesting variations rather than deviations. It is towards such an ideal that the Multiculturalism Directorate, program officers and consultative committees throughout the provincial systems of government are aspiring. There is still much to be done, but multiculturalism is an idea whose time has come.

Chapter 3

The New Challenge of Student Assessment and Placement

Ronald J. Samuda

The problems of ethnic minority student placement and education have become matters of universal concern in the industrial countries of Europe, North America and Australia where the growth of immigration has made for multiracial societies. In Canada and the United States, especially, the increase in recent immigrants coupled with the policies of multiculturalism and fair citizenship have forced schools to examine the issues of assessment and placement of students with diverse backgrounds and needs. Awareness is increasing that conventional tests and assessment procedures are both inappropriate and inadequate for helping teachers and counsellors understand students who have newly come from alien cultural backgrounds. There is thus an urgent sense that innovative approaches and tools must be found.

The Situation in Great Britain

A brief review of the situation in Great Britain may help to reveal some of the problems of student assessment and placement. It was not so long ago that under the Butler Act of 1944, the three-part school system of Secondary Grammar, Secondary Modern, and Secondary Technical schools was regarded as adequate for satisfying educational needs. The implications of such a system in terms of social class differentiation and conflict was, in the 1950s, not yet an issue. Accordingly, the streaming of children into three different types of education at the end of elementary school was simply regarded as a way of handling differential ability of learning. As a part of the Butler Act, the so-called 'Eleven Plus' testing programs were widely regarded as an effective and appropriate way to sort out students into different educational paths.

Throughout the 1950s and until the comprehensive school system emerged, British teachers would administer and hand-score examinations in English, mathematics, and academic aptitude, and use the composite scores as the basis for recommending students for one of the three types of schools. While both the public and the educators were aware that this system upheld as well as reflected the hierarchical and socioeconomic class divisions that constituted British society, only a few questioned it. In fact, it was taken as a foregone conclusion that children from the slums of Lower Broughton, for example, would never make it into grammar schools. The odd student might get into technical school and become a draftsperson or technician, but the majority ended up in the lower streams of 'secondary modern' institutions. If a student managed to qualify for the grammar school, a later opportunity might present itself to allow him or her into a university, but that happened very rarely. By and large, these assessment strategies, while seemingly objective, were partially responsible for keeping people of various social classes 'in their place'. In doing so, the educational system provided the rationale for perpetuating the social, economic, and occupational strata of British society.

Such assessment strategies were designed and based on the assumptions that an individual's intelligence and learning capability were inborn and fixed, and that an IQ test could precisely measure these qualities. It was also believed that intelligence tests were free from cultural influence. An IQ score, in other words, was thought to be a 'true' measure of a person's intelligence, regardless of his or her cultural and educational background. It was not considered that individuals growing up in socially and educationally impoverished environments may have scored poorly simply because they were unfamiliar with the content and problem-solving approaches on which these tests were based.

It was not until relatively recently that psychologists began to examine the relative structure of IQ tests, and to recognize that the development of learning abilities is related to factors other than in-born ability, such as socioeconomic status, culture, and mother tongue. Studies of the assessment and placement of ethnic minority immigrant children in Britain, such as that by Judith Haynes (1971) and Bernard Coard (1971), reveal how social and economic barriers in British schools were further compounded by the arrival on the scene of non-white immigrants from former British colonies. Indeed, the traditional tests used to assess student capabilities and learning potentials were sadly inadequate to deal with a drastically changed student population with diverse cultural and linguistic orientations.

Despite a persistent anti-test sentiment over the past 20 years and the increasing awareness that when used indiscriminately, standardized tests often create inequities in education, many teachers and psychologists still use them as a means of appraising learning potential, including that of culturally different ethnic minority students. As a group, non-white students do not score as highly on most standardized tests as their white counterparts. Some groups interpret this from a racist point of view, such as Enoch Powell and his supporters (Coard, 1971); others regard it as an indication of the long-standing inequities suffered by Third World immigrants. In any case, the most devastating effect is that minority students in Britain were often permanently placed in special education classes or schools for the mentally retarded because they were unable to obtain the required high scores. Standardized tests have also been used to justify their disproportionate numbers in vocational and technical education programs with minimal intellectual stimulation. In the country that produced one of the pioneers of individual psychology and mental testing, Sir Frances Galton, one might expect that better assessment procedures would be used.

The Situation in North America

In North America we face similar problems in assessing and placing minority students, especially in areas where large numbers of new immigrants have settled. Schools are ill-prepared to cope with the difficulties that confront them. The respective situations of Toronto,

Ontario, and Dade County of Greater Miami, Florida, may serve to reveal the scope of these problems.

Between 1968 and 1978, close to half a million people from South Asia, Africa, and the Caribbean came to settle in Canada. A significantly large percentage of these new arrivals chose to make their homes in Ontario, especially Toronto. The result is that this city faces a unique challenge in educating a fast-growing and changing population. Today, almost half the student population in Toronto schools comes from homes with a cultural and linguistic milieu that is neither English nor French, the two traditional mainstreams of Canadian society. The emergence of such a large multiethnic group coupled with the implementation of an ideology of multiculturalism, has created a sizeable and complex task for the schools to handle.

Similar problems but ones that are even more explosive and complicated by deeply entrenched racial conflicts exist in the United States. Court cases such as that of *Larry P. versus Wilson Riles* in California indicate the seriousness of the problem of inappropriate assessment and placement. This case revealed that black children were being placed in classes for the mentally retarded on the basis of assessment procedures totally unsuited to their ethnocultural backgrounds (Samuda, 1975). One can gain some insight into the issue by looking at the socio-psychological problems that have fallen on Dade County in Florida. Since the Communist takeover of Cuba in the late 1960s, south Florida has been inundated by the arrival of over half a million Cubans. More recently, Greater Miami has had to cope with the sudden influx of over 100,000 people from Mariel Bay, as well as an estimated 40,000 Haitians. The plight of these Creole-speaking Caribbean refugees, as well as the problems of accommodating and supporting them, have been only sporadically reported by the press. The Dade County educational system and neighbouring county boards face the formidable task of educating large numbers of Hispanic and Haitian children, as well as lesser but significant numbers of immigrants from Vietnam, Pakistan and Russia.

Accommodating Ethnic Minority Students in Ontario Schools

What are the major difficulties in accommodating ethnic minority students? The answer is related in several ways to the present orientation of schools and the special needs of newly arrived students. For one thing, the educators who run the schools — mainly middle-class whites — are themselves products of a social and pedagogical structure that reflects the values, attitudes, and expectations of the dominant groups of Canadian society. Second, the education that students receive in these schools reinforces the values, language, and socialization patterns of the majority, and bestow social and cultural advantages on the children who belong to this group. Thus, the schools as they exist now favour a definite type of student and alienate others.

For some fortunate individuals, early influences and environmental conditions provide an almost perfect correlation between home and school, and therefore a relatively easy transition to the social and curricular organization of the latter. Is it any wonder that such students achieve well? However, for those whose environmental circumstances have been different — socially, economically, linguistically, and/or culturally — there is little accommodation. These students are sometimes labelled disadvantaged, deprived, or handicapped, which can lead to negative and damaging effects for the individuals involved. Frequently there is a tacit implication of relative and endemic deficiency in those who fail to exhibit standards of behaviour or academic levels of achievement considered normal, especially in the area of literacy.

In some research (described and elaborated upon more fully in chapter 7) into the testing and placement of minorities in Ontario (Samuda and Crawford, 1980), we found that the term 'special education' had become a catch-all title for a miscellany of programs that cater to students who are intellectually subnormal, physically or psychologically handicapped, or suffering from learning disabilities such as dyslexia. In many school systems, special education represents the administration's attempt to accommodate all students who differ from the norm in one way or another. It is into this broad catch-all category that the ethnic minority student who is unable to keep pace with his or her majority counterpart is placed. This is not to say that there are no minority students who are truly biologically, physiologically, or neurologically impaired. Unfortunately, however, the concept of special education classes has become so stigmatizing that parents fear the negative connotations that inevitably accompany such a placement. The belief that 'different' means 'deficient' is still very prevalent in the placement of minority children in England, Canada, and the United States, although happily it is on the decline.

The need to accommodate ethnic minorities has highlighted the school system's inadequacy in dealing with students who deviate from the accepted cultural norm. Essentially, we are still faced with the task of finding a way to identify an atypical individual's level of academic potential and performance in order to place him or her in a particular niche within the educational system. However, in our efforts to deal with this issue, we need to seek solutions for more than the problems of assessment and placement. We must also recognize that teachers themselves traditionally have been trained in a mode that emphasizes and perpetuates an essentially ethnocentric view of society. Educators, whether they be administrators, counsellors, or teachers, have been trained to fit the student to the system, not the other way around.

In our study of assessment and placement practices in Ontario, teachers often told us they'd treat students all alike, by which they meant that students were given exactly the same treatment, regardless of their ethnicity or individual background. It is sobering to consider that such practices have been universally followed. Yet the fact is that teachers have been trained to value the culture of the majority and to emphasize the norms that they perceive to be 'Canadian'; seldom have they been provided with the training or professional experiences that would encourage, enhance, and optimize a perspective of cultural pluralism. How, then, can they now be expected to cope with a new student population that requires special pedagogical considerations because of tangible factors such as language and customs, and intangible ones such as motivational patterns, communication modes, and ways of coping with the world?

Instead of responding to the new realities of our multicultural society, the Canadian school system and teacher-training institutions persist in perpetuating traditional methods. In our study, we found that 90 percent of the educators situated in areas of high ethnic concentration reported that the assessment of immigrant students who do not possess school documents comparable to Ontario report cards was their main concern. How, for example, does one place a 15-year-old male newly arrived from Pakistan, with no creditable form of school transfer papers, who speaks little or no English, and whose level of academic achievement cannot be measured by any of the existing battery of tests? The problem is not easily solved. To place him in an elementary school would be insulting and unfitting; however, to place him in a class matched to age also presents obvious problems. Sometimes immigrant students arrive with disadvantages such as intermittent schooling, yet suddenly they must adjust to a new country, learn a new language, deal with a sometimes hostile and unwelcoming environment, and try to fit into a pattern where often there are neither models nor peers to identify with.

When we asked the participants of our study to suggest alternative programs and methods that might improve the accuracy and quality of placing immigrant students, the answers were limited in scope. Some felt that school transfer documents should be made mandatory for all new students. Others suggested that transitory reception classes for newcomers be established. A significant proportion (21 percent) of teachers who belonged to boards with a high ethnic minority concentration favoured an assimilation program. By contrast, teachers in more heterogeneous regions tended to favour the creation of 'holding centres' where the new arrival would have to assimilate before he or she could enter the schools. These teachers often indicated a resentment that they and the school system had to cope with immigrant students, and generally held the view that it was the immigrants' responsibility to adopt Canadian ways and become assimilated as quickly as possible in the majority culture. Such views clearly are at odds with the essence and policy of multiculturalism in Canada.

In response to our structured questions, many teachers and administrators recommended the following: 1) more careful screening of immigrants by immigration authorities, 2) mandatory culturalization of children at the preschool level, 3) intensive immersion classes in the English language, 4) more resource staff and teachers, 5) more guidance counsellors, 6) more special education classes, 7) more special education teachers, 8) better-quality testing using local norms and culture-free tests, and 9) testing in the mother tongue. Individuals varied in the number of recommendations they made, as well as in the strength of their opinions on one or more of the issues. Generally speaking, educators who worked with many immigrant students showed more sensitivity to their needs and were less insistent that they bear the responsibility of assimilation.

Let us examine the issues and implications raised by these responses to the problems of testing, counselling, and placing ethnic minority students in Canadian schools. The issues seem mainly to be:

1. the assumptions underlying an understanding of cultural pluralism in teacher-training;

ty.ty.ty.ty.ty.ty.ty.ty.ty.ty.ty.ty.ty.ty.ty.ty.

 Chapters 8 and 9 are specifically geared to summarize the advances presently underway to change the emphasis generally from a dependence on standardized norm-referenced models towards more culturally relevant modes of dynamic assessment. These two chapters focus on the innovations presently proposed to fill the vacuum, and provide an overview of mental capacity testing to take the place of the more static modes of norm-referenced assessment procedures. Since we have so pointedly indicated our critical views of the traditional norm-referenced knowledge based norms, we believe that it is also our duty to suggest new and more appropriate approaches. In presenting these two contrasting models, in chapters 8 and 9, it is our intention to demonstrate examples of more culturally fair alternatives.

Chapter 4

Psychometric Factors in the Appraisal of Intelligence

Ronald J. Samuda

I. Introduction

Almost without exception, articles and textbooks on educational and psychological testing recommend that test buyers and users exercise the utmost judiciousness when selecting and administering tests and when interpreting test scores. Recently, this good advice has been reiterated in connection with the testing of ethnic minority groups. Psychologists and test makers have associated the discontent expressed by educators with the assessment (especially intellectual) of minority individuals with the longtime misuse of standardized tests by teachers, counsellors, admission officers, and other education professionals. What Harold Seashore said two decades ago is, unfortunately, still largely true:

> The biggest problem today is not the tests themselves... It is getting a supply of competent professionals to interpret and make proper use of the tests. For every $500.00 a school spends on the tests themselves, it should spend $15,000.00 on salaries for personnel to supervise and interpret the tests (in Goldman, 1961, p.2).

In the introductory section of the 'Guidelines', Fishman and his associates expressed the same sentiment. They contended that responsible educational authorities should recognize that placing tests in the hands of unskilled personnel is as unwise as allowing cars or other highly technical and powerful tools to be handled without proper training and guidance. They stress a particular necessity for caution when educational and psychological tests are administered to members of minority groups (1964, p. 130).

Reliability and Validity

Undoubtedly, one of the most important aspects of a test is the degree to which it is valid — that is, the extent to which it actually measures what it was intended to measure. Ebel (1961) has called validity "one of the major deities in the pantheon of the psychometrician" (p. 640). Another essential aspect is reliability. Together, validity and reliability determine the usefulness of a test since a test that does not provide consistent measurement has no value. Although "no test can be valid unless it is reliable" (Wesman, 1952), reliability alone does not ensure validity. Gronlund illustrates the nature of the relationship between reliability and validity as follows:

> As with a witness testifying in a courtroom trial — the fact that he consistently tells the same story does not guarantee that he is telling the truth. The truthfulness of his statements can be determined only by comparing them with some other evidence. Similarly, with evaluation results, consistency is an important quality but only if it is accompanied by truthfulness, and truthfulness, or validity, must be determined independently. Little is accomplished if evaluation results consistently provide the wrong information (1971, p. 76).

Reliability has been defined as "the consistency of scores obtained by the same individuals when re-examined with the same test on different occasions, or with different sets of equivalent items, or under other variable examining conditions" (Anastasi, 1958a, p. 71). If, for example, an individual scores 116 points on an intelligence test on one occasion, and 84 points on the same test administered under the same conditions two weeks later, then the reliability of the test is highly suspect. No test, of course, can be perfectly reliable, for psychological measurements, like physical measurements, are affected by a number of sources of variance or error. These sources of error have been identified as trait instability, sampling error, administrator error, scoring error, health, motivation, degree of fatigue and luck in guessing (Mehrens and Lehmann, 1969, p. 33). Thus, the reliability of a test must be indicated so that users are aware of the degree to which it will be accurate. A measure of reliability is expressed in the form of a coefficient ranging from 0 to 1.0, with the most typical values falling somewhere between 0.85 and 0.90.

It is not the purpose of the present discussion to examine in any detail the different types of reliability coefficients: it is sufficient to state that there are various ways of estimating them, including searching for internal consistency and using test-retest and interform techniques (see Anastasi, 1968a, pp. 78-85). Rather, we will focus attention on factors that affect the reliability coefficient, and the implications of these factors for the test results of ethnic minority students.

In addition to sources of error, various factors are known to influence the reliability of a test. Durost and Prescott (1962) have categorized these factors according to their effect on the different types of reliability coefficients. Test length (the fewer the items, the lower the reliability), item difficulty, group heterogeneity (the more heterogeneous the group, the higher the reliability), and, most importantly for the purposes of this discussion, spread of scores, all affect a test's reliability. While the range of ethnic minority test scores are spread across the entire distribution, they do tend to cluster at the lower end of the scale with little differentiation among them. Wesman (1952) has shown that the narrower the range of scores, the lower the coefficient of reliability. He concludes that:

> A test may discriminate with satisfactory precision among students with wide ranges of talent but not discriminate equally well in a narrow range of talent. A yardstick is unsatisfactory if we must differentiate objects varying in length from 35.994 inches to 36.008 inches... It should be obvious, then, that no reliability coefficient can be properly interpreted without information as to the spread of ability in the group on which it is based (in Gronlund, 1968, p. 197).

Minority children, then, are consistently assessed by tests that do not indicate the value of the reliability coefficient for their group. The tests only indicate how reliable they are according to sample groups upon which reliability was first established. As a result, for groups that differ from the sample group the actual effectiveness of a test "will tend to be lower than the reported reliability coefficient appears to promise" (Fishman *et al.*, 1964, p. 131). High reliability coefficients are only high for the reference group and those groups that approximate it. The coefficients will tend to be much lower for groups that are more homogeneous and have a smaller range of talent than the reference group. In its recommendations, the 'Guidelines' emphasizes the fact that:

> The sensitive test user should be alert to reliability considerations in regard to the particular group involved and the intended use of the test. In assessing reports... he will not be satisfied with high reliability coefficients alone. He will consider not only the size of the reliability samples, but also the nature and composition of the samples and the procedures used to estimate reliability. He will try to determine whether the standard error of measurement varies with score levels and whether his testing conditions are similar to those of the reliability sample. He will ask whether

the evidence on reliability is relevant to the persons and purposes with which he is concerned. He will know that high reliability does not guarantee validity of the measures for the purpose in hand, but he will realize that low reliability may destroy validity (Fishman *et al.*, 1964, p. 133).

With regard to the concept of validity, while it has always been recognized as an essential and indispensable characteristic of a test, it has suffered from a lack, or more precisely, from an abundance of definitions (Ebel, 1961). What constitutes a valid test, and how is its validity to be measured? In order to answer this question a joint committee involving the American Psychological Association, the American Educational Research Association, and the National Council on Measurement and Education proposed some guidelines, first in 1954, and then extended in 1973, called the *Standards for Development and Use of Educational and Psychological Tests*. The validity of a test may be defined as "the degree to which the test is capable of achieving certain aims" (French and Michael, in Gronlund, 1968, p. 166). Thus if one of these aims is to measure Jane's ability to spell, the test she is given must have good content validity; if another aim is to establish her chance of entering college, the test used must have good predictive validity; finally, if a characteristic such as creativity is to be measured, the test used must have good construct validity. This does not mean that a test may fulfill only one aspect of validity; rather, depending on its purpose, one facet of its validity will be emphasized over others. The *Standards* recognize three types of validation procedures: content validity, criterion-related validity and construct validity. These are detailed below.

Content Validity. This type of validity "is demonstrated by showing how well the content of the test samples the class of situations or subject-matter about which conclusions are to be drawn" (French and Michael, in Gronlund, 1968, p. 166). Thus a test has good content validity if its items relate well to the particular objectives to be assessed. The appropriateness of a test item can only be determined by careful and critical examination. Furthermore, in the selection of test items, efforts must be made to ensure that all possible relevant sources (textbooks, curricula, experts, etc.) have been sampled so that all major aspects of the area under consideration are covered and any extraneous factors that could lower the content validity are minimized. Such a validation procedure is particularly essential for evaluating achievement tests.

Two major assumptions are made in this validation procedure with respect to scholastic aptitude or mental ability, namely: 1) that test takers have been exposed to and are familiar with the universe of information from which test items are drawn; and 2) that the language of the test is the language of the test takers. In the case of the Stanford-Binet test, for instance, children are asked to identify 'common objects' presented in the form of pictures or toy models, to explain why certain objects are employed in daily living, and to interpret pictorially presented situations (Anastasi, 1968a). However, while the 'common objects' such as books, periodicals, and art objects used by the Stanford-Binet may certainly be familiar to children from middle-class families, they may be almost completely unknown to less advantaged children. A child of the slums who is asked: "Why do we have books?" may have no answer to a question that has no relevance in his or her daily life. Taylor (1971) has pointed out that many common words in the English language have very different meanings for blacks than they have for whites. Angoff and Ford (1973) found that blacks can answer correctly more items that deal with modern culture. Klineberg (1935b) reported that when West Virginia rural blacks were asked to give the opposite of a word, no answer was given because they did not know the meaning of 'opposite'. He remarked that if these people "were required to take the Otis test as a written examination, in the usual manner, they would naturally make a zero score on all the 'opposite' items" (p. 169).

Furthermore, in the Stanford-Binet and many other standardized group intelligence tests, strong emphasis is placed on the definition of abstract words, on sentence completion, on analogies, and so on, all of which presuppose a certain mastery of the comprehension and usage of standard English. Many instances have been reported in which the speaker of a black vernacular gave 'nonsensical' answers to test questions because he or she did not understand what was required or was unfamiliar with the examiner's pronunciation.

Criterion-Related Validity. This type of validity "is demonstrated by comparing the test scores with one or more external variables considered to provide a direct measurement of the characteristic or behaviour in question" (French and Michael, in Gronlund, 1968, p. 167). Criterion-related validity is generally predictive in nature. For instance, in intelligence tests, academic achievement is the criterion against which IQ scores are validated: it is predicted that a high IQ score forecasts success in school, while a low score indicates a relatively low chance of success. The degree to which intelligence tests have good predictive validity, however, depends upon the degree to which both the criterion and the test score are devoid of contaminants. Fishman and his associates (1964) identified three categories of factors that can impair a test's predictive validity with respect to ethnic minority test takers.

The first category concerns those factors that can directly influence test scores. The literature abounds in studies that have demonstrated how external variables such as nutrition, self-concept, anxiety, and motivation can affect the performance of children on tests that supposedly measure their intellectual functioning. Whereas as early as 1935 Klineberg illustrated that speed of performance directly affects test scores, he specifically proceeded to show that speed, upon which the large majority of tests depend in more or less pronounced degrees, is basically a culturally oriented concept. He states:

> The attitude toward speed varies greatly in different cultures and not all peoples will work on the tests with equal interest in getting them done in the shortest time possible. Peterson and his associates (1925) have noted this relative indifference to speed among Negroes and the writer found that the injunction to 'do this as quickly as you can' seemed to make no impression whatsoever on the American Indian children on the Yakima reservation in the state of Washington (1935b, p. 159).

Scores have been shown to increase when good rapport exists between the examiner and examinee. In the case of minority children, the race of the examiner greatly influences their performance, especially when they are being tested for intelligence. Likewise, familiarity with testing procedures, the testing centre, the test format, test instruction, and test-taking skills also affect the result to a certain extent.

The second category of factors relates to the criterion itself — the school grade. Do grades really represent a true and accurate measure of a child's (particularly a minority child's) scholastic aptitude? Or are they subject to the influence of other variables that are unrelated to academic success? "Grades are likely to reflect motivation, classroom behaviour, personal appearance, and study habits, as well as intelligence and achievement" (Fishman et al., 1964, p. 136). In addition, other variables such as the teacher's knowledge of the child's IQ score, financial status of the family, area of residence, number of siblings, and so on, contribute to a large extent to the formation of stereotyped notions about a given individual's expected performance in school, his or her potential to achieve, and the way in which he or she is rated. A number of studies (see Rosenthal and Jacobson, 1968) have documented the fact that teachers' expectations not only colour their judgements of their students but also influence the students' own perceptions of themselves, their levels of aspiration, and their achievements.

Finally, criterion validity may be lowered whenever the period between the administration of the test and the obtainment of the criterion measure is lengthy. Fishman and his associates state:

> An illness, an inspiring teacher, a shift in aspiration level or in direction of interest, remedial training, an economic misfortune, an emotional crisis, a growth spurt or retrogression in the abilities sampled by the test — any of these changes intervening between the testing and the point or points of criterion assessment may decrease the predictive power of the test (1964, pp. 136-137).

Construct Validity. This type of test validity "is evaluated by investigating what qualities a test measures, that is, by determining the degree to which certain explanatory concepts or constructs account for performance on the test... Essentially, studies of construct validity check on the theory underlying the test" (French and Michael, in Gronlund, 1968, p. 167). Traits such as intelligence, motivation, interest, and creativity are not observable, and thus cannot be measured directly. Thus, in order to obtain information as to whether individuals possess a certain trait, it is essential to build a theory specifying its characteristics. Generally, it is hypothesized that those who possess a particular construct, such as intelligence, behave differently from those who do not. By observing the two extremes — an extremely intelligent person and an extremely stupid one — a list of differentiating characteristics can be established. Maslow has provided an extensive picture of their respective behaviours: generally speaking, "an extremely intelligent man, when compared with an extremely stupid man, solves his problems, intellectual and personal, more rapidly... he behaves generally in a manner that we call more efficient, more functional, more intelligent" (Maslow, 1944, p. 85). Thus a theory is built specifying how intelligent people behave, and individuals are classified accordingly. Because the concept of intelligence is still a concern of major importance, a detailed examination is now necessary.

II. The Concept of Intelligence

The advent of World War I made large-scale testing a reality of civilian life. Due primarily to the pioneer work of Otis, U.S. Army psychologists developed the tests that came to be known as the Army Alpha and Beta, which were administered to over a million soldiers in an attempt to sort and classify them according to intellectual levels and capacities. By the time World War II began, mass testing had become an established practice everywhere in the United States, and its production a booming and lucrative business. Used extensively by schools, colleges, and employers (Goslin, 1965), intelligence tests now play a vital part at almost all stages of a person's life. From preschool days through to postgraduate years, tests are administered for grouping and course-selection purposes, for placement in special education classes or institutions, for career orientation, for college entrance, and for admission to various professions. A person's IQ score largely determines the kind of education he or she receives and, ultimately, the kind of position attained in society.

What is an Intelligence Test?

An intelligence test provides, in the form of a symbol such as the IQ, a global, overall estimate of a person's intellectual ability. In the case of the original test developed by Binet and Simon, the score was a relative one expressed in terms of mental age. As Maslow remarked, "it could say only that little Jacques had more intelligence than little Pierre and less intelligence than Anatole" (1944, p. 89). It was Stern who introduced the notion of the *intelligence quotient*, the value produced when a child's mental age (MA) is divided by his or her chronological age (CA). The following formula was derived:

$$IQ = \frac{MA}{CA} \times 100$$

Tyler compared mental age to "the size of a boy's suit or a girl's dress. We tell people how big Susie is physically when we say that she wears a size 10. We tell them how big she is mentally when we say that her MA is 10" (1963, p. 44). The 1960 revision of the Stanford-Binet test provided, besides various refinements, a similar computation of the IQ as the one used in group intelligence tests. The IQ is no longer merely a quotient, but rather a standard score with a mean of 100 and a standard deviation of 15. Therefore, "what an individual IQ really tells us is how many standard deviations above or below average a person is" (Tyler, 1963, p. 45). The popularity that the IQ has received over the years is to be deplored, for it was and still is frequently misused and its meaning repeatedly misinterpreted.

The Various Definitions of Intelligence

Intelligence is a concept that has always been a major concern of psychology. Given this importance, it is startling to report that, to date, there is no consensus on the definition of the term. Over the years many definitions have been proposed: so many, in fact, that Spearman (1927) felt that it had become "a mere vocal sound, a word with so many meanings that finally it had none." When, in 1921, the *Journal of Educational Psychology* published a series of articles on intelligence written by prominent psychologists, little agreement could be found among the fourteen distinct definitions that emerged (Tyler, 1969). The same ambiguity that existed over 60 years ago is still apparent today. To illustrate, the following is a list of some of the ways in which intelligence has been defined:

1. The capacity to judge well, to reason well, and to comprehend well (Binet and Simon).
2. The ability to carry on abstract thinking (Terman).
3. The capacity to do well in an intelligence test (Boring).
4. The ability to undertake activities that are characterized by difficulty, complexity, abstractness, economy, adaptiveness to a goal, social value, emergence of originals, and to maintain such activities under conditions that demand a concentration of energy and of resistance to emotional forces (Stoddard).
5. The aggregate or global capacity of the individual to act purposefully, to think rationally, and to deal effectively with the environment (Wechsler).
6. The degree of availability of one's experiences for the solution of immediate problems and the anticipation of future ones (Goddard).
7. Innate, general, cognitive ability (Burt).
8. The outcome of the interplay of innate potentiality and of such conditions as good emotional adjustment and appropriate educational stimulation (Vernon).

If we examine this list, we notice a number of interesting character-istics. First, most of the definitions try to be all-encompassing and use vague, undefined, even undefinable terms that reveal very little. Second, overemphasis is placed on the ability to reason abstractly. Third, all the definitions tend to regard intelligence as an entity. As Wesman remarked: "We have all too often behaved as though intelligence is a physical substance, like a house or an egg crate composed of rooms or cells; we might better remember that it is no more to be deified than attributes like beauty or speed or honesty" (1968a, p. 267). Finally, most of the definitions fail to recognize that what is considered an act of intelligent behaviour is inescapably linked to and determined by the values and standards of society. Intelligence is a culture-bound concept, inseparable from any given setting or environment. For an Australian aborigine, for example, intelligence within the context of the environment could be defined as a composite of the various skills and knowledge of folkways that ensure survival — accuracy in the use of a boomerang, the ability to find water, and so on. Any society with a more naturalistic and primitive mode of life than that found in the industrialized West will place greater emphasis on manual skills than on purely intellectual accomplishments. To say that one society is more intelligent than the other has no meaning, since the valued qualities and requirements for intelligence are different.

The Various Theories of Intelligence

There have been many theories of intelligence, from Plato's chariot with horses and charioteer to Guilford's cube. Basically, modern attempts at defining its nature can be classified into two groups: the *two-factor* theory and the *multifactor* theory.

Briefly stated, the first theory can be traced to Galton's distinction between what he called *general ability* and *special abilities* (Burt, 1958, 1968). This distinction was based on the belief that mental tests measure, to some extent, a basic intellectual ability, which Spearman later called *g*. The more intelligent a person is, the more *g* he or she possesses. Tests of reasoning or tests requiring an individual to establish relationships between things were thought to measure *g* most effectively (Tyler, 1956). Besides this universal or general capacity, which was believed to be 'pure' intelligence, there was a specific factor, *s*, for each different minor type of ability. Spearman's followers, Burt and Vernon in England and Humphreys in the United States, devoted much effort to organizing the multiplicity of specific factors discovered by various investigators into a logical system. This resulted in the hierarchical models of Burt and Vernon, where Spearman's *g* is placed at the top of a pyramid containing various levels of subdivisions (Guilford, 1967, p. 58).

The multifactor theory, as the name suggests, differs in that it does not link all mental abilities to a common factor. Thurstone, the leading exponent of this theory, claimed that intelligence was multifaceted. He identified eight facets or specific independent abilities, which he called primary mental abilities (PMA), as follows: verbal comprehension, word fluency, number, space, memory, general reasoning, and speed. Thurstone also observed that some degree of intercorrelation exists among the primary abilities, since those who excel at verbal comprehension also tend to evince a facility for word fluency (Linden and Linden, 1968a, pp. 71-74). Espousing Thurstone's approach, Guilford (1967) proposed his now-famous structure of intellect model (SI) in the shape of a cube. The SI model comprises three dimensions: content (four categories); operations (five categories); and products (six categories). The cube thus contains 120 (4 x 5 x 6) possible cells, each representing a hypothetical mental ability. Guilford claimed that out of the 120 factors, 82 had already been identified.

This brief summary of the two major schools of thought concerning the structure of intelligence is by no means exhaustive, and the reader is advised to consult the above references to gain a more comprehensive view of this highly complex subject.

Apart from the theories mentioned above, there are two that suggest new ways to assess minority students. These are Cattell's theory of *fluid and crystallized intelligence* and Sternberg's *componential intelligence,* both of which are explained in Chapter 8.

It is not surprising that the editor of the 1969 symposium *On Intelligence,* W.B. Dockrell, found that "intelligence as a concept is alive and well", when the participants of the conference included the famed Burt, Vernon and Jensen. Yet such an assumption is highly debatable, especially in light of the recent controversy over the relation between race and IQ, which if nothing else has uncovered the fallacies in the present IQ tests. First among these fallacies is the claim that intelligence can be measured by tests when, as we saw earlier, intelligence has not yet been satisfactorily defined. At best, IQ tests reflect the constructor's personal view of what constitutes intelligent behaviour. Then there is the question not of whether Burt's or Guilford's or Boring's model is the correct one, but rather whether the concept of intelligence itself is appropriate and useful. Guilford defends this question but qualifies his statement:

> The term 'intelligence' is useful, nonetheless. But it should be used in a semi-popular, technological sense. It is convenient to have such a term even though it is one of the many rather shifty concepts we have in applied psychology. It would be very desirable, for purposes of communication and understanding, to specify a number of intelligences — intelligence A, intelligence B and so on (1956, p. 290).

The Concept of Intelligence in Historical Perspective

How did intelligence tests come into existence? How does one explain the fact that IQ tests, as they currently exist, reflect a belief that innate potential remains fixed throughout an individual's lifetime and can be measured? The answers to these questions can be found in the archives of psychology, a field that acquired the status of a science when the first psychological laboratory was opened by Wilhelm Wundt at Leipzig in 1879.

The legacy left by the earliest psychologists is mainly one of methodology, for they contributed little to the testing of intelligence as we understand it now. Sir Francis Galton has been credited as being the father of individual psychology and mental measurement. An eminent explorer, scientist and scholar, Galton undoubtedly was one of the most versatile thinkers of his time, and made valuable contributions as diverse as the Galton whistle for detecting sensitivity to high tones and fingerprint identification. In view of the fact that he came from a family of longstanding wealth and prominence, it is not surprising that he developed an early and intense interest in the study of heredity;

specifically, the hereditary aspects of what he called genius. In 1869, Galton published his first major work, *Hereditary Genius: An Inquiry into Its Laws and Consequences*, which undisputedly bore the influence of his cousin Charles Darwin's *The Origin of Species* (1859). In this book, he proposed to show that genius tends to run in families (a small number of families), and hence that it is determined by inheritance and influenced only insignificantly by the environment.

> The arguments by which I endeavour to prove that genius is hereditary consists in showing how large the number of instances in which men who are more or less illustrious have eminent kinsfolk. I feel convinced that no man can achieve a very high reputation without being gifted with very high abilities; and I trust that reason has been given for the belief that few who possess these very high abilities can fail in achieving eminence (p. 49).

Galton's conviction that nature held absolute power in determining one's development was in complete opposition to the position taken by the eighteenth-century French philosopher Helvetius and his followers, who firmly believed that differences in people were due to differences in education: *l'éducation peut tout*. Galton exemplified the hereditary factor with his studies of one-egg and two-egg twins, which he later included in his second major work, *Inquiries into Human Faculty and Its Development* (1883). Both books unequivocally reflect his belief that since mental traits are inherited and remain unaltered by environmental forces, only superior persons should reproduce and survive, in order to improve the human race. In the introductory chapters to *Hereditary Genius* and *Inquiries into Human Faculty*, one reads:

> I propose to show in this book that a man's natural abilities are derived by inheritance, under exactly the same limitations as are the forms and physical features of the whole organic world. Consequently, as it is easy, notwithstanding those limitations, to obtain by careful selection a permanent breed of dogs and horses gifted with peculiar powers of running, or of doing anything else, so it would be quite practicable to produce a highly gifted race of men by judicious marriages during several consecutive generations (p. 45).

and

> My general purpose has been to take note of the varied hereditary faculties of different families and races, to learn how far history may have shown the practicability of supplanting inefficient human stock by better strains, and to consider whether it might not be our duty to do so by such efforts as may be reasonable, thus exerting ourselves to further the ends of evolution more rapidly and with less distress than if events were left to their own course (quoted in Peterson, 1925, p. 74).

In 1884 Galton set out to classify people in his laboratory at the Kensington Museum in London. Over 9,000 people were tested by means of simple sensory and motor tests, for which Galton believed that the ablest (that is, the most intelligent) would demonstrate the highest sensory discrimination. For a small fee, a person could acquire information concerning his or her height, weight, breathing power, keenness of vision and hearing, memory, strength of pull and squeeze, and reactions to colour, time and other variables. However, these tests did not prove as successful as Galton had expected, since they did not enable him to make any important generalizations concerning individual differences. As Hunt remarked: "Had Galton's types of tests proved efficient in differentiating those who would achieve with distinction from those who would not, the use of tests to determine those who should reproduce themselves would have been only a short step" (1961, p. 12).

The field of psychometrics began in Galton's anthropometric laboratory. Using physics as his model, Galton set out to devise a scientific instrument that would help him accelerate nature's task of "supplanting inefficient human stock by better strains". From Quetelet, the Belgian mathematician, Galton borrowed a concept related to physical traits and applied it to psychological traits. Quetelet's concept of the average man (nature's ideal) was based on observations that human physical characteristics such as height tend to approximate a bell-shaped probability curve. In order to explain why psychological traits tend normally to remain distributed throughout the population, Galton conceptualized the notion of regression to the mean, without which the stability of the bell-shaped curve would be impossible. The inevitable consequence of a theory that assumes that intelligence is and remains normally distributed is that it automatically dooms 50 percent of the population, at all times, to being below average.

Assisted by Karl Pearson, his student and biographer-to-be, Galton introduced such statistical concepts as standard deviation units to represent all possible scores, the theory of correlation, and the principle of regression to the mean (or regression to mediocrity, as he called it).

In contrast to Galton's approach, the French at that time were devoting their attention to the study of mental retardation and emotional and social maladjustment. Especially creditable were the work of the physician Esquirol, the psychiatrist Itard, and the creator of the Vineland Training School for the Mentally Retarded, Edouard Seguin. The psychologist Binet and the physician Simon together published the first successful test of intelligence in 1905 with the aim of identifying the defective, mentally retarded child from the normal child. The two men wrote:

> Our purpose is by no means to study, to analyse and to disentangle the aptitudes of persons inferior in intelligence. That will be the object of a later work. Here we limit ourselves to the evaluation and quantitative determination of their intelligence in general. We shall determine their intellectual level; and to give an idea of this level we shall compare it with that of normal children of the same age, or of an analogous level (quoted in Peterson, 1925, p. 167).

The Binet-Simon scale was created in response to the practical and urgent demand of the French minister of public instruction for the creation of special education classes for children who could not benefit from regular classroom instruction. The original scale comprise 30 simple, quick, and precise tasks or subtests "bearing principally on the faculty of judgment". Unlike the Galtonian tests, which Binet and Simon criticized for being too sensory and too simple, this scale tapped what they believed to be the fundaments of intelligence — the ability to judge well, to comprehend well, and to reason well. Although Binet accepted and adopted the term 'intelligence' as popularized by Galton and Spencer, he strongly disagreed that it was a fixed quantity, believing instead that it could be improved by training. To support his statement, he cited the progress made by children identified as mentally retarded during their first year of enrollment in special education classes. In the nature versus nurture debate, Binet recognized the importance of nurture upon test performance and the necessity of controlling the cultural factors pervading his tests — factors that had been demonstrated to favour upper- and middle-class children. He identified these factors as "home-training, attention, motivation, language, habit of looking at pictures and scholastic exercise". By the time the second edition of the intelligence scale was ready (1908), Binet and Simon had realized that their test did not measure just intellectual capacity. They remarked:

> It is something far more complex that we measure. The result depends first, on the intelligence pure and simple; second, on extra scholastic acquisition capable of being gained precociously; third, on scholastic acquisitions relative to language and vocabulary which are at once scholastic and extra-scholastic, depending partly on the school and partly on the family circumstances (Binet and Simon, 1916, p. 259).

James McKeen Cattell first introduced intelligence tests to the United States. A self-proclaimed disciple of Galton, Cattell returned to the U.S. from Europe imbued with the belief that intelligence was hereditary: fixed and determined by genetic structure. Supporting Galton's view that in order to improve the human race 'inefficient human stock' should be supplanted by 'better strains', Cattell offered each of his children one thousand dollars to marry the child of a college professor (Sokal, 1971, p.630). As the first professor of psychology to be appointed in the United

States (a claim disputed by Sokal in 1971), Cattell soon became extremely influential in spreading the testing movement. At the University of Pennsylvania, he published his classic article "Mental Tests and Measurements" (1890) in which the term 'mental test' appeared for the first time. Later, as director of the psychological laboratory at Columbia University, he administered tests similar to Galton's to a hundred freshmen in an attempt to show that mental ability could be evaluated and academic achievement predicted. However, his data collected over a period of four years failed to support his views.

Another instrumental American figure in the field of testing was G. Stanley Hall. Although he never met Darwin or worked with Galton, Hall felt that the theory of evolution was, in his words, "the thing for me" (Hunt, 1967, p. 176). As the first president of Clark University, Hall's commitment to the theory of inherited and fixed intelligence left its mark on the numerous students he taught, many of whom later became the pillars of the testing movement in the United States — Henry H. Goddard, F. Kuhlmann, Lewis Terman, and Arnold Gesell. Goddard translated the Binet-Simon scale into English in 1908 to use it with the feeble-minded at Vineland Training School in New Jersey. But it was another admirer of Galton, Lewis Terman, at Stanford University, who used the scale on normal individuals in the American population and modified it. Published in 1916 and revised twice (in 1937 and 1960), the Stanford-Binet test soon became the most widely used scale of intelligence in North America.

The purpose of this historical summary has been to show how Galton's concept of intelligence and his method of measuring it by means of simple tests evolved. Galton's theory of hereditary genius became incorporated into America, seemingly a more egalitarian society than that of Victorian England, because the early American psychologists — Cattell, in particular — had studied and worked with him rather than with Binet (Hunt, 1967).

Of course, racist interpretations of human differences predate Galton. Although its origins are difficult to establish, what is evident is that among the writings advocating the incontestable superiority of the white race (Aryans particularly) de Gobineau's *Essay on the Inequality of the Human Races* was not justification for an otherwise unjustifiable policy of social and political actions. Using 'high reputation' as his criterion of 'high ability', Galton came to the conclusion that the ancient Greeks surpassed all other races, while blacks were judged intellectually inferior to Anglo-Saxons and Jews were seen as "specialized for a parasitical existence upon other nations" and "not capable of fulfilling the varied duties of a civilized nation by themselves" (in Montagu, 1974, p. 410). As a result of Galton's views, Pearson strongly advocated that

Jewish immigration to England be restricted (see Pearson in Montagu, 1974, p. 419). In the United States, Carl Brigham (1923), upon examining army intelligence test results, successfully urged the government to encourage immigrants from Northern European countries but to drastically limit the entry of Alpine and Mediterranean individuals, who he believed were responsible for the decline in 'American intelligence'. In due fairness to Brigham, it should be mentioned that he later deplored his earlier position; however, his original findings and interpretations were consistent with the views of his time and with the doctrine of 'Nordic superiority' as propounded in Schultz's *Race and Mongrel* (1908) and Grant's *The Passing of a Great Race* (1916).

In the eyes of the hereditarians, intelligence is an irreversible and inescapable condition and any attempts to raise it by corrective training (for instance, compensatory education) are bound to fail. Not unlike Calvin's religious elect, Galton's 'eminent men' are those who will, of necessity, make it to the top of the social ladder. Galton's Calvinistic approach to the psychology of human differences has been accepted for so many years that one tends to regard his theories as commandments, often forgetting that they can be and have been challenged by other theories and other evidence.

Chapter 5

Nature versus Nurture

Ronald J. Samuda

Introduction

The nature versus nurture issue has been prominent for a long time. Sir Percy Nunn reminds us that it was Shakespeare's Prospero who, speaking of Caliban as "A devil, a born devil, on whose nature/Nurture can never stick" (*The Tempest*, IV, i), first established the distinction — as we understand it now — between the two terms. Used by Sir Francis Galton in his *Inquiries into Human Faculty* (1883), these were to be the accepted terms thereafter (Nunn, 1945, p. 113).

Both sides of the heredity-environment controversy have supported their positions with collections of evidence. Early hereditarians undertook to demonstrate their case by recounting the histories of twins who behaved predictably alike, and by citing the appalling record of the Jukes family: "out of about 1,000 persons in five generations, 300 died in infancy; 310 spent 2,300 years in almhouses; 440 were wrecked by disease; 130 were convicted criminals (including 7 murderers); and only 20 learned a trade" (Nunn, 1945, p. 115).

At the other extreme, proponents of the environment side of the controversy accepted wholesale John Locke's doctrine of the *tabula rasa* — that is, the mind begins as a clean slate and is imprinted with ideas brought in by way of the senses. If, according to this theory, a child was put in the right kind of environment, she or he would grow up to become the right kind of adult. Differences between people were related, wholly and simply, to education. In Helvetius's words, "enough is ascertained to prove, beyond a doubt, that if education does not perform everything, there is hardly anything that it does not perform" (Nunn 1945, p. 114). This is also the behaviourist's position, as in this classic proclamation:

> Give me a dozen healthy infants, well-formed, and my own specified world to bring them up in and I'll guarantee to take any one at random and train him to become any type of specialist I might select--doctor, lawyer, artist, merchant-chief and, yes, even beggar-man and thief, regardless of his talents, penchants, tendencies, abilities, vocation and race of his ancestors (Watson, 1963, p. 104).

The present trend seems to be a shift away from radical and global positions to a more moderate and conciliatory stance. As more information is gained about the effects on the fetus of nutrition, intrauterine conditions, maternal care, and so on, the idea that is gaining momentum is that both the environment (in the broadest sense) and heredity can influence the nature of an individual. Cynthia Deutsch refers to this relationship as *interpenetration*, a term which, in her opinion, emphasizes the "modifiability of nature as well as nurture":

> The interpenetration discussed involves the operation of environmental influences on the product of genic influences. However, modern genetics teaches that genic operation itself is responsive to environmental variation. Experiments show that incubating larvae from the same genetic strain at a different temperature will result in adult individuals of a different colour. The environment, then, affects the biological attributes of the organism by influencing the operation of the gene (1968, p. 61).

We will now discuss both the nature and the nurture positions in turn.

The Hereditarian Argument

The early hereditarians seldom caught the attention of the public. Their theories of mental heredity, studies of twins and foster children, formulas, and esoteric debates rarely moved beyond the pages of scientific journals or the floors of academic forums. By contrast, their modern counterparts have enjoyed much publicity in national and international newspapers, magazines, popular television shows, and so on. Undoubtedly, the man who put the hereditarians on the map was Arthur Jensen with his theory in 1969 of the persistent differences in test scores between black and white Americans on IQ tests.

Two successive aspects of the theory of mental heredity have existed in the United States. At first, heredity and environment were considered to be not only antithetical to one another but mutually exclusive. Then, as it became clear that one inherits *potential*, not unalterable traits, the heredity-environment question became: in what *proportion* do genetic and non-genetic factors contribute to intelligence?

Before we proceed further, it is necessary to define some technical terms: genotype, phenotype, and heredity. To understand the meaning of *genotype*, we will begin at the point at which the sperm unites with the ovum. The fertilized egg, which is a single cell, has a nucleus that contains chromosomes — stringlike structures composed of a vast number of minute particles called genes. Genes exist as pairs, one half of a pair inherited from the mother and the other half from the father. The way the genes are arranged and behave in the cells determines how the end product, the individual, will turn out. The ways in which they can be combined are almost limitless. As Jennings remarked: "Different individuals are made as it were on diverse recipes; and the diverse recipes give different results... No two individuals, in such an organism as man, are concocted on the same recipe (save in the rare cases known as identical twins)" (in Watson, 1963, p. 51). It is this unique 'recipe' — that is, one's unique set of genes — that constitutes genotype. Gottesman describes the genotype as "the totality of factors that make up the genetic complement of an individual" (1968, p. 29). It is created at the moment of conception, and therefore is fixed at birth. Hirsch (1970) has estimated that there are over 70 trillion potential human genotypes.

Phenotype refers to "the totality of physically or chemically observable characteristics of an individual that result from the interaction of his genotype with his environment" (Gottesman, 1968, p. 29). Dobzhansky describes phenotype as follows: "The phenotype is the appearance of the individual — the structure and functions of his body. The concept of the phenotype subsumes, of course, not only the external appearance, but also the physiological, normal and pathological, psychological, socio-cultural, and all other characteristics of the individual" (1964, p. 58). The phenotype is not fixed, and can vary with time.

The interaction between genotype and phenotype, between the unobservable and the observable, can be illustrated by an experiment by Cooper and Zubek (1958), as reported in Pettigrew (1964). After breeding two genetically distinct strains of rats (an intelligent strain and a dull strain) for 13 successive generations, Cooper and Zubek placed groups of both strains into three different environments: 1) the natural habitat of the rat; 2) a restricted environment (a barren cage with only a food box and water pan); and 3) an enriched environment (a cage with swings, bells, tunnels, decorated walls, etc.). Results showed that in the natural environment the learning ability of bright rats was significantly higher than that of dull ones. (Maze error scores were 117.0 and 164.0 respectively; the lower the score, the higher the ability to solve the problems). In the restricted environment, both strains performed equally poorly (scores of 169.7 and 169.5, respectively. In the enriched environment, again the difference in scores was negligible, with the performance of both strains now high (111.2 and 119.7). This experiment demonstrated how similar genotypes (bright rats) may have different phenotypes (their performance in the three different environments), and how different genotypes (bright rats and dull rats) may have similar phenotypes (their performance in the restricted and enriched environments).

Gottesman (1968, p. 29) described a study conducted by Sinnott, Dunn and Dobzhansky (1958) with similar implications. Genetically identical Himalayan rabbits (similar genotypes) presented different phenotypes when reared in different environments. The rabbits reared under natural conditions developed white bodies with black extremities; those reared in warm cages developed completely white bodies. Gottesman concluded that:

> Given uniformity of trait-relevant environment, almost all observed phenotypical variance in a trait must stem from variability in the genotypes. Given uniformity in that part of the genotype relevant to the trait under consideration, almost all the observed phenotypical trait variance must stem from variability in the environments. Given heterogeneity for both genotypes and environments — the situation which prevails for human populations--the observed trait variability must be attributed to some combination of genetic and environmental variances (1968, p. 32).

As described by Jensen, the concept of *heritability* is "the proportion of phenotypic variance due to variance in genotypes" (1969, p. 42). More precisely, heritability indicates (in the form of a number ranging from 0 to 1.0) how large a role the genetic make-up (genotype) plays in the total amount of the variation of a trait (for example, skin colour) in a particular group of people at a particular time. Heritability is not a property of an individual or of a trait; it is a property of populations (Fuller and Thompson, 1960). Hunt and Kirk define and estimate heritability as follows:

> Heritability is the correlation of the unobservable, theoretical, genotypic variance of a trait with the observed, and measured, phenotypic variance of a trait... Since the genotype is a logical construct that is not observable, estimating heritability demands that investigators find ways to estimate the genotypic variance of a trait from observables. The simplest index of heritability, originally invented by Frances Galton, estimates the genotypic variability through measures of the trait in parents, based on the average measure for the two parents and correlates these measures with measures of the trait in the offspring of these parents, based on the average measure for the children of each couple. The higher the correlation berween such measures for parents and children, the greater the heritability (1971, p. 274).

If the number expressing heritability is large, the trait in question is highly heritable; that is, genes account for much of the variance. For example, Jensen (1969) claimed that for whites the heritability coefficient for intelligence was between 0.80 and 0.85. This would mean that intelligence is a highly heritable trait in Caucasians: i.e., 80 to 85 percent of the variation in IQ is due to heredity, and only 15 to 20 percent to environmental factors.

In investigations of the respective influences of environment and heredity on measured intelligence, it has been customary to compare the characteristics of related and unrelated persons. Erlenmeyer-Kimling and Jarvik have summarized by means of correlation coefficients the work carried out over the past 50 years on the relationship between mental functioning and genetic potential. From 52 studies collected in eight countries, they concluded that "a marked trend is seen toward an increasing degree of intellectual resemblance in direct proportion to an increasing degree of genetic relationship, regardless of environment communality" (1963, p. 1477). Although they did not reject the possible influence of the environment on intelligence, these researchers remarked that the consistency of their compiled data left them no choice but to support the hereditarian stand in the nature-nurture controversy. Jensen's 'Table 2' (1969, p. 49), in which he lists the various correlations observed between related and unrelated persons, is essentially based upon the summary developed by Erlenmeyer-Kimling and Jarvik.

Hereditarians argue that if the environment played a major role, then monozygotic (identical) twins, who share the same genes and thus have the same heredity, should have significantly different IQs if reared in different environments. Jensen (1969) cited three major studies of white monozygotic twins involving 232 white subjects (116 pairs) separated from six months to two years after birth, and raised over the entire range of socioeconomic levels. These studies, Jensen reported, revealed a close correlation between pairs in terms of IQ: 0.86 for the 53 pairs of twins in Burt's (1966) research, and 0.77 both for the 14 pairs studied by Newman, Freeman and Holzinger (1937) and the 44 pairs studied by Shields (1962). Thus, all three studies seemed to indicate that twins obtain very similar IQ scores, even when each half of a pair is raised in a different environment. Commenting on Burt's (1966) data, Hernnstein remarked that the correlation of about 85 percent "is more than usual between ordinary siblings or even fraternal twins growing up together with their own families" (1971, p. 55). Jensen further pointed out that in the same study, the correlation of IQ was almost as high as that of height (0.94) and weight (0.88). Hence the claim that differences in IQ can be explained in great part by differences in environmental conditions seems to be refuted by this evidence.

Studies of unrelated children reared in the same environment (generally a foster home) have also been extensively used to demonstrate the hereditarian position. If the environment dominates, unrelated children whose environmental conditions are almost identical should possess very similar IQ scores. The table of correlations compiled by Erlenmeyer-Kimling and Jarvik shows that for children in this situation the median correlation is only 0.23. As further evidence, Jensen (1969) cited Leahy's (1935) investigation, which yielded a 0.20 correlation, and Burks' (1928) research, in which the average IQs of foster children and natural children living in carefully matched environments were compared. The comparisons favoured the natural children, who produced higher scores. It was also found that the foster children tended not to resemble their foster parents in intelligence, unlike biological parents and children. A 15-year study conducted by Skodak and Skeels involving 100 adopted children further revealed that, despite their improved environments, these children seemed to gravitate more toward the IQs of their natural parents than those of their adoptive ones. Although they refrained from interpreting their findings in a hereditarian light, these researchers nevertheless noted the "increasing correlation between child IQ and true mother IQ with increasing age" (1949, p. 114).

There seems to be no consensual estimate of the exact heritability of intelligence. Figures vary from a high of 88 percent (Burt, 1958) to a low of 60 percent (Woodworth, 1941). However, most hereditarians do recognize the influence of the environment — insignificant as it may appear — on test results. Burt identified three ways in which the influence of environment is felt:

> (a) The cultural amenities of the home and the educational opportunities provided by the school can undoubtedly affect a child's performance in intelligence tests of the ordinary type since so often they demand an acquired facility with abstract and verbal modes of expression; (b) quite apart from what the child may learn, the constant presence of an intellectual background may stimulate (or seem to stimulate) his latent powers by inculcating a keener motivation, a stronger interest in intellectual things, and a habit of accurate, speedy, and diligent work; (c) in a few rare cases illness or malnutrition during the prenatal or postnatal stages may, and almost from the very start, permanently impair the development of the child's central nervous system. The adjusted assessments may do much towards eliminating the irrelevant effects of the first two conditions; but it is doubtful whether they can adequately allow for the last (1958, p. 9).

On the whole, then, except for physiological and nutritional handicaps, hereditarians feel that differences in the results of intelligence tests can be explained in terms of genetic make-up; that is, the "innate amount of potential ability with which a child is endowed at birth sets an upper limit to what he can possibly achieve at school and in after life" (Burt, 1968, p. 17). According to this view, endeavours to raise scores by modifying environmental conditions (such as by means of compensatory education programs) are not only futile but inexorably doomed to failure (Jensen, 1969). In fact, Hernnstein (1971) went so far as to predict the return of "aristocrats, privileged classes, unfair advantages and disadvantages of birth" if an attempt were made to make the environment as good and as uniform as possible for everyone. Hernnstein contended that lowering the effects of the environment augments the heritability of intelligence, as well as the prospect of a society built on inborn differences:

> The higher the heritability, the closer will human society approach a virtual caste system with families sustaining their position on the social ladder from generation to generation as parents and children are more nearly alike in their essential features. Greater wealth, health, freedom, fairness and educational opportunity are not going to give us the egalitarian society of our philosophical heritage. It will instead give us a society sharply graduated, with ever greater innate separation between the top and the bottom, and ever

more uniformity within families as far as inherited abilities are concerned. By removing arbitrary barriers between classes, society has encouraged the creation of biological barriers. When people can freely take their natural level in society, the upper classes will, virtually by definition, have greater capacity than the lower (1971, p. 64).

The Environmentalist Argument

Environmentalists refute the hereditarians' concept of genetically determined intelligence, and instead maintain that differences in performance can be explained in terms of environmental advantage or deprivation. It is generally agreed today that both nature and nurture interplay and elicit the observed racial differences in IQ scores; however, most environmentalists and hereditarians disagree over the *degree* of importance of each factor.

Broadly stated, this view is that the question of differences in intelligence scores is one not of race, but of class and caste. The environmentalist studies those factors (physical, biological, psychological, and sociocultural) that membership in a lower class and caste entails, and which cannot be disregarded when making racial comparisons. Because the surroundings, knowledge, and experiences of the lower classes are so disparate from those of the middle and upper classes, this view holds that the success of the lower classes in school (typically a middle-class-oriented institution) cannot be ensured without a vast program of remediation and compensation. One eminent psychometrician, in defending the virtues of the SAT, remarked to a skeptic: "What's wrong with being middle-class? Everybody wants to be middle-class." But what does it really mean to be of the upper class, middle class or lower class? In comparing the three major types of stratification systems — class, caste, and estate — Mayer defines a *class* system as one that is

> ... based primarily upon differences in monetary wealth and income. Social classes are not sharply marked off from each other nor are they demarcated by tangible boundaries. Unlike estates, they have no legal standing, individuals of all classes being in principle equal before the law. Consequently, there are no legal restraints on the movement of individuals and families from one class to another. Unlike caste, social classes are not organized, closed social groups. Rather, they are aggregates of persons with similar amounts of wealth and property, and similar sources of income (1959, p. 8).

Along the same lines, Mueller and Mueller noted that "if 'social class' possesses any sociological meaning, it signifies a hierarchy in the distribution of the privileges of life. In fact, the measurement of the social distance between the respective classes is a measure of these differentials" (1953, P. 486).

A *caste* system is the most rigid type of social stratification, consisting of closed social groups arranged in a fixed order of superiority and inferiority. An individual born into a particular social caste cannot move easily into a higher one: not unlike one's eye colour or height, one's caste cannot be changed (Mayer, 1959). In the United States, blacks have been in the unusual position of suffering from both a class system and a caste system based on colour, forced into a stratification system in which a white individual is, and remains, socially superior to any black individual, regardless of education, occupation, or wealth. The sharply demarcated colour line led the black American community to develop a separate but similar class structure separated into its own upper, middle and lower levels. However, the obvious limited economic and educational opportunities for blacks mean that each black class does not rank with its white counterpart in terms of wealth (Mayer, 1959). In this caste-class system, blacks emerge the victims and the losers. Drake wrote that:

> Negroes in America have been subject to "victimization" in the sense that a system of social relations operates in such a way as to deprive them of a chance to share in the more desirable material and non-material products of the society which is dependent, in part, upon their labor and loyalty. They are "victimized" also because they do not have the same degree of access which others have to the attributes needed for rising in the general class system — money, education, "contacts," "know-how"... The "victims," their autonomy curtailed, and their self-esteem weakened by the operation of the caste-class system, are confronted with "identity problems." Their social condition is essentially one of "powerlessness" (1966, p.4-5).

It was during the 1930s and 1940s that several investigators put to rest the notion that equal opportunity in the distribution of the privileges of life prevailed in the United States. Extensive studies of geographically diverse communities (Lynd and Lynd, 1929, 1937; Warner and Lunt, 1941; Davis, Gardner and Gardner, 1941; Warner, Havighurst and Loeb, 1944; West, 1945; Warner *et al.*, 1949; Hollingshead, 1949) documented the existence of a social stratification, and the reality that success was not solely the result of an individual's effort and merit, but greatly depended upon his or her inherited position, wealth, social connections, formal education, and other advantages unrelated to personal qualities and achievements. Mayer

(1959) also contended that a racial caste system denies a large segment of the population equal participation in the distribution of opportunities and wealth.

The Index of Status Characteristics (ISC) developed by Warner and his associates divided the American population into social classes on the basis of occupation, income, type of house and dwelling area. One needs no statistical evidence to support the observation that when these criteria are adopted, minorities in general, and blacks in particular, are relegated to the lowest level of the social scale. The traditional black dwelling area is the overcrowded and spatially isolated ghetto, characterized by run-down and vastly inferior housing, poor public services, inadequate medical facilities, and low-quality schools.

Despite some significant advances over the past few decades, blacks are still concentrated in the low-income sectors of the economy and still form the core of the blue-collar force. In comparison to whites, they receive significantly lower salaries, which are made even smaller by the fact that "non-white family heads in 1960 had a smaller median income than whites for every educational level... the average income for a non-white family with a male head who had finished high school was less than that of a white male head who had finished only the eighth grade" (Drake 1966, pp. 17-18). Moynihan (1965) also drew attention to the fact that the rate of unemployment for non-whites was more than twice as great as that for whites.

Within the Canadian context, several studies have shown similar patterns of unemployment and relegation to low-income jobs for visible minorities. A three-year study of Third World immigrants to Canada found that they experienced higher rates of unemployment, earned less money, and often could not find work in their chosen field (Henry, 1986).

Cultural Deprivation of Minorities

Both the hereditarians and the environmentalists agree that minorities generally score lower on tests of intellectual performance, but they disagree as to the cause of the deficit. Whereas hereditarians believe that genes are at the root of the problem, environmentalists contend that the variables that relate an individual's background to his or her performance must be identified. The home, cultural patterns, language, cognitive skills, and so on must be explored, and a strategy of intervention must be devised in order to prevent, arrest and reverse the effects of deprivation. This cultural-deprivation frame of reference deserves closer attention.

An impressive number of studies dating from the early 1920s have presented evidence that supports a theory of cultural deprivation and casts serious doubts upon, even if it does not invalidate, the credibility of the genetic inferiority model. The pioneering work of Klineberg was of fundamental importance in introducing a new approach to the problem of racial differences in intelligence. For the first time, the widely accepted belief that blacks were genetically inferior was challenged, and the environment was offered as the causative agent. In *Race Differences*, Klineberg categorically asserted that no research yet had revealed any scientific proof of racial differences in intelligence (1935b, p. 345). Gordon's study of canal-boat and gypsy children living in England showed, as early as 1923, the effects of an intellectually deprived environment on intelligence. Here, it was found that poor school attendance, coupled with the high mobility and illiteracy of their parents, relegated these children to the borderline of feeble-mindedness. Means of 69.6 for the canal boat children and 74.5 for the gypsies were obtained on measures of intelligence, and these means dropped sharply with age. In the United States, mountain children of Anglo-Saxon heritage were found to exhibit the same signs of retardation and age decrement in IQ as Gordon's subjects. Studies by Asher (1935) in Kentucky, Wheeler (1932) in Tennessee, and Sherman and Key (1932) in the Blue Ridge Mountains, conducted on subjects living in isolated and economically and culturally impoverished communities, showed that poor performance on standard intelligence tests had to be accounted for by poverty and the lack of stimulation in the environment. Shimberg (1929) also showed that a gap existed between the test scores of urban and rural white children, not only in the United States but also in Europe whenever city and country people were compared (Klineberg, 1931).

Some researchers found ample evidence of high intelligence and ability in black children: Jenkins (1948) found that "at least sixteen published studies... give an account of Negro children possessing IQs above 130; twelve of these report cases above IQ 140" (in Wilcox, 1971, p. 103). Jenkins also noted that for one female child who tested at IQ 200, no trace of white ancestry could be found. This observation contrasted sharply with the theory of William Shockley that for every one percent increase in white blood, there would be a gain of one IQ point.

Further undermining the theory of genetic differences in intelligence were the results of army tests given during World War I, which revealed that blacks from the states of Pennsylvania, New York, Illinois, and Ohio attained higher scores than whites from Mississippi, Kentucky, Arkansas, and Georgia (Klineberg, 1935b).

Other studies in the 1930s also demonstrated that a richer environment could raise the test scores of blacks. Klineberg (1935a) tested the IQs of 3,000 Harlem schoolchildren who were matched by sex, age, schools attended, socioeconomic status, and birthplace (all were born in the South) but who differed in the number of years they had lived in New York City. Without exception, those blacks who had most recently arrived from the South scored the lowest, and the longer the period of residence in New York, the higher the score obtained (1935a). Lee (1951) arrived at a similar conclusion following a study on Philadelphia-born and Southern migrant black students. In the face of these results, the theory of selective migration (brighter persons migrate to the cities and to the North), which has been used to explain the superior scores of urban and northern black children, gave way to the more adequate explanation that an improved environment results in improved test scores (Freeman, Holzinger, and Mitchell, 1928).

The study under the direction of Skodak and Skeels (1949) of 100 adopted children of inferior socioeconomic birth who were placed in homes of above-average economic, educational and cultural status has already been mentioned as providing support for the hereditarian position. It was true that, as in similar studies (for example, Burks, 1928), these children's IQs tended to resemble the IQs of their biological parents more closely than those of the adoptive parents. However, the mean IQ of the biological mothers was 85.7 compared to 106 for the children: a difference of over 20 points that must reflect the influence of a rich environment. This study also showed (Table 12, p. 110) that out of the 63 children and their mothers who took the 1916 version of the Stanford-Binet intelligence test, 52 children but only 19 mothers scored above average (95-134). Such findings seem to be inconsistent with a position that states that genetic make-up has the greatest influence on intelligence. The authors concluded (p. 116) that "maximum security, an environment rich in intellectual stimulation, a well balanced emotional relationship, intellectual agility on the part of the foster parents — all these and other factors contributed to the growth of the child."

Several other investigations (Collins, 1928; Haggerty and Nash, 1924; Havighurst and Breese, 1947; Pressey and Ralston, 1919; Standiford, 1926) demonstrated an apparent correlation between parental occupation and a child's intellectual level. The higher the father's occupation on the social scale, the higher the child's IQ score. Traditionally, children whose parents are professionals or work at a managerial level score higher on intelligence tests than those whose parents are skilled or unskilled labourers. Terman and Merrill (1937), Seashore, Wesman, and Doppelt (1950), and others have found that a difference of approximately 20 IQ points exists between the upper and lower ends of the social scale. The mean IQ of children with parents in the low occupational categories is 95, compared to a mean of 115 for offspring of professional or managerial parents.

Simply stated, the cultural deprivation theorists have formulated the following basic assumptions: 1) the environment plays a major role in the development of cognitive skills and in the learning process; 2) some types of environments are more stimulating to cognitive development than others; and 3) the proper task for early childhood educators of disadvantaged children is to identify stimulation deficiencies in the environment (Deutsch and Deutsch, 1967). Minority children from lower-class backgrounds score lower on intelligence tests because their environments lack those attributes that are essential for academic success, which white, middle-class milieus already possess.

The typical dwelling area of most deprived black children, investigators have found, is the urban ghetto; a spatially isolated, overcrowded community that lacks the fundamental amenities. The typical household is noisy, disorganized, and contains more relatives and siblings (often illegitimate) than that of the average white family (Keller, 1963). There are more unstable and broken homes due to the father's desertion or absence, with the result that boys are often raised in predominantly matriarchal atmospheres and are deprived of contact with male role models, especially successful ones (Deutsch, 1967; Ausubel and Ausubel, 1963). Housing and surrounding buildings are substandard and usually located in areas where there is "little opportunity to observe natural beauty, clean landscapes or other pleasant and aesthetically pleasing surroundings" (Deutsch, 1967, p. 44). Inside, the homes have few pictures, books, toys, and other objects that can provide a child with tactile, visual, and aural stimulation. Finally, children of lower socioeconomic levels receive more physical punishment than children of higher levels (Milner, 1951).

According to Davis and Havighurst, considerable differences exist in childrearing practices between social classes. However, except in the areas of feeding and cleanliness training, in which blacks, regardless of class, were more permissive in the former and stricter in the latter, Davis and Havighurst found no evidence of colour differences in childrearing practices. They observed:

> Middle-class families are more rigorous than lower-class families in their training of children for feeding and cleanliness habits. They generally begin earlier... place more emphasis on the early assumption of responsibility for the self and on individual achievement... are less permissive... in their regimen... they require their children to take naps at a later age, to be in the house at night earlier, and, in general, permit far less free play of the impulses of their children... middle-class children are subjected earlier and more consistently to the influences which make a child an orderly, conscientious, responsible and tame person... middle-class people train their children early for achievement and responsibility (1946, pp. 707-708).

In general, the environment of a lower-class child was found to be less verbally and visually stimulating than that of a middle- or upper-class child. Deutsch (1967) noted that the lower-class environment is a noisy one (due to continuously running television sets, crying babies, screaming children etc.) but the noise is not meaningfully related to the children themselves. As a result, their auditory discrimination (which Deutsch found to be related to reading ability) attention span, memory span and responsiveness are markedly diminished.

Lower-class children's concept of time is also affected. Their concentration is poor, and they are less able to handle abstract concepts. With regard to the last point, Hess et al. (1968) related poor ability to conceptualize abstractly to maternal language style. The researchers found a significant correlation between the mother's language abstraction and the child's performance, and concluded that "there is an abstraction factor in the middle-class mother's language which may have far-reaching implications for the subsequent intellectual development of the child" (p. 168). The language of a lower-class working mother was found to be more restricted, less linguistically subtle and elaborate, less complex syntactically, less abstract, and less imaginative. Thus Hess and his associates agree with Bernstein's (1960) theory of a dichotomy between formal (middle-class) and public (lower-class) language. Handicapped by these early deficits, a lower-class minority child enters school with a marked disadvantage and falls victim to the cumulative deficit phenomenon described by Deutsch (1967). Unlike the middle-class child whose home, with its hidden curriculum, provides the basic school-related skills, the typical disadvantaged child sees school as a strange and discontinuous environment. Unable to catch up with intellectually nurtured, school-oriented, and achievement-motivated peers, such students fall further and further behind as time passes.

How should the consistent results showing a correlation between socioeconomic status and intelligence level be interpreted? Are poor people poor because they are dull, or dull because they are poor? Whereas proponents of a genetically determined level of intelligence elect the first alternative, environmentalists favour the second. However, both the hereditarian and the environmentalist positions seem to rest on certain fallacies.

Fallacies of the Hereditarian Position

The scientific basis for the existence of racial differences in intelligence rests on four premises. The first premise is that the concept of intelligence is well and universally understood. The second premise is that IQ tests provide a true and reliable measure of intellectual functioning, and that differences in test scores reflect differences in intellectual potential. The third premise is that whites and blacks represent two racially distinct groups and that each is homogeneous within itself. The last premise is that the effects of the variance in physiological, sociocultural and economic conditions on *both groups* can be ignored. The first two fallacies have been discussed in chapter 4. We now proceed to discuss the other two.

Before any inference can be made that racial differences exist in test performance, we must first understand the meaning of 'race', and then try to establish whether black Americans constitute a racial group distinct and separate from that of white Americans.

Biologically, a race is a subspecies or variation in the single species to which all people belong — *Homo sapiens*. The theory of evolution states that whatever diversity exists among these subspecies can be attributed to the diversity of the environments in which different groups originally lived. Briefly stated, natural selection is the process by which most changes within the genetic constitution of a population occur, and only those possessors of genotypes that are best suited to a particular environment survive to pass their genes on to the next generation. Gottesman remarks that "many of the characteristics observed in current races are the results of adaptation to ancient environments" (1968, p. 23). Thus, the dark skin colour of Africans, for instance, can be explained in terms of the necessity for protection from intense sunlight, while the pale skin of Nordic people made it possible to absorb even the faintest rays of the sun in order to manufacture vitamin D (Pettigrew, 1964).

Genetically speaking, all human beings are alike: it is the way in which the genes *cluster* and *organize* that differentiates them. Thus, race is a result not of the *types* of genes present in a population, but of the *frequency* with which a particular genetic composition is found in a particular population. In the words of Boyd, a race is "a population which differs significantly from other human populations in regard to the frequency of one or more of the genes it possesses" (1950, p. 201).

There are likely as many race taxonomies as there are investigators interested in compiling them. Gottesman (1968, pp. 12-13) lists the works of Boyd (1950), Coon, Garn, and Birdsell (1950), Garn (1961), and Dobzhansky (1962), in which from six to thirty-four different races are described. On the other hand, Montagu (1952, p. 46) opposes the classification of races, on the basis that it runs counter to the process of evolution, but favours the position that races are "different kinds of temporary mixtures of genetic materials common to all mankind." Serological experiments have permitted the organization of races along the lines of blood types: Africans, Caucasians, and Orientals differ in the frequency of the genes for blood types A, B, and O. Bodmer found that "in Oriental populations, for instance, the frequency of the gene for the blood type B is 17 percent, while it is only 6 percent in Caucasians. This means that type B individuals are generally three times as common in most of Asia than they are in Europe" (1972, see Fig. 1, p. 89).

However, Mayr pointed out, "biologically, it is immaterial how many subspecies and races of man one wants to recognize" (1963, p. 644). What is more important, in the context of the present discussion, is the fact that there is no such thing as a 'pure' race. The possibility that a racially distinct group of people has not been interbred with the rest of humankind seems remote and, as Dunn and Dobzhansky (1952) emphasized, "nothing can be more certain than that pure races in man never existed and cannot exist" (in Pettigrew, 1964, p. 62). Where, then, does the black American stand biologically? In the gene pool of the American 'Negro' or 'coloured' individual are the genes of two of the major races, African and Caucasian. Conversely, the *white* American must also claim some African ancestry, although quantitatively less. Pettigrew gives the following account of the relative percentage of Caucasian blood to be found in the black American:

> A series of investigations over the years provide comparable estimates of the genetic influence of cross-racial mating upon Negro Americans. Early studies lacked modern blood system genetic methods and relied upon morphology and the reconstruction of ancestral lines. This research estimated that the percentage of Negroes with at least one known white forebear ranged between 72 and 83 percent (Wirth and Goldhamer, 1944). With a large sample of fifteen hundred Negroes, Herskovits in 1930 arrived at more detailed figures. He calculated from the reports of his subjects that roughly a seventh (14.8 percent) had more white than Negro ancestors, a fourth (25.2 percent) had about the same number of white and Negro ancestors, almost a third (31.7 percent) had more Negro than white ancestors, and the remainder (28.3 percent) had no known white ancestor. In addition, a quarter of the sample's Negroes (27.2 percent) claimed one or more known Indian forebears (1964, p. 68).

Glass and Li (1953) estimated that the number of white genes present in the black American of today reaches 30.56 percent; Roberts (1955), upon re-examining their data, arrived at the lower figure of 25 percent. From researchers such as Pollitzer (1958), who calculated the 'genetical distance' between whites and West Africans, whites and Charleston blacks (Gullah), and whites and blacks from other parts of the United States, it can be concluded that, genetically, the average American black is about as far removed from pure Negroid types as he or she is from pure Caucasian types.

If black Americans cannot be said to belong truly to the Negro race, then it seems incongruous to call any individual who has the remotest trace of Negro ancestry 'black'. It is also an error to make 'racial' comparisons in test performances, as if black and white American subjects belonged to totally separate and scientifically determined races. As Gottesman concluded, "if you choose to call the white individual with a Negro grandfather a Negro, then logic would require you to call the 'average' Negro in New York or Baltimore, white" (1968, p. 22).

The fallacy behind the hereditarians' position is that they ignore the present biological reality and place disproportionate emphases on skin color and external features such as hair, nose, and lips. If the distinctive external characteristics of blacks were removed, it would be impossible to determine their race with certainty. Therefore, to associate mental qualities simply with physical qualities seems rather nonsensical because "no one asks whether there are mental and temperamental differences between white, black, or brown horses" (Montagu, 1952). For instance, if the theory that brain size is related to intelligence were correct, then the Neanderthal, whose brain size was 75 cubic centimeters larger than that of *Homo sapiens*, would have to be considered mentally superior to us.

Even if one assumes that it is possible to draw a clear line between blacks and whites, the failure to adequately control certain environmental, cultural, and sociopsychological variables still invalidates any interpretation of intellectual superiority or inferiority of one group compared to the other. In fact, any procedure that attempts to compare two groups in order to see if they are equal or if one is 'better' is doomed from the very start for the following reasons.

It is standard procedure for investigators interested in comparing the intellectual performance of blacks and whites to choose, as their representative sample, groups matched in various factors such as sex, age, amount of schooling, parental education, socioeconomic status, parental occupation, family size, and so on. By controlling these factors as much as possible, it is believed that differences in test results will more accurately reflect differences in intellectual attainment and ability. The *a priori* assumption, of course, is that the historical and cultural circumstances in which the two groups were raised can be ignored, and that similar educational, professional, and economic opportunities have been open to both.

Several investigators have drawn attention to the scarcity of adequate instruments for measuring environments. Anastasi remarks that the *Mental Measurements Yearbooks* contain a section on socioeconomic scales, but few entries are included. Moreover, most of the available variables are crude and superficial. It is only since the late 1950s that serious efforts have been made to develop sophisticated indices of environmental variables for specific purposes (1958, p. 579). Bloom concurs with this view, and also notes that "our catalog of tests of individual differences is enormous, whereas our instruments for measuring environmental differences consist of a few techniques for measuring social class status and socioeconomic status" (1958, p. 185). In addition, the tendency of the existing scales is to classify environments globally as good or bad, desirable or undesirable, favourable or unfavourable. Wolf (1964) opposed this one-dimensional view of environments and devised a testing procedure that stressed not so much the physical characteristics of the home and the parents' occupational status, but rather the interactions between parents and children as far as the development of intelligence is concerned (see Bloom, 1964, pp. 78-79). Although several techniques exist that identify an individual's social-class status (e.g., Warner's evaluation of participation and Index of Status Characteristics; Sim's SCI Occupational Rating Scale), the occupational level of the major breadwinner has proved to be a simple and fair approximation of social status.

The fact that blacks and whites have not been given equal occupational opportunities is well documented. Demographic studies repeatedly have shown that black workers, in proportion to whites, are grossly underrepresented in the professional, managerial, sales, and crafts occupations, although they have made substantial gains in better-paying white-collar jobs since 1960 (Bouvier and Lee, 1974). Hauser (1966) estimated that such occupational gains represented only half that of the white population. Wide discrepancies between the two groups still exist, as is evident from the unemployment rates. Some figures released by the U.S. Bureau of the Census (U.S. Department of Commerce, 1973) should help to demonstrate the gulf that exists between the two groups. The census showed that in 1972, 10 percent of the black labour force, compared to 5 percent of the white labour force, were unemployed. Other figures indicate that an almost constant 2:1 ratio of black-white unemployment has existed for a long time. Blacks also face more frequent and longer periods of unemployment, and perform more part-time than full-time work (Fein, 1966).

Wages, naturally, are commensurate with occupation. The high concentration of blacks in blue-collar jobs has created an income gap that is further aggravated by the fact that minority wage earners are consistently underpaid due to their low levels of educational *attainment*. It is true that the median income of black families has increased remarkably from $2,807 in 1950 to about $6,700 in 1970 (Bouvier and Lee, 1974). However, during 1970 the median income of whites reached $10,236. Further investigations into the census data reveal that "part of the explanation for the narrowing of the gap in income between whites and blacks is attributable to the working wife... Many more black than white wives work" (Bouvier and Lee, 1974, p. 3). Furthermore, blacks do not receive the same remuneration as whites for performing the same job (Drake, 1966).

For instance, black teachers with four years of college education, or black carpenters, firemen, and truck drivers, all with four years of high school education, received substantially smaller salaries than their whites counterparts (Bouvier and Lee, 1974, p. 7). Hauser (1966) reported Siegel'e monetary estimate of the earnings of a black American:

> The difference between nonwhite and white earnings in 1959 of males 25 to 64 years old was $2,852.00 as reported in the Census. Of this difference, $1,755.00, or 62 percent, is attributable to the differences in the regional occupational, and educational distribution of whites and nonwhites. Thus, even if nonwhites had achieved the same regional, educational, and occupational distribution as whites, nonwhites would still have earned only $1,097.00 or 38 percent below the level of whites. The average cost of being a Negro in the United States in 1960, then, was about $1,000.00 in earnings (in Parsons and Clark, 1966, p. 84).

Similarly, research in Canada has consistently revealed earning differentials between certain ethnic groups (especially visible minorities) and white mainstream Canadians. Reitz et al. (1981) reported that incomes for both West Indian and Portuguese males were lower than those of other groups by about $3,000. Furthermore, even when education, work experience, and knowledge of English were controlled, income differences between black West Indians (men and women) and their white Canadian counterparts remained constant. Likewise, a study of a specific group, graduates with MBA degrees, found that people of visible minority origin earned $3,000 less than white Canadians (Ontario Human Rights Commission, 1983).

Educational Factors. Blacks, especially in the southern United States, have a long history of limited educational opportunities. Hauser (1966) provides pertinent data on this topic. Although illiteracy among blacks declined from 30.4 percent in 1910 to 23 percent in 1960, it was still three times as great as that of whites (7 percent). Until 1960 white children of elementary- and secondary-school age not only attended school in greater proportion than black children of the same age but spent more years in school. By the early 1970s, however, the proportion of blacks attending school had doubled, and the number of school years completed had increased vastly (Bouvier and Lee, 1974). But the education of whites also progressed steadily over the same period of time, thus also reducing the possibility of substantially narrowing the interracial gap. As a consequence of wider illiteracy, lower school enrollment, and fewer years of schooling of blacks compared to whites, black family heads find themselves in a situation where the quantity and quality of their education is dangerously below par. As Edwards observed, "the low level of educational achievement for such a large proportion of non-white family heads has obvious implications for the cultural life to which the Negro child is exposed in the home and doubtless for the type of motivation the child receives for achievement in school" (1966, p. 289).

Differences between the educational attainment of blacks and whites are not only quantitative but qualitative. The black school-child is likely to receive a lower level of instruction and lesser amount of homework than his or her white counterpart. Deutsch (1967, p. 117) observed that the typical black school generally spends an inordinate amount of classroom time (80 percent) on matters of discipline and organizational details, thus seriously re-ducing the amount of time devoted to actual teaching. She estimated that students in such schools receive one-half to one-third the ex-posure to learning of their white counterparts.

Teachers, especially whites, regard slum schools as having low prestige and therefore consider an assignment in one of them as be-ing only temporary, pending the availability of a better vacancy (Green, 1971; Haubrich, 1963). As Becker's study of the career pat-terns of Chicago public school teachers illustrated (Cloward and Jones, 1963, p. 191), predominantly black schools are characterized by unusually high staff turnover. The recruitment of qualified staff for such schools poses a serious challenge to administrators, who often have no alternative but to hire young, inexperienced, and mobile teachers whose employment opportunities are limited. Indeed, it is difficult to convince anyone that creative, effective, satisfying, and remunerative teaching can be done in schools that are overcrowded, inadequately furnished, and poorly financed. Jencks estimated that 15 to 20 percent more a year is spent on the average white school-child than the average black schoolchild (1972, p. 28).

If, as Canady (1943) suggested, one of the requirements of comparing blacks and whites is "identical or not significantly differ-ent environmental conditions — especially educational opportunity" (in Wilcox, 1971, p. 94), then it is clear that no meaningful interracial comparisons of intelligence can be made, because the two groups have had such disparate education and educational opportunities.

Even if all the other variables we have so far discussed could be controlled, the psychological effects of prolonged membership in a lower caste would still corrupt, and hence nullify, any comparisons between minority and majority groups. Those effects have been explored extensively: poor self-concept, identity conflicts, submission to white dominance, fear of white competition, high anxiety level, sensitivity to the race of the examiner, poor motivation to achieve, low aspirational levels, fatalistic attitude, and so on. *There is an indelible stigma attached to being black in America.* Unlike other races that can meld more easily into the mainstream, blacks have always been too conspicuous to blend in successfully. Even if he or she is a successful businessperson, lawyer, professor or politician, a black person is first and foremost *black*. American public opinion, despite a recent favourable trend, has always been reluctant to admit that blacks are as intelligent as whites. Pettigrew reports that "in 1942, only 42 percent of white Americans believed the two groups to be equally intelligent; by 1944, the figure was 44 percent; by 1946, 53 percent; by 1956, 78 percent" (1964, p. 195).

In conclusion, there seems, at the moment, hardly any basis for attempting to make valid interracial comparisons of test performance. Rebutting Eysenck's challenge that experimental evidence of nurture's influence be brought forth, Rex summarized his position as follows:

> Since, however, the crucial variable is the difference between white and Negro history and the fact that Negro history involves the fact of slavery, experiment would mean subjecting the group of Negroes to white experience. The empirical study which holds constant, size of income, type of neighborhood and length of schooling in the United States of the present day, therefore, should in theory be supplemented for an experiment in which the peoples of Africa conquer, capture and enslave some millions of European and American whites under conditions in which a very large proportion of the white population dies and in which the white culture is systematically destroyed and in which finally a group of emancipated whites living in 'good neighborhoods' are then compared to their Negro masters. It is not sufficient to brush aside this assertion, merely by saying that we should not draw conclusions from 'hypothetical experiments'. The fact is that the differences in the history of Negroes and whites are a factor of immense significance and that any statistical reasoning which leaves them out can reach no conclusions of any value whatever (1972, pp. 170-171).

Fallacies of the Environmentalist Position

The theory of cultural deprivation or disadvantage also contains its problems. Frank Riessman's widely read book, *The Culturally De-*

prived Child (1962), has been credited with popularizing the term 'cultural deprivation'. Although Riessman refutes the notion that lower socioceconomic groups have no culture of their own, he nonetheless uses the term to describe those groups that "lack many of the advantages (and disadvantages) of middle-class culture" (p. 3). By cultural deprivation he means "those aspects of middle-class culture — such as, education, books, formal language — from which these groups have not benefited." Although the term was accepted in everyday parlance, several educators and writers, including Clark (1963a) and Mackler and Giddings (1965), opposed it from the beginning. Various other terms were suggested for characterizing the child who does not fit into the mainstream culture. He or she has alternatively been called disadvantaged, underprivileged, socially deprived, socially disadvantaged, educationally deprived, and socially rejected. Clark and Plotkin reiterated the need for a moratorium on the usage of euphemisms such as cultural deprivation. "Serious adverse effects in social planning, educational policy and research follow from its wide acceptance. Conceptual and theoretical confusion is generated by the loose definition of the term. The deficiencies of the concept far outweigh whatever advantages are gained by its continued use" (1972, p. 69).

Actually, the term 'culturally deprived' literally means either lacking a cultural background — an impossibility since no individual is devoid of culture — or belonging to a culture that is deemed deficient and constitutes a handicap for its members. With respect to blacks, cultural deprivation means that their culture is regarded as not being conducive to the kinds of attitudes, skills and knowledge required by white schools and white society at large. Mackler and Giddings state that whenever the words 'culture' and 'deprivation' are used together, "they suggest very incorrectly that a culture can of itself be deprived or that a culture can somehow deprive its members who depend upon it of the goods, skills, and behaviours, which are necessary for survival and adjustment" (1965, p. 609). Cultural deprivation, in their opinion, represents one of those tags or labels that "do not help to banish the myth of Negro inferiority" but maintain and entrench it.

A common misconception is that black slaves arrived in America culturally naked. Consequently, it is seldom realized that, although blacks and whites have lived as compatriots for over 300 years, they do not share the same culture (Canady, 1943, in Wilcox, 1971). The diversity of folkways that such a wide assortment of slaves (from

West Africa, Angola, Madagascar and other areas) brought to the United States has, despite constant attempts to annihilate it, remained surprisingly strong and has deeply influenced the lifestyle of American blacks. Canady reported that:

> Although the American Negro's accommodation to European custom has been far-reaching, nevertheless, Herskovits finds that many forms of his present-day behavior are readily recognizable as of African origin, that is, manifestations of the carry-over of aboriginal customs. For exemple, Africanisms in religious beliefs and practices, music, dance, folklore, attitudes and certain aspects of motor behavior are generally observable in the United States (in Wilcox, 1971, pp. 95-96).

Not withstanding its African origin and Caucasian-influenced transformations, American black culture is a sequela of slavery. The high concentration of ex-slaves and their descendants in the 'black belts' of the United States led to what St. Clair Drake called the 'ghettoization' of blacks:

> The ghettoization of the Negro has resulted in the emergence of a ghetto subculture with a distinctive ethos, most pronounced, perhaps, in Harlem, but recognizable in all Negro neighborhoods. For the average Negro who walks the streets of any American Black Ghetto, the smell of barbecued ribs, fried shrimps, and chicken emanating from numerous restaurants gives olfactory reinforcement to a feeling of 'at-homeness'. The beat of 'gut music' spilling into the street from ubiquitous tavern juke boxes and the sound of tambourines and rich harmony behind the crude folk art on the windows of store-front churches give auditory confirmation to the universal belief that "We Negroes have 'soul'." The bedlam of an occasional brawl, the shouted obscenities of street corner 'foul mouths', and the shine of police sirens break the monotony of waiting for the number that never 'falls,' the horses that neither win, place, nor show, and the 'good job' that never materializes. The insouciant swagger of teenage drop-outs (the 'cats') masks the hurt of their aimless existence and contrasts sharply with the ragged clothing and dejected demeanor of 'skid-row' types who have long since stopped trying to keep up appearances and who escape it all by becoming 'winos'. The spontaneous vigor of the children who crowd streets and playgrounds (with Cassius Clay, Ernie Banks, the Harlem Globe Trotters, and black stars of stage, screen, and television as their role models) and the cheerful rushing about of adults, free from the occupational pressures of the 'white world' in which they work, create an atmosphere of warmth and superficial intimacy which obscures the unpleasant facts of life in the overcrowded rooms behind the doors, the lack of adequate maintenance standards, and the too prevalent vermin and rats (1966, pp. 9-10).

Put simply, it is impossible to equate black lower-class culture with middle-class culture. Eels and his coworkers (1951) recognized the influence of cultural differences upon the test performance of minority groups. These researchers' attempt to design a culture-free test did not succeed, but nevertheless it represented an effort to eliminate or at least attenuate the disadvantage suffered by minority groups in tasks foreign to them. Klineberg (1935b) related several accounts of how different modes and ways of living could affect test results. As an example, he cited his experiences with the Dakota Indians, whose custom was not to answer a question in the presence of someone who does not know the answer (p. 155). This custom is very different from the mainstream customs of encouraging people to ask questions as much as possible.

Not surprisingly, a culture can only be found wanting whenever the yardstick that is applied to it is basically ethnocentric in its gradations. Advocates of the cultural-deprivation thesis have posited that "the customs and values and the language of one's group are superior to those of other groups and are the 'right' and 'good' standards by which the behavior of all persons ought to be measured" (Mercer, 1971, p. 317). Therefore, they have focused on "describing Negro behaviour not as it is, but rather as it deviates from the normative system defined by the middle-class" (Baratz and Baratz, 1970, p. 32). They have stressed the negative and pathological aspects of black culture, and confused equality with sameness.

The philosophical basis of a theory that postulates cultural deprivation is the 'average child', who is subject to the same laws and principles as Quetelet's average man' (see chapter 4). Any departure from this mean is expressed in terms of deviance. Naturally, the mean or norm is embodied in the values, standards, experiences, and knowledge of the white middle class, of which the school is a mirror. Any failure to measure up to so-called normal behaviour or to meet success as prescribed is attributed not to genetic factors in this case, but to the familial, social, and cultural milieu in which the child lives. As Baratz and Baratz remarked: "Both the genetic model and the social pathology model postulate that something is wrong with the black American. For the traditional racists, that something is transmitted by the genetic code; for the ethnocentric social pathologists, that something is transmitted by the family" (1970, p. 32).

If, as Hunt (1967) succinctly stated, "the difference between the culturally deprived and the culturally privileged is, for children, analogous to the difference between cage-reared and pet-reared rats and dogs" (in Passow *et al.* 1967, p. 202), it follows that in order to protect the child from the invidious influences of the environment, measures must be taken to alter the thinking, communication, and behaviour patterns of a group whose orientations differ so markedly from those of the middle class. Since middle-class children do well in school partly because it is simply an extension of their home (Cloward and Jones, 1963), intensive remedial and compensatory programs must be implemented so as to bring 'substandard' children up to the normal level. For such an enterprise to be successful, however, it should begin before school, at the earliest possible stage of the child's life. What is being advocated, in fact, is that underprivileged parents abandon their childrearing practices for 'better' ones, and relinquish their parental duties to the care of social scientists, linguists, psychologists, and so on. As the originators of the Early Training Project remarked, "the general strategy of our research is based upon the fact that, short of a complete change of milieu for children in infancy, we have yet to demonstrate that it is possible to offset in any major way the progressive retardation that concerns us" (Gray and Klaus, 1965, pp. 887-888). Ideally then, the infant should be taken away from its parents and brought up in the kind of environment conducive to academic performance and success. Ideally then, ethnic groups should trade the customs, patterns, mores and attitudes that keep them culturally distinct for those of the middle class. However, the futility of attempts to turn ghetto children into middle-class children has been well expressed by Gordon and Wilkerson:

> The unexpressed purpose of most compensatory programs is to make disadvantaged children as much as possible like the kinds with whom the school has been successful, and our standard of educational success is how well they approximate middle-class children in school performance. It is not at all clear that the concept of compensatory education is the one that will most appropriately meet the problems of the disadvantaged. These children are *not* middle-class, many of them never *will* be, and they can never be anything but second rate as long as they are thought of as potentially middle-class children... At best, they are different, and an approach which view this difference as something to be overcome is probably doomed to failure (1966, pp. 158-159).

An impressive amount of evidence indicates that black mothers are responsible for producing "linguistically and cognitively impaired children who cannot learn" (Baratz and Baratz, 1970, p. 36). As mentioned earlier, Hess *et al.* (1968) have related the lower-class child's poor ability to conceptualize abstractly to maternal language style. Hunt too adopted the view that the parents are poor linguistic models for their children (1968, p. 31). But Baratz and Baratz have denounced what they call the 'inadequate mother hypothesis' and claimed that:

> One of the chief complaints leveled against the black mother is that she is not a teacher. Thus one finds programs such as Caldwell's (1968) which call for the 'professionalization of motherhood' or Gordon's (1968) which attempts to teach the mother how to talk to her child and how to teach him to think (1970, p. 37).

The apparent failure of compensatory or enrichment programs to remedy cultural deprivation has been viewed in very different lights. Hereditarians see in it additional proof that genes play a much more significant role in intelligence level than is generally conceded. However, opponents of the social pathology model attribute the failure of Head Start and similar programs to the dehumanizing implications of a theory that rejects the concept of cultural pluralism, and postulates the white, middle-class lifestyle as the only viable way. Moreover, they denounce such a position as a theory of distortion and "a built-in rationalization for the educator who fails to teach minority children effectively" (Clark and Plotkin, 1972, P. 65). Educational institutions and society in general, not parents, must answer for the difficulties of minority children, especially black children. "There is no question," Clark and Plotkin state, "that the uncritical attitude towards deprivation in the child relieves school administrators and teachers from their primary function of education" (1972, p. 65). They further contend that: "The possibility that the failure may stem from budgetary deficiencies and other more direct educational inadequacies such as teacher attitudes and training, inadequate supervision, bureaucratic rigidity, and outmoded curricula and materials is short circuited by the prevailing concept of cultural deprivation" (1972, p. 56).

Ultimately, comparisons across cultures and across ethnic groups involve value judgments. Academic achievement (as well as professional, socioeconomic, and political success in the U.S. and in Canada) seems to demand some adherence to the endemic Puritan ethic that pervades North American society in general. As long as society remains the way it is, the middle class individual of any ethnic group will have advantages over those on the lower levels of the socioeconomic ladder; the persevering and industrious Oriental will outstrip the Native American because of differences in value orientation. We are still a far way from righting the balance, and from recognizing the equal value of the ethnic minority individual's culture. Despite movements towards multicultural policies, and the attempts to institute a fairer distribution of educational and occupational opportunities, the structural bias within the social systems remains intact and the school reflects that bias in no uncertain terms. We need to train a different kind of teacher with the awareness and information contained in the following chapters.

Chapter 6

Understanding and Coping with Individual Differences

Shiu L. Kong

There is a tendency among practising teachers to label and to stereotype minority students. In conducting a study of teacher attitudes, one persistent theme seemed to be generally held as being fair and democratic, and could be summarized as "we treat them all alike" (Samuda and Crawford, 1980). These educators were obviously reacting to the massive influx of linguistically and culturally different minorities pouring into the urban educational systems over the past three decades. There was a tendency, too, for teachers to characterize certain ethnic groups as having particular traits and interests. It was not uncommon for teachers to expect Oriental students to excel in the areas of mathematics and science. Similarly, ethnic minority immigrants from the Azores and from the West Indies were often shunted into classes for the vocationally oriented occupations.

This chapter is intended to emphasize the fact that individual differences exist *within* all ethnic and cultural groups. Understanding should extend beyond environmental circumstances of language and culture; it should embrace the essentials of individual differences. Administrators, teachers, and counsellors need to be aware, too, that 'treating them all alike' can have deleterious consequences in terms of a student's success at school and job satisfaction in the workplace.

Differences and Equality

A fundamental belief of democracy is that all people are equal under the law and in terms of human rights. In reality, people are unequal in a wide range of traits, some of the more important being sex, personality, physical build, intellectual capacity, temperament, aptitude, and motivation. People also differ in terms of their environment. Every child is born into a social context marked by such factors as socioeconomic status, culture, ethnicity, and parental attitude. These factors influence — for better or worse — an individual's development as he or she grows up.

Conflicts arise from the discrepancy that exists between our beliefs in social equality and the fact that many differences do exist. In interpersonal relationships, these conflicts are sometimes resolved through understanding and accommodation; at other times, they are accentuated because of prejudices or behavioural restrictions regarding how people should relate to each other.

In a caste society, people of one class treat those of another class according to established manners and values. In most western countries, however, people generally regard each other as being more or less on the same level and accept each other on mutually respectful terms. In our daily encounters with others, we intuitively sense the differences or similarities between them and ourselves and adjust our behaviour according to these perceptions. We tend to accept or accommodate the opinions and actions of people we know and understand, even if we disagree with those opinions or actions. We make allowances for deviant behaviour (according to our own standards) of people we love, and criticize and deride those whom we dislike.

It is within human institutions that are based on the concept of equality, that conflicts between this theory of equality and the reality of individual differences become critical. The public school is a case in point. In the classroom, a teacher is expected to treat 30 or so students equally, using the same teaching methods, materials, and learning expectations. Yet all teachers know that extensive differences in abilities, interests, achievements, temperaments, and aspirations exist among students attending the same grade. After spending some time with a group, a teacher discovers that student A is more capable or learns faster than student B, and that the two should probably be treated differently. But it is necessary to know much more than the simple fact that the students are different in their ability to learn. To what extent are they different? Why are they different? Is it the teacher's responsibility to enlarge or to reduce this difference? These are some of the perplexing questions confronted in the classroom.

Some of these questions have been investigated by psychologists in studies of individual variability and group variability. Differences can be described in two ways: (a) in terms of the kind or category (such as differences in body size or intelligence); and b) in terms of quantity or extent (such as A is two inches taller than B). While in everyday language we say that Barbara is smarter than Sue, in the language of psychology we would say that Barbara is more intelligent than Sue, or that Barbara has an IQ of 130 and Sue an IQ of 110. Even more specifically, we could say that Barbara's verbal IQ is higher than Sue's, but that they have the same performance IQ. This means that Barbara can more easily or imaginatively perform tasks involving the use of language, but that both girls are equal in tasks such as arranging blocks into certain patterns.

It becomes obvious that by using specific measuring tools and techniques we can identify individual differences more precisely and reliably. Whereas our everyday observations are often influenced or biased by our own likes and dislikes, to the extent that cultural and other related factors play a role, psychological measurements tend to be more objective. However, the quality being measured by a test is also restricted by the nature of the specific test being used. A pound of mass or weight gains in the way in which it is defined. A kilogram is a different measure of mass than a pound.

Two sources of problems can arise from the use of 'objective' psychological measurements to determine individual differences. The first relates to the level of accuracy that can be attained by these tests, for many problems must be overcome before measuring instruments and techniques will be perfected. At the present stage, interpretation of test results must be done by specialists giving careful consideration to the limitations inherent in a particular test. The second problem lies in our tendency to overgeneralize or to expect too much from test results. For example, if we find out that Bill has an IQ of 150 we may tend to regard him as a superior person, able to do anything — or, we might assume from his inability to do certain things that intelligence tests are useless. Recognizing these two sources of problems can help us use tests and their results more carefully and productively.

With these considerations in mind, let us now proceed to discuss individual differences in learning. In general, psychologists study differences between individuals for the sake of gathering data; examining as many facets of human variability as they can. The result is an accumulation of facts about how people differ from one another and some speculations on factors that contribute to these differences. In education, we are most concerned with finding out how students differ in those psychological traits that are directly related to learning.

It has been established that by the time children enter school at approximately five years of age, significant differences exist among them in terms of intelligence (general ability), academic aptitude (specific learning capacity in various subjects), interest, learning style, and basic knowledge in reading and mathematics. Such variability is seen not only among pupils from widely different backgrounds, such as might be found in an urban school, but also among those from relatively homogeneous suburban neighbourhood environments. Hildreth (1950), for example, reported that in a group of seven-year-olds, grade norm scores ranged from the first to the sixth grade level. For a group of ten-year-olds, the range was from the first to the ninth grade level. These initial differences thus widen as children grow older and proceed to higher grades, as is well substantiated in *The Non-Graded Elementary School* (Goodlad and Anderson, 1959).

Similarly, in a study of the achievement in mathematics of 71 Grade 9 students, Ketcham and Fitzgerald (1963) reported grade equivalents ranging from 4.4 to 16.6. Data collected in a province-wide study of student achievement in Ontario revealed extensive overlapping of aptitude and achievement scores in English and mathematics obtained by the student populations of Grades 7, 8, and 9 on tests originally designed for the latter. For example, 14 percent of the Grade 7, 27 percent of the Grade 8, and 36 percent of the Grade 9 student population in the city of Toronto obtained scores on the *Canadian English Achievement Test* equivalent to the top 25 percent of the Grade 9 student population in the entire province of Ontario (Toronto Board of Education, 1962). In studying the progress rate of 40 intellectually superior first-grade pupils learning mathematics with programmed texts, Suppes and Hansen (1965) reported that, at the end of 26 weeks, the fastest learner had completed approximately 6,000 more problems than the slowest one. The achievements in mathematics by the two students differed by approximately one-and-a-half grades.

Within a regular class where children are grouped together mainly by age, individual differences of all kinds and extents exist. Yet present learning conditions in our schools do not facilitate meeting individual needs. In fact, the educational system almost seems to discourage teachers from using a one-to-one or even a small group approach. Our school organization, teacher utilization, classroom organization, curriculum design, and examination and certification systems seem to be planned for processing human beings *en masse*.

Of course, there is no justification or need for an exclusively individualized approach to teaching and learning. In fact, studies in human ecology, cognitive development and socialization show that people need to interact in various kinds of activities. There is also evidence that group forces exert an important motivating influence in many social situations, including the classroom. When managed properly, such forces can facilitate school learning.

In order to accommodate individual differences in learning, it is necessary for teachers to understand the ways in which children vary, as well as the factors that contribute to such differences.

Factors in Academic Achievement

Differences in Intelligence. Generally, teachers can determine whether a student is academically able by using such cues as alertness, comprehension ability, questions and answers, and the quality of his or her work. For psychologists, intelligence is a theoretical construct that involves standardized measurements of abilities in symbolization, language use, concept formation, and problem solving. Although psychologists cannot as yet agree on what exactly is intelligence, they have come to understand it quite well in the 90 years of intense study since the French psychologist Alfred Binet designed the first intelligence test.

Binet's original intention was not to design a test of intelligence, but one that could correlate with academic success of children in the same grade. However, his test was so successful that it was quickly adopted in Great Britain and the United States, where psychologists converted it into a scale that provides a single index of measurement. This scale was called the Intelligence Quotient, or IQ. Subsequent studies have provided descriptions of what IQ scores measure or mean, and how they correlate with performance in various tasks, including general school achievement. Although useful, these descriptions are not conclusive, and they have generated controversies about IQ usage and testing. Since some of these controversies are based on erroneous arguments from people who do not quite understand the concepts and operations of intelligence tests, it is important that teachers acquire a proper perspective on the subject.

IQ tests fall into two general categories: individual tests and group tests. Individual tests, such as the Stanford-Binet and the Wechsler scales, generally provide the most reliable and valid results within the limitation of the concept of intelligence quotient. Group tests, on the other hand, are susceptible to all kinds of confusing variances.

Although IQ tests yield a single score, they do not measure a single ability, but rather a combination of abilities. It is here that controversies arise. If we look at the Stanford-Binet scale as an example, we find not only that there is a wide range of different tasks required for a particular age group, but that the tasks are also quite different for different age groups. How can such a variety of tasks yield a constant value for the intelligence quotient? The answer given by test designers is that even though the tasks are different, their scores correlate moderately well, and the variety of tasks helps to ensure test reliability. Nevertheless, the identification of intelligence factors has been the subject of a great deal of study for almost a century. The results of these studies offer many insights into the nature of intelligence, but because some of them involve very complex and cumbersome analyses, they are not very useful for teachers. Arthur Jensen (1969) has come up with a simple classification of the abilities that make up intelligence. In this classification, intelligence is divided into two dimensions called Level I and Level II. Level I abilities include association learning and rote memory, and relate to the performance of such tasks as memorizing specific content, using an alphabetical code, and communicating in a foreign language. Although these tasks are by no means simple (try to imagine doing simultaneous translations of speeches made by Members of Parliament), they require little or no reasoning or problem-solving. Level I abilities are chiefly associated with the mastery of the basic skills included in the elementary school curriculum.

Level II abilities include abstract thinking and reasoning, which are needed to solve new problems. They relate to the performance of such tasks as reading comprehension and the application of abstract principles in subject fields. It has been found that Level II skills are less successfully taught than Level I skills. On the basis of extensive research, Jensen believes that Level II abilities are largely hereditary in origin (Jensen, 1969, 1970, 1973; Jensen and Figuera, 1975). Even teaching by the discovery method and training in problem-solving skills do not seem to improve Level II abilities, because they relate to solving problems or situations that are very different from one another, such as supplying meaningful analogies, stating similarities and differences, and solving abstract problems that do not seem to have general principles. Jensen's claims in this respect have created considerable controversy among psychologists.

As a whole, the IQ is not necessarily a stable fixed value, but changes during childhood and adolescence. Longitudinal studies such as that of McCall, Applebaum, and Hogarty (1973), revealed that Stanford-Binet scores, on average, change 28.5 points between the age of two-and-a-half and 17, with the highest change being 40 points! The environmental factor in thought to be most influential, for it was found that scores of children of lower socioeconomic status tend to drop. According to a study by Tyler (1965), children of high socioeconomic status have an average IQ of 110-115 at four years of age, and they maintain this or a slightly higher score when they are adults. By comparison, urban disadvantaged children have an average IQ of 95 at four years of age, but drop gradually to 80-85 by adulthood. We will discuss why this may occur when we deal with differences in socioeconomic status in the next section.

When a large number of people are tested, one can expect to find that the distribution of IQ scores displays a continuous range of variability approximating a normal curve. This indicates that intelligence, at least as determined by IQ tests, owes its origin to diverse factors. As revealed by a classic study (Terman and Merrill, 1937), approximately 64 percent of all IQ scores fall between 85 and 114. A teacher with a class of 35 children at any grade can thus expect considerable variability.

From time to time it has been charged that the IQ tests currently used favour middle-class whites. Even though content analysis of most of these tests does not support such charges, it is true that children who learn English as a second language and therefore have a limited verbal comprehension cannot be tested reliably with IQ tests written in English. Despite all kinds of controversies and diffi- culties, the fact remains that IQ scores, when properly derived, re- main the most reliable predictors of school achievement. As such, they can indicate to a teacher what kind of achievements an individ- ual student can be expected to attain. Since the scores can be im- proved through enrichment (Bransford and Stein, 1984; Haynes, 1981; Wickelgren, 1974), knowing the IQ of a student can also help a teacher create a set of conditions favourable to the student's development.

Differences in Socioeconomic Status

One of the criteria most commonly used to describe the differences between people is socioeconomic status, or social class. There is actually a fine distinction between these two terms, although they are used interchangeably. Socioeconomic status is material-oriented and usually refers to one's occupation and income, educational level, and the kind of neighbourhood one lives in. By contrast, social class is not necessarily related to wealth, but indicates a person's status and social prestige within the community. Often, such prestige is in- herited from one's family.

As our social structure and occupational characteristics change, it is a mistake to use simple wealth as an indication of socioeco- nomic status, especially when we relate wealth to academic achievement. There is no question that a person's family income de- termines the kind of material environment in which he or she grows up, including exposure to such educationally relevant stimuli as travelling, home computers, private lessons, and so on. However, as we shall see, variables such as interpersonal warmth, security, car- ing, parental modelling, verbal stimulation, opportunity for linguistic and emotional expression, and motivation are much more important to optimal development, and hence are more influential on cognitive growth and academic success. As many of these factors are more imbedded in some cultures than in others, a student's cultural back- ground is educationnally relevant. The education level of the parents also is an important factor in his or her academic progress (Stevensen et al., 1978). Since highly educated parents take a more direct interest in their children's education and are more inclined to volunteer for school activities and services (Shipman et al., 1976), teachers often find them more cooperative and helpful.

Contrary to a common belief that people of different socioeconomic status have different values regarding education, researchers have found that the majority of parents, whether of high or low socioeconomic status, recognize the value of education and want their children to progress as far as possible educationally (Hess, 1970). However, few parents of low socioeconomic status are familiar with the school setting and still less with what to do to help their children to develop fully. It is therefore apparent that, as far as education is concerned, differences in socioeconomic status are not so much differences in material well-being but, rather, in knowledge and methods of childrearing. A teacher who knows this can work with parents so that they can cooperate and help with the education of their children.

Children need security and plenty of interpersonal interactions in order to learn. They also need models. There is ample proof from research (Hess, 1970; Laosa, 1978; Steward and Steward, 1974) that parents who provide a rich cognitive environment seek opportunities to interact with their children as often and as extensively as they can. Such parents answer their children's questions, encourage and support their explorations, and generally provide an appropriate context of meaning so that they can gradually assimilate new experiences on their own terms. When these parents interact with their children, they do so specifically and precisely. They name objects and explain events as the child perceives them. They explain causal relationships. They encourage aspirations and planning, and discuss future activities. They impose discipline in terms of specific demands, accompanied by clear instructions on how to meet those demands. They act as models for such activities as reading, effective communication, critical thinking, and community involvement. They set examples of social fellowship in their daily lives. They not only allow their children to observe, but involve them as participants.

By contrast, many parents who are disadvantaged socioeconomically have neither the time nor the resources to carry out any of these activities, often being too wrapped up in their own problems. Their interactions with their children may be intense emotionally, but lack regularity and predictability. The effects that these two kinds of parenting have can readily be inferred. It is obvious that children who grow up in cognitively rich environments are more likely to possess security, confidence, and plenty of opportunities to plan activities that they can carry out purposefully. Those from disadvantaged homes live in a state of tense uncertainty, and their activities may be sporadic and aimless.

A good example to illustrate the difference between the two kinds of environment is an experiment that was carried out using an 'Etch-a-Sketch' board. Some readers may know the Etch-a-Sketch, a commercial toy that resembles a small television screen. It has two knobs that can be rotated. One knob when turned etches a horizontal line on the screen, moving either right or left; the other knob etches a vertical line either upwards or downwards. Turning both knobs simultaneously results in curved, wavy, or diagonal lines. Thus, one can etch all kinds of figures by turning the two knobs in different ways.

In this experiment, using mother-child pairs from various socioeconomic backgrounds, the mother was asked to operate one of the knobs while her child operated the other. Together, they were to etch an assigned figure such as a square, a rectangle, a flight of steps, or a house. Before the game began, the mother was given the assignment and shown how to use the Etch-a-Sketch. It was then her responsibility to explain to her child both how to operate the toy and ultimately how to complete the game.

When the game was over there was a follow-up discussion on some of the events that occurred during it. The results showed that the typical socioeconomically disadvantaged mother was egoistic, demanding, and displayed few resources and little patience in showing her child what to do. She would start the game without checking whether the child fully understood it or not. She blamed the child whenever a mistake occurred, including when the mistake was hers. If the game was not successful after two or three attempts she would abandon it, putting all the blame on the child and accusing him or her of being stupid. In most cases, she seemed so anxious about completing the game successfully that she neglected the process as well as her child's needs and personal esteem. The game usually ended up leaving a negative and sometimes hostile feeling in both mother and child, with no indication of learning on the part of the latter.

In contrast, the typical educated mother of high socioeconomic status would use both visual and verbal demonstrations to show what was needed to be done and how to do it. She would make sure that her instructions were adequate by testing the child with appropriate questions, and would commence the game only when she was sure that it was clear. When a mistake was made, she would apologize if it was hers, or, if it was the child's, give encouragement to try again. If the mistake was caused by a lack of understanding rather than motor coordination, she would stop the game and cover the relevant points again. Throughout the course of the game, there would be verbal communication to provide reinforcement and sharing. It was clear that her focus was on the child, his/her learning, and the emotional sharing between the two of them. In this case, a successful performance, though important, became a means to an end. The child learned not only how to use the etching device but, more importantly, how to cooperate in an activity with another person.

Although there is a whole range of styles between the two extremes presented above, we believe that this example offers teachers a good reference for reflecting on their own classroom style. For those who work in schools where a good proportion of students come from low socioeconomic homes, the challenge is exciting. There is evidence that students readily model themselves after their teachers and, given warm, caring and personal interactions, can be well motivated to learn when expectations are held for their progress (Kleinfeld, 1975; St. John, 1971).

In teaching a class containing students from different socioeconomic backgrounds, teachers should be sensitive to their natural emotional undercurrents, and accommodate and respect individual differences rather than make frequent comparisons and attempt to measure everyone by a single standard.

Gender Differences and Sex Roles

Most teachers in high schools can tell you that male and female students on the whole achieve in different ways, yet a systematic survey of the research literature reveals that boys and girls do not differ in intellectual functioning (Maccoby and Jacklin, 1974). The observed differences in academic performance are largely the result of sex-role differences perceived by both adults and by the children themselves. These perceptions can influence variables that are relevant to achievement, such as motivation, aspiration, attitude, and learning style, so that by the time children reach high school age, marked sex-related differences may exist.

There is a common observation that girls read better than boys, while boys have superior mathematical abilities. Although research evidence reveals that girls do read better than boys at various school levels, cross-cultural comparisons indicate that such differences are the result of social-cultural rather than biological factors. For example, Johnson (1976) studied the reading performance of second-, fourth-, and sixth-graders in the United States, Canada, Great Britain, and Nigeria. His results revealed conflicting trends of superior performance between the United States and Canada on the one hand, and Britain and Nigeria on the other. So far, we have not come up with a well-founded explanation as to why such differences favour one sex in one country and the other sex in another country.

In mathematics, the same forces are apparent. When certain variables such as interest level and rate of exposure are controlled (Fennema and Sherman, 1977), in the upper grades boys are still found to outshine girls in mathematics, partly because of perceptual differences that developed in the early years. Early in life girls are taught to believe that mathematics is not for them, and adolescent girls tend to bypass optional courses in this area. More recently, research revealed that gender differences in mathematics were evident among elementary school children (Benbow and Stanley, 1980).

We must recognize the fact that subtle gender biases pervade our society, including its schools. Since the emergence in the 1960s of the feminist movement, educators have become much more sensitive to the need to eliminate sexism in the curriculum and in other aspects of education. However, a prejudice that has dominated our culture for hundreds of years cannot be changed easily. For example, despite efforts made by authors and publishers, a study analyzing 100 children's books published between 1972 and 1974 revealed that women's roles were still not being represented accurately and fairly (Stewig and Knipfel, 1975).

It appears that in order to actualize the potentialities of every student, it is necessary for teachers not only to take into account a student's abilities, but also to be aware of the circumstantial factors that may have adversely affected his or her attitudes, interests, and motivation to learn. By understanding these factors, a teacher can initiate long-term corrective measures designed to help students dispel erroneous perceptions and beliefs about themselves.

Differences in Cognitive Style

Perhaps the most educationally relevant individual differences have to do with *cognitive style*. Cognitive style is an important aspect of learning that affects the interactions between student and teacher and therefore must be monitored carefully. It refers to two related aspects: 1) the way in which individuals process information in perception and learning; and 2) the various strategies that they use in carrying out tasks. *How* a person uses information in learning or in solving problems is the focus, rather than how well he or she does so. Of course, a particular cognitive style can produce better-quality results when it is well matched to the requirements of a particular task.

The following list represents some of the cognitive styles identified and studied by Sigel and Coop (1974):

- Attention to the global features of a stimulus versus examination of its fine details.
- Division of stimuli into a few large categories versus many small ones.
- Intuitive inductive thinking versus logical deductive thinking.
- Quick, impulsive response behaviour versus slow, painstaking problem-solving behaviour.
- A tendency to classify objects on the basis of either 1) observable characteristics, 2) similarities in function, time or space, or 3) common possession of some abstract attributes.
- A tendency to impose one's own structure on what is being perceived, versus that of allowing the specific features of the perceived object and its background context to structure one's perception.

Each of these cognitive styles and its variations can lead to a difference in learning results in terms of speed, precision, and quality. The first two aspects, speed and precision, are explained in terms of *conceptual tempo*. The third is explained in terms of *psychological differentatiation*. We shall now see how each of these aspects functions to influence learning.

Conceptual tempo refers to the degree to which people are impulsive or reflective in deciding a response when two or more alternatives are possible. When placed in a test situation where only one of several similar answers to a question is correct, a cognitively impulsive student acts quickly, sometimes making a selection even before examining all the given alternatives (Kagan and Kogan, 1970). In contrast, a cognitively reflective student studies all the alternatives before selecting a response.

A truly cognitively impulsive student is quick in response but is likely to make errors because of not taking the time to consider the problem carefully, while the truly cognitively reflective student takes more time to respond but makes fewer mistakes. However, there will also be those individuals who are both fast and accurate, and others who are both slow and inaccurate. That is, some people respond quickly because they are skillful and efficient, not because they behave impulsively, and, some respond slowly because they do not know how to achieve the task, not because they are reflective (Bentler and McClain, 1976; Haskins and McKinney, 1976). Thus, one may raise the question of whether the term 'cognitively impulsive' is appropriate, since many quick responders are not impulsive, but unusually able or decisive in their actions.

Many factors impinge on the formation of conceptual tempo, but it is believed that parental modelling and domestic socialization are significant influences. It should be noted that being conceptually impulsive or conceptually reflective simply reflects a behavioural style: there is no indication that one style is superior to the other in terms of performance effectiveness or learning efficiency. The important point is that success in problem-solving or learning is determined not by speed of response, but by the match between the strategy used and the demands of the task involved. Teachers of minority students therefore should respect the individual cognitive style of each rather than attempt to impose changes.

Conceptual tempo is related to the performance of many school tasks, such as early reading progress (Kagan and Kogan, 1970; Sunshine and DiVesta, 1976). This is because reading requires careful and accurate discrimination of similar yet different visual symbols such as 'd' and 'b', 'p' and 'q', 'if' and 'it', 'was' and 'saw', etc. Children predisposed to differentiate fine detail and to examine first impressions carefully are likely to read more accurately than those who respond crudely and casually.

For students who lack an effective cognitive style for learning, it is possible to provide training for the acquisition of more efficient problem-solving skills. For example, a successful experiment was carried out by Meichenbaum and Goodman (1971) to train fast but inaccurate responders to talk to themselves in order to guide their own actions in the process of problem-solving. The teacher would first model a task performance while providing a verbal explanation of what was being done, step by step. Then students were asked to perform the same task while the teacher instructed them aloud.

Next, both teacher and student would perform the task together while instructing themselves aloud. When consistent success was achieved, the self-instruction spoken aloud would be reduced first to soft whispers and finally to silent speech. The idea was to train the impulsive and careless student to approach learning or problem-solving more systematically and carefully, through explicit modelling and self-instructed practice.

Psychological differentiation refers to the manner in which a person recognizes and selects the salient points in perception. This is also referred to as a *global* versus *analytical* perceptual style, or as *field-dependent* versus *field-independent* (Witkin *et al.*, 1977). People who are field-dependent usually have difficulty in discriminating stimuli from their immediate contexts. As a result, their perceptions are easily affected by manipulation of the associated context. For example, a field-dependent student is easily confused about a familiar melody if the accompanying music is changed, or may find it difficult to recognize a well-known figure pattern if it is embedded within intersecting lines. By contrast, people who are field-independent are more analytical. Because they can separate the perceived stimuli from the background, their perceptions are more consistent and not easily changed with variations in the context.

In the educational context, field-dependent students prefer to learn in groups with ample opportunity for interaction. They work hard to please their teachers and therefore are easily motivated by praise and encouragement. Because they are less analytical in orientation, they need more explicit directions and instruction, exact definition of ideas, and clear delineation of relationships. As a group, they tend to be warm, tactful, considerate, affectionate and well-liked. They are also more malleable. By comparison, field-independent students prefer individualized approaches, independent learning, and research projects. They tend to formulate their own goals and to respond to intrinsic reinforcement. They are independent-minded and prefer to develop their own learning strategies once they know what is required of them. Socially, field-independent people tend to be analytical and impersonal in their interactions with others. As a result, they are less susceptible to group pressures, less conforming, and less sensitive to other people's feelings.

Students who differ in these ways do not necessarily differ in overall academic achievement, but each kind does have certain preferences and can perform better in certain kinds of subject matter and tasks than in others. Different perceptual styles may also lead to different preferences in occupational choice: in general, field-independent student favour mathematics and the sciences, while their field-dependent peers perform better in social studies and the humanities. Accordingly, field-independents tend to orient toward careers that require theoretical, analytical skills and systematic organization, whereas field-dependents favour occupations involving social skills and people.

Given these differences in orientation, preference, and perceptual style, it can be seen that psychological differentiation directly influences learning. It also affects teaching. In other words, teachers too are field-dependent and field-independent, and as such assume different teaching styles and teacher-student relationships, and vary in the way they perceive students and events. Although it is unclear whether students learn better with teachers whose styles resemble their own, or a combination of both types, research evidence shows that awareness and consideration of cognitive style on the part of teachers enable them to attain better results (Doebler and Eicke, 1979). The point is that being aware of one's own idiosyncrasies and the needs of others can form a basis on which better interpersonal relationships can be built. In this regard, it is important for teachers to realize their responsibility to respect a student's cognitive style and to enhance its effectiveness in learning, rather than to compete with it and attempt to make it conform with their own.

Providing for Diversity

The obvious range of student abilities, aptitudes, learning styles, and aspirations within the same classroom calls for the provision of diversity in learning and social development. Unfortunately, the majority of teachers are mostly concerned with covering the prescribed curriculum and maintaining a standard of achievement. What may constitute the most challenging task of teaching is upholding standards of excellence, *while at the same time providing for student diversity especially as it is influenced by cultural and ethnic minority group factors.*

The curriculum content and the expected standards of achievement, including the rate of progress, can be easily communicated to students. Within the limits of these requirements, it should be possible to engage each student in self-regulated learning so that he or she can proceed through the school year according to individual capabilities and will. In order to implement self-regulated learning, it is essential that the teacher help students to change their views of learning success: to learn to view success as a systematic way of exceeding their own standards rather than simply as a comparison of their performance with an external standard. As long as students are proceeding positively towards the attainment of a set curricular goal, it is reasonable to allow them to regulate their own day-to-day progress. By doing so, the teacher helps them to assume the responsibility for planning and monitoring their own learning.

Learning requires full personal involvement, and one learns best if one is in control of one's own learning situation. Control of the learning situation means seeing significance in what is being learned, understanding the limits and expectations, and feeling in command of the relevant activities and rate of progress. For many years, teachers erroneously believed that if they allowed students to set their own daily or weekly learning goals, the students would set such low standards that they would experience no gain at the end of the year. Research evidence shows, on the contrary, that when children are allowed to monitor their own standards they tend to set moderate but attainable learning goals that go slightly beyond their current performance levels (Covington and Beery, 1976). In addition, research in mastery learning (Bloom, 1976) has suggested a variety of methods by which a prescribed curricular standard can be reached with appropriate accommodation of differences in learning rates. For example, slow-learning students could be allowed to have additional time for instruction and practice, while their faster-learning peers are given opportunities for enrichment programs or elective projects. As long as sufficient time and assistance are provided, the majority of students can attain the same prescribed performance standards in most school subjects within the time set for a course.

To allow for diversity also means allowing for cultural differences in learning style, including modes of communication and self-expression. We saw earlier that children differ in a wide range of skills, including expression. Some express themselves best through the use of words, while others may be more effective using other media. Within a single medium of expression, such as writing, some students may prefer to write long detailed essays, while others may favour short summaries that are to the point. A teacher can encourage this individualism by allowing students to set their own goals and to present their work in a variety of ways or media.

Providing for diversity in teaching and learning is important, not only because of individual differences, but also because diverse expressions communicate richness in concept and in perception which themselves constitute important 'content' for learning and socialization. Diversity in operation as well as in product fosters further diversity, which reflects and accommodates the wide range of needs and expectations of people in a society. In a pluralistic society that values differences within unity, teaching for as wide a range of expressions as possible in an essential way to uphold this social value. In education, diversity is best served by teaching individual students well, and by helping every one of them to learn, develop, and aspire in his or her own way.

Promoting Personal Excellence

Personal excellence exists in an interpersonal context. Students are often motivated to excel by group forces that have some special meaning for them. From the principles of human development, we know that such important skills and qualities as language, values, perception, and knowledge develop and grow on the basis of interpersonal relations. In order to accommodate individual differences in education, therefore, we must adopt a two-pronged approach to teaching. On the one hand, teachers should encourage and facilitate individual learning; but on the other hand, they need to create a sense of community or togetherness among the members of a class. Not only should each student develop a personal sense of purpose and an awareness of self, but he or she must also learn to relate to and work with others in group situations.

This dual task of the teacher is perhaps more critical today than it has ever been. Increased mobility and urbanization have produced conflicting effects on human relationships. Our quest to fulfill individual goals often takes us in directions away from others, yet we also need to feel part of a group. No one can argue with these differing needs, and it is one of the school's most important tasks to teach young people how to balance them.

As teachers, how do we interpret the concept of equal opportunity in education? Suppose you are a high school teacher who is confronted by a father who asks: "Why can't my son go to university? I pay taxes just like everybody else." If you know that his son cannot even meet Grade 10 standards, you might answer: "I am afraid, sir, that your son doesn't have the abilities needed by a univer-sity-bound student." You are quite certain about this point since all the records and your own observation support your judgement. Your conscience is clear. Back in the classroom, you present 30 students with the same material and ask them to do the same assignments. Moreover, you mark their assignments with the same standards and expectations in mind for all. Suppose that same father attended your class, and at the end of it asked you: "You said that my son is not like other students. So why do you teach them all in the same way?" Again, your answer may be quite simple: "Look, there are 30 students and just one of me. I plan my lessons to suit the aver-age student. By doing this, I am trying to meet the needs of the largest sector of my students. I do also try to allow for individual differences by asking different students different kinds of questions. But I basically have to teach this way because this is how our school is organized; otherwise you would have to pay higher taxes!"

Although this is a hypothetical situation, the questions and an-swers are real enough. John Gardner (1963) in his book *Excellence - Can We be Equal and Excellent Too?* asks: "What do we mean when we say 'Let the best man win?' Can an egalitarian society tolerate winners?" The dilemma is clear. If we ignore individual differences in ability, motivation, and performance, and if we protect the slow and curb the swift, we will end up promoting mediocrity, in which case the very survival of our society will be at stake. On the other hand, if we emphasize competition and encourage the best person to win all the time,we will cater to the middle class elite at the expense of ethnic minority students.

The same dilemma exists on a smaller scale in our classrooms. One of the most significant discoveries of educational research is that among the large number of school dropouts there are students of all levels of ability and performance. Precisely what causes bright as well as less able students to drop out of school is difficult to de-termine. However, it is reasonable to speculate that schools, by ca-tering too much to the average student, have failed to satisfy the needs of non-average students.

The present urgent task of education is to develop a way of teaching and learning that will fulfill the quests for equality and ex-cellence at the same time. For an individual to be equal to others and yet to strive for excellence are not necessarily contradictory needs. As one sets out to achieve excellence, one is likely to estab-lish goals relative to one's own ability and level of aspiration. At the same time, external standards of excellence provide one with a frame of reference with which to compare one's personal goals. Therefore, as long as a person is not prevented by others from working toward his or her goals, they can be reached.

There should be little doubt that equal opportunity in education should be interpreted within the context of an individual's own concept of excellence. In other words, one should be entitled to as much educational opportunity as one's abilities and aspirations require. If this opportunity is assured, there is no need to demand that all people must be given exactly the same education.

How can our schools help children to develop both a sense of equality and a self-motivated desire to attain excellence when there are so many differences among them? What can teachers do to enable every student to achieve his or her own standard of excellence within the limitations of the curriculum and existing classroom conditions? Such a complex and fundamental issue, which does not appear to have an easy solution, might well cause a teacher to feel discouraged and despairing. But when one looks at some of the new developments that are emerging in education, it is hard not to become hopeful and excited. From this perspective, let us look at some innovations that promise more individualized teaching in schools.

Innovations to Accommodate Individual Differences

To begin with, our school organization has undergone considerable changes in the last two decades, and is still changing as we move into the future. Unfortunately, the basic organization that we have inherited from the nineteenth century remains largely intact. For example, we still group children together by age and confine learning activities to the classroom. There are, of course, sound economic and social reasons for this kind of organization, but few sound educational reasons. As we saw earlier in this chapter, grouping children by age results in a class with a wide range of abilities, interests and performance levels. In addition, the conventional classroom, bound by four walls, severely restricts diversified learning activities. For example, learning that involves multisensory experiences and direct observation of natural phenomena is virtually impossible. In some situations the physical limitations also prohibit grouping children by interest.

However, despite these limitations, many important experiments have been conducted to create a more flexible and responsive environment within the conventional organizational structure of the classroom. For example, many schools now practice continuous progress plans where individual students are permitted to move up to a higher grade when they prove that they are ready for it. In fact, one version of the continuous progress plan also takes into account the fact that students do not necessarily progress equally in all subjects, so that a multigrade timetable is possible. Arrangements are made for non-average students, whether exceptionally bright or handicapped, to participate in a number of different educational environments during the week. Open-concept schools are designed in such a way as to allow for a blending of group instruction and individual learning.

As long ago as 1962, Harold Shane reported on 35 different plans for grouping children together for learning that could be arranged within the conventional school structure. The educational literature is full of debates on the merits and demerits of such plans. However, all are based on certain assumptions that must be examined very carefully. For example, in ability grouping it is assumed that students with similar abilities will benefit more from each other's company than students with different abilities, yet there is no psychological evidence to support this assumption. In fact, a comprehensive report (Goldberg *et al.*, 1966) showed that ability grouping in itself has no significant effect on academic achievement. What matters is what we do with the groups and how we use interpersonal dynamics to foster learning. Grouping by ability or interest merely provides a presumably more favourable setting in which some unique activity may take place.

Along with school organization, educational goals and curriculum design have also undergone considerable changes in recent decades. The goals of education have, in fact, shifted so drastically that unless teachers make an effort to deliberate on their implications they could be working against the very goals that the educational system is intended to achieve. As an illustration, a recently published set of goals for secondary education in Ontario (Stephenson, 1980) listed 13 goals for the development of every aspect of life, only three of which pertained directly to academic learning. Yet in practice, many teachers, perhaps influenced by old-fashioned administrators or by ingrained habits through years of teaching, still regard academic learning as the only purpose of schooling.

A serious effort of sensitization to the need for change is required. In Ontario, as in many areas of North America, a significant change in curriculum design began in the early 1960s (Frye, 1962). From the ideas that were put into practice, four basic requirements to facilitate individualized education have emerged:

1. A core of basic concepts around which specific instructional programs may be organized and flexibly implemented.
2. Emphasis on direct discovery experiences and the inductive process of learning.
3. Emphasis on the resource centre, which contains books, reference materials, audio-visual equipment, learning kits, life materials, human resources, programmed materials, computer terminals and modular programs for students to use at will.
4. Emphasis on the development of all aspects of human potential and life skills.

These concepts of curriculum design enable both student and teacher to approach learning from diverse standpoints, guided by personal interest, ability, and the initiative to explore what lies beyond the immediate environment. The curriculum becomes a frame of reference within which students are free to set up individual learning goals. The teacher accordingly becomes an organic part of the learning environment, serving as a resource person and encouraging students during the course of their learning ventures. Instead of merely being responsible for the organization and presentation of a fixed body of facts, teachers are now also responsible for adapting themselves to the diverse requirements of the learners, and coordinating their activities with matching facilities. It almost goes without saying that to discharge these responsibilities effectively, they must develop a personal knowledge of and a trustful relationship with every student under their care.

There are also many innovations in instructional design that can help teachers cater to individual needs. An example is the Contingency Contracting System, which incorporates realistic, individually set learning goals, absolute standards of performance, clearly defined objectives, and an evaluation policy that reflects all of these elements. For the larger portion of curriculum content, every student in the class follows a similar work pattern. In addition, however, each is allowed to undertake one or a number of individual learning 'contracts', for which small sections of the curriculum are set aside. The contracts may be large or small, but each involves three important facets:

1) A clear statement, usually formulated by the student, of the task to be done.
2) A statement of the standard or quality of work required as a result of a negotiation between the student and teacher.
3) A statement of the reward (credit, mark, etc.) that will be given to the student when he or she has completed the requirements.

Contingency contracting means that students can match their skill level with a selected task difficulty along a continuum of progress. The learning, therefore, is non-competitive. Students know what is required of them, are clear about what needs to be done to meet those requirements, and are able to control the opportunity for success by manipulating the amount and quality of their own efforts relative to the task. They develop a task orientation in which the emphasis is on accomplishment rather than on response to an externally imposed assignment. But the real merit of contingency contracting is that they can approach a learning goal at a rate and with the kind of activity that they find most suitable.

Another innovative instruction technique is Mastery Learning, which attempts to break up the learning of a body of knowledge or a concept into small tasks. These tasks are then organized into a sequentially ordered unit so that one task is prerequisite to another, and more complex tasks are composed of simpler ones. When learning material is arranged in a hierarchy of this kind, each student can proceed to learn at his or her own rate. The teacher first assesses all students to decide at which point they should enter the sequence, and instruction then begins at the level above those steps that have already been mastered. In this way, everyone is credited with what they already know so that no time is wasted on familiar tasks. This also means that members of a class can work at many different levels at a given time during the school term.

With mastery learning materials, students can either work alone or in small groups. During a class period, some members of the class might work independently while the teacher attends to the individual needs of others. However, it must be pointed out that certain school subjects are more amenable to a sequenced organization than others. In some subjects, such as literature and social studies, teachers might find themselves creating an arbitrary or artificial hierarchy of material that, by its nature, cannot readily be classified in this manner. In addition, some students simply are incapable of working independently without extensive training and unless their confidence is built up.

In addition to instruction systems, new technologies also offer immense opportunities for individualized teaching and learning. Perhaps the most versatile educational technology, and one that will be increasingly available in the future, lies in the area of computer-assisted instruction. Computer-assisted instruction is a system that allows a student to interact with a computer terminal in much the same way as with a tutor. With good programming a computer can act as the best of tutors, storing all the pertinent facts about a student's capabilities, work habits, motivational needs, and performance level, and able to accommodate every facet of these learning needs.

Basically, there are two types of computer-assisted instruction programs: drill programs and tutorial programs (Suppes and Momingston, 1972). In a drill program, the classroom teacher handles the conceptual teaching of a new topic or subject content, and the computer then provides the opportunity for individual students to 'drill' or practice what has been learned. A tutorial program, in contrast, provides basic instruction as well as the necessary drill sessions.

As an educational tool, computer-assisted instruction has many advantages. It can serve as a teacher-substitute in many academic aspects of the curriculum, if it is available whenever a student requires it and allows him or her to practise and review material over and over again. This way, the instruction is highly individualized since the student determines when he or she is ready for the next step. The computer also provides immediate feedback, such as positive reinforcement for success or more drills if is required. Finally, it is capable of being humorous and interactive however much it is being belaboured by the slowest learner. For more inspired and capable students, it offers the excitement of being able to write instructional programs themselves. Often the pay-off from such an activity is not only learning and achievement but invention. As we move into the future, the extensive use of computer-assisted instruction, along with other educational innovations, promises to provide the maximum range of diversity in learning for all students to proceed at their own pace and in a manner that is most appropriate and satisfying for them.

Summary

We saw earlier how human beings vary in many respects, and that there will be extensive differences among the students of a class grouped by age. As long as our present school organization prevails, these individual differences will increase in every dimension as children proceed to higher grades. Intelligence, socioeconomic background, gender, sex roles, and cognitive styles all account for educationally relevant individual differences, and affect learning and development implications for teaching.

Conflicts arise when teachers are expected to teach all students equally despite their obvious differences in interests, abilities, learning style, and aspirations. Such conflicts can be resolved by a realistic interpretation of equal opportunities for learning: that is, that all students should be provided with the opportunity and guidance to work out a set of personal goals and standards of excellence that are uniquely appropriate to their own capabilities and aspirations. The fundamental responsibility of contemporary teachers is to help students (especially those that differ markedly from the mainstream) establish such goals and standards, and to guide them in learning.

The question of how to personalize teaching in our present school system was examined in relation to the realities of our educational environment. There is no doubt that prevailing conditions somewhat restrict teachers from relating to students on a personal level. However, there are strong indications that many of the restrictions are vanishing and are being replaced by new systems of organization, curriculum design, and instructional methods and technologies that promise more flexible and favourable conditions.

We believe that ultimately teachers are personally responsible for understanding and accommodating the conditions and special needs of an increasingly complex population of students under their care. The cultural diversity that has been occurring, especially since the early '60s, has intensified the need for more awareness and a more appropriate program of pre-service and in-service teacher training. What is needed is that, if we are to achieve a modicum of educational equity, teachers must become sensitive to both the evolving needs of individual students, and the changing conditions and technologies that are emerging to enable them to fulfill their learning potential.

Chapter 7

Institutionalized Racism and the Assessment of Minority Children: A Comparison of Policies and Programs in the United States and Canada

Jim Cummins

Institutionalized racism can be defined as ideologies and structures that are used to systematically legitimize unequal division of power and resources (both material and non-material) between groups that are defined on the basis of race or ethnicity (see Skutnabb-Kangas and Cummins, in press). Discrimination can be brought about both by the ways in which particular institutions (e.g., schools) are organized or structured, and by the (usually) implicit assumptions that legitimize and perpetuate that organization.

An example of institutionalized racism in the educational system can be seen in the fact that in the United States until the 1970s there were three to four times as many black and Hispanic students in classes for the educable mentally retarded as would be expected on the basis of their proportion in the school population (Mercer, 1973). This overrepresentation was brought about both by the organization of curriculum and teaching practices to reflect middle-class dominant group values and experiences, thereby promoting academic difficulties among minority students, and by the subsequent selection of students for special education on the basis of IQ tests that incorporated the same cultural and linguistic biases as the classrooms (see Cummins, 1984; Samuda, 1975). This structure was legitimized by the assumption that IQ tests were valid indicators of minority students' academic abilities, and that their school failure was an inevitable consequence of mental inferiority due to one or more of the following factors: genetic inferiority, bilingualism, linguistic deficiency, or cultural deprivation (see Hakuta, 1986, for a review). In other words, standardized achievement and IQ tests 'located' the cause of minority students' educational difficulties within the students themselves, thereby screening from critical scrutiny the interactions that the children experienced within the school system. In this way the institutionalized racism reflected in the use of standardized tests and the assumptions that legitimized this use were contributing directly to the educational disabling of certain ethnic groups.

The data regarding the massive overrepresentation of minority children in special education classes have been available for almost 20 years. To what extent have policy-makers, academics, and school administrators in both the United States and Canada instituted policies and programs to redress institutionalized racism in the assessment process? Have the multiculturalism policies in various provinces and school systems made Canadian educators more sensitive to this issue than their American colleagues, whose social policies are more overtly oriented to rapid assimilation of minorities? Alternatively, has the American concern for equality of educational opportunity during the 1960s and since resulted in a greater resolve to eradicate bias in testing? To what extent have educators in both countries taken account of the research data available on issues related to minority children's language development and bilingualism?

We will first briefly review the conceptual issues that must be addressed when developing programs and policies regarding assessment of minority students, and the research that bears on these issues. Next, the policy response in both countries will be analyzed. Finally, directions for eradicating institutional racism in the assessment process will be outlined.

Issues and Research

During the past 15 years the number of students in both the United States and Canada whose home language is different from that of the school has grown dramatically. In an increasing number of major urban school systems, more than half the students have learned English (or French, in Quebec) as a second language or speak a nonstandard variety of English.

What are the implications of these demographic changes for special education, particularly for psychoeducational assessment? To what extent are typical IQ tests culturally and linguistically biased? How can psychologists tell if a student's difficulties are due to a genuine learning disorder, as opposed to a lack of proficiency in English? How long should educators delay psychoeducational assessment of such students, and what are the implications of a delay for those with genuine learning problems? What advice should be given to immigrant parents regarding language use — specifically, should parents of children with learning problems be advised to use English as much as possible at home? For minority parents, the issues are equally complex and problematic. How much confidence should they place in the judgement of experts regarding the causes of their child's learning difficulties? Should they accept the frequent contention that the use of a different language at home is contributing to these difficulties? How can they help their child with homework when they themselves may not be fluent in the school language?

Research relating to these issues will be reviewed under three categories: 1) the extent to which typical IQ tests are biased against minority students; 2) the length of time it takes students to learn different aspects of English; and 3) issues related to bilingualism and home language use.

In an analysis of more than 400 psychological assessments of minority students (Cummins, 1984), subjects were found to perform very much below norms on the Wechsler Intelligence Scale for Children Revised (WISC-R), the most commonly used individual IQ test in North American schools. Performance was significantly more depressed on the verbal parts of the test than on the non-verbal parts.

On the *Information* subtest, which attempts to assess what children have learned as a result of their previous experiences, minority children obtained a median scale score of 4.9 compared to the norm of 10.0. Seventy percent obtained a scale score of 6 or below compared to only 16% for the test norming sample, while more than one-third (34%) scored 3 or below, compared to 2.5 percent for the norm. This pattern of results is hardly surprising when one considers the content of the test. Questions such as "How many pennies in a nickel?" and "Who discovered America?" and "How tall is the average Canadian man?" all depend on experiences specific to a middle-class North American milieu. Minority students typically have not had these experiences. In this study it was found that scores on the *Information* subtest were usually entered into computation of the child's IQ despite obvious cultural and linguistic bias in the test.

How Long Does it Take to Learn English?

Of central importance to the issue of appropriate use of IQ tests among immigrant students is the question of how long it takes them to develop English academic language skills (e.g., vocabulary knowledge) equivalent to those of native speakers on whom the norms are largely based. Several conclusions about academic achievement seem warranted on the basis of the research on the learning of English as a second language. First, it is necessary to distinguish between the acquisition of *conversational* skills, and those skills required for *academic success*. Very different time periods are required to achieve peer-appropriate levels in these two aspects of second-language proficiency. Specifically, conversational skills often approach native-like levels within about two years of exposure, whereas for academic proficiency, it appears that a period of at least five years, on average, may be required (Cummins, 1984). This pattern can be attributed to the fact that in face-to-face conversation the meaning is supported by a range of contextual cues (e.g., the concrete situation, gestures, intonation, facial expression, etc.) whereas this is seldom the case for academic uses of language, as in reading a text.

In the Cummins (1984) study it was found that psychologists often failed to take account of the difference between these two aspects of proficiency. Because minority students often *appeared* to be fluent in English, there was a tendency to assume that they had overcome all language problems and that IQ tests administered in English would be valid. The data clearly show that this assumption was unfounded.

In short, the research evidence suggests that verbal psychological tests tend to underestimate minority students' academic potential until they have been learning the school language for at least five years. Thus, for students who have been speaking it for less than this period, it becomes extremely problematic to attempt diagnoses of learning disabilities, since any genuine problems are likely to be masked by as yet inadequately developed language proficiency.

Bilingualism and Home Language Use

A large number of research studies show that bilingualism in itself does not exert any negative influence on children's academic development. In fact, there are many studies suggesting that when both languages continue to develop, bilingual children's school progress and intellectual growth are enhanced.

However, educators have frequently advised immigrant parents to use the school language at home on the grounds that exposure to a different language will confuse the children and impede their school progress. Parents who accept this advice are likely to expose their children to poor models of English. Furthermore, if the parents' English is not well founded, then the intellectual and emotional quality of communication in the home may well suffer.

There are currently a large number of research studies showing clearly that what matters most for immigrant students' academic success is not the language being used in the home, but the quality of communication between adults and children (see Cummins, 1984, for a review). Thus, if parents want their children to reap the personal and academic benefits of full bilingualism, they should use their own language as much as possible. Educators should advise parents on ways to expose their children to a rich linguistic environment (e.g., reading and telling stories, discussions, etc.) through their mother tongue. Children who come to school with a solid conceptual foundation in Chinese, Italian, Portuguese, etc., will have little difficulty transferring this foundation to the school language. On the other hand, the child who comes to school fluent in surface aspects of English but with little conceptual foundation will likely experience considerable academic difficulty.

By the same token, there is no validity to the common assumption among psychologists and other educators that children with learning difficulties should be excluded from heritage language (mother tongue) classes or bilingual programs. The research data show positive transfer and mutual reinforcement of academic skills across languages. It surely makes sense to develop children's academic potential through the two linguistic channels that mediate their out-of-school experience with the world.

The policy response in the United States and Canada

In the United States, the field of bilingual special education has emerged from efforts dating to the mid-1960s to promote equality of educational opportunity for students from social and cultural minority groups. The underachievement of black, Hispanic, and Native American groups has been documented by the Coleman Report (Coleman et al., 1966) and many subsequent studies. As noted above, research has also shown that minority students were more than three times as likely to be placed in classes for the educable mentally retarded as would be expected from their numbers (Mercer, 1973). Culturally- and linguistically-biased psychological assessment procedures were established as a major culprit in this overrepresentation. Litigation in the United States increasingly established the right of minority students to a non-biased assessment, which, in the case of students from non-English-speaking backgrounds, involved assessment through the primary or dominant language (e.g., Diana vs. State Board of Education [1970] in California). This provision was explicitly incorporated into Public Law (PL) 94-142, which guaranteed to all handicapped children in the United States an education appropriate to their needs. Children were required to be assessed in their most proficient language "unless it is clearly not feasible to do so."

Concurrent with this increasing concern for nondiscriminatory assessment was the emergence of bilingual education as a programmatic response to the underachievement of non-native English speakers. The Bilingual Education Act of 1968 provided funds for a limited number of bilingual programs in order to explore their effectiveness in reducing underachievement, primarily among Hispanic students. However, it was not until after the 1974 Lau vs. Nichols decision by the U.S. Supreme Court that bilingual education was established by the Office of Civil Rights as the favoured remedy to redress minority students' educational difficulties. Controversy continues unabated regarding the extent to which bilingual education is appropriate and effective in promoting minority students' educational development (Hakuta, 1986).

The field of 'bilingual special education' is a natural outgrowth of the increasing prominence during the 1970s of both bilingual education for language minority students and special education for the handicapped. In the United States, the primary users of bilingual special education are language minority students who are suspected of being either educationally handicapped or gifted in some way. The establishment of the field has resulted in recent years in considerable research and development funds being allocated to issues of assessment and the exploration of programming for handicapped (and gifted) minority students.

Despite the clear policy response in the United States, the available evidence suggests that the initiatives in bilingual special education undertaken during the past decade have been only marginally successful in redressing problems. While overrepresentation of minorities in classes for the educable mentally retarded has been virtually eliminated, there has been a corresponding increase of overrepresentation in learning disability (LD) classes (Dew, 1984; Tucker, 1980). Ortiz and Yates (1983), for example, report a 300% overrepresentation of Hispanic students in LD classes in Texas. Other studies show major disjunctions between policy and practice when it comes to fair assessment (Garcia and Yates, 1986; Maldonado-Colon, 1986). Significant knowledge gaps on the part of psychologists have also been identified regarding issues such as limitations of standardized tests, bilingual language use in the home, and patterns of language development (Cummins, 1984).

In short, the structure of discrimination within the American educational system has largely maintained itself, despite apparently strong legal and educational provisions to institute equality of opportunity. It appears that although policy, legal, and programmatic initiatives are necessary for real change to occur, they are not sufficient. Educators must redefine their roles so that their interactions with minority children and communities challenge the societal power structure, rather than simply reflect it (Cummins, 1986). This process appears not to have taken place to any major extent.

In Canada, many of these same issues are increasingly being discussed by educators and policy-makers, but up to this point there has been a marked lack of policy and research initiatives such as those that have been undertaken in the United States. Special education initiatives have been implemented in several provinces with provisions similar, in most respects, to those embodied in PL 94-142. However, legislation (e.g., Bill 82 in Ontario) makes virtually no reference to nondiscriminatory assessment of minority students; no courses are offered in Canadian universities on issues related specifically to bilingual special education; and research or theoretical papers devoted to the special education of minority students are virtually absent from Canadian special education (or mainstream education) journals. It is worth noting that in contrast there has, however, been considerable research on special education issues related to mainstream students in French immersion programs. Although the number of students in such programs is very much less than that of minority students in the general educational system, research on French immersion appears to be a considerably greater priority. This is presumably because parents of children in immersion are members of the dominant middle-class group, and know how to access the power structure to have their priorities acted upon.

To what extent have multicultural education policies influenced assessment and placement of minority students in Canada? Very little, it appears. The Ontario Ministry of Education commissioned a survey of policies and programs with respect to testing, assessment, counselling, and placement of minority students in the late 1970s (Samuda and Crawford, 1980). This report, which is discussed more fully in chapter 8, documented the fact that a large majority of school boards had no policies or special provision regarding these issues.

Ethnocultural community groups have been expressing concerns about discriminatory assessment and streaming of minority students into vocational programs since the early 1970s. First, the Dante Aligheri Society raised these issues with the Toronto Board on behalf of Italian students; more recently, Portuguese, Greek, and black parents have voiced similar concerns. In the late 1970s several boards of education adopted policies of delaying formal educational and psychological assessment of minority students until they have been in Canada for at least two years. However, this period was based on assumptions of how long it takes children to learn English, rather than on any empirical data. As noted above, the data suggest that a much longer period (at least five years on average) is required for immigrant students to catch up to native speakers in academic aspects of English, although they may acquire relatively fluent conversational skills within two years.

During the period that multicultural policies were being developed and implemented by a number of the larger urban school boards in Ontario, the province was also developing its special education legislation, Bill 82. However, the two processes appear to have proceeded independently, with minimal discussion of the extent to which the identification and assessment provisions of Bill 82 might discriminate against minorities.

In support documents dealing with the bill, discussion of questions related to nondiscriminatory assessment is limited to vague cautions such as: "Where a child's language is other than English or French, a reasonable delay in the language-based aspects of assessment should be considered." A more recent memorandum to school boards gives somewhat greater recognition to potential problems: if a pupil's first language is other than English or French and/ or the pupil has facility in neither of these languages, consideration should be given to postponing assessment, or, where possible, conducting it in the child's first language. (Policy/Program Memorandum No. 59, p. 2).

However, no suggestions are given as to what constitutes a 'reasonable' delay, nor are pitfalls associated with first-language assessment considered. There appears to have been no obvious response at a policy level to the findings of the Samuda and Crawford (1980) report showing that many school boards across the province fail to pay even lip-service to Ministry guidelines regarding the testing of minority students. Apart from a handful of school boards, there is little evidence that minority students' cultural and/or linguistic backgrounds are systematically being taken into account in the identification and placement process. Similarly, although Bill 82 mandates parental participation in Identification, Placement and Review Committee (IPRC) meetings, little evidence exists of sustained consideration of how to ensure this in a meaningful way when the parents do not speak fluent English and/or do not understand the purpose or consequences of placement decisions.

The lack of consideration of non-discriminatory assessment in the drafting of Bill 82 raises some disturbing questions. For example, was the issue ignored because those who drafted Bill 82 were genuinely ignorant of it, or because they considered it to be unimportant or marginal? The first supposition is hardly credible, since the issue was highlighted in most of the major academic journals in special education and school psychology during the previous decade. Thus, it may be that it was simply an awkward one that was more convenient to ignore than to deal with. The lack of awareness among ethnocultural groups and opposition parties to the implications of the legislation for minority children certainly facilitated this strategy.

The bill constitutes a prime example of how institutionalized racism can inadvertently be perpetuated at a policy or legal level.

In short, academics, policy-makers, and to some extent administrators on school boards have tended to show little sensitivity to issues concerned with nondiscriminatory assessment, despite the evidence from the United States and Canada that typical psychological assessment procedures significantly underestimate the academic potential of minority students. No specific training has been or is currently being provided for psychologists on issues related to bilingualism and minority language development, again despite considerable evidence that misconceptions about the effects of bilingual language use in the home and the learning of heritage languages at school are common among psychologists and other educators. Institutionalized racism with respect to assessment has remained virtually unchallenged at the levels of policy and legal provision, professional training and certification, and (with a few exceptions) school board programs.

Directions for change

Implications for Educators

Implementation of strategies to reverse discriminatory assessment policies is likely to be complex, since these policies are rooted in the very organization of school systems and in the conceptualization of entire fields such as special education and school psychology, where the normative 'medical model' of scholastic dysfunction still predominates. The research data (e.g., Ortiz and Yates, 1983) suggest that the structure within which psychological assessment takes place orients the psychologist to locate the cause of the academic problem within the minority students themselves, and that policy changes alone are unlikely to significantly alter this structure.

For educators, the first step towards change is to shift the focus of assessment from the individual child to the child's entire learning environment, i.e., the interactions that he or she has both within and outside the school. It is virtually inevitable that assessment will be disabling when the only tools at the assessor's disposal are psychological tests (whether in the child's first language or English). Since the tests focus only on psychological processes, educational difficulties will, of necessity, be attributed to psychological dysfunctions. To challenge such disabling, the assessment must focus on the extent to which: 1) children's language and culture are incorporated within the school program; 2) educators collaborate with parents as partners in a shared enterprise; and 3) children are encouraged to use both their own and the school language actively within the classroom to amplify their experiences and interactions. In other words, the primary focus should be on improving the educational interactions that minority children experience.

Second, educators should *never* advise parents to switch to English in the home. The assumption that "learning two languages will confuse children" has been totally discredited by the evidence. If parents are completely fluent in English, then use of English in the home is not a problem; however, if this condition is not met, then the quality of communication in the home is likely to suffer. Educators should inform themselves about which patterns of language use in bilingual homes are less desirable (e.g., lack of consistency in use of each language) and discuss these issues with parents. However, advice should be aimed at helping parents develop their children's conceptual foundation in both languages. This is especially the case if a child is experiencing academic difficulties.

In addition, all school boards should devise explicit policies regarding assessment and placement of minority students that take account of the research data. Failure to do so would be to prompt litigation from community groups on the grounds of violation of the Charter of Rights and Freedoms.

School boards should consider adopting a model similar to the multicultural consultant model used by the North York Board of Education in Ontario. In that board, professionals assess children's educational and conceptual background in their first language. This model also involves the training of paraprofessional assessment translators who administer assessments for children from less numerous minority groups under the supervision of the multicultural consultant.

Steps should also be taken to ensure meaningful parental participation in placement decisions. Currently, many minority parents have little idea of what a psychological assessment entails; they do not understand terms such as hyperactivity, learning ability, etc., even when attempts are made to translate these terms into their own language. In short, they are suspicious about the entire process, and are concerned — perhaps with some justification — that their children may be given a one-way ticket to a special education class.

Implications for Minority Parents

In view of the lack of training of many psychologists on issues related to bilingualism and second-language development, parents should be wary about blindly accepting the interpretation and advice of educators with respect to assessment and placement issues. Minority communities can play a major role in pressuring school boards and universities to seriously address the issue of the assessment of their children. Specifically, they should consider writing to directors of boards of education and/or government policy makers to seek answers to questions such as the following:

1. What *specific* training have psychologists and other special educators received on issues related to bilingualism and minority students' development?
2. What are the board and government policies regarding the psychological assessment of children from bilingual backgrounds?
3. To what extent do board and government policies (if they exist) reflect the research showing that verbal IQ or achievement tests are likely to seriously underestimate minority students' academic potential until they have been learning the school language for at least five years?
4. What steps have been taken to ensure meaningful parental participation in placement decisions when the parents do not speak English and may have little understanding about the entire special education process?

Conclusion

It has been suggested that we still have a considerable way to go in adapting special education assessment and placement procedures to the changing multicultural reality across North America. Little confidence can be placed on norms developed for most tests currently in use (e.g., the WISC-R), for they are discriminatory and potentially damaging to minority students' academic prospects. What is equally damaging is the fact that current research knowledge regarding bilingualism is often not reflected in the assumptions and behaviour of special educators and psychologists. This knowledge base is also not reflected in classroom interactions. In view of this situation, and of the well-documented past abuses of psychological tests, minority parents should be skeptical about the opinions of the experts, and should also pressure boards of education and provincial or state governments to ensure that their children's rights are not being violated.

Chapter 8

Student Assessment and Placement in Ontario Schools

Ronald J. Samuda

The issues and problems of minority student assessment and placement are not unique to any one country or any one system. The recent and unprecedented influx of immigrants into areas like Dade County in Southern Florida and Toronto in Ontario, Canada, has forced educators to examine their standard practices in the use of tests to determine program placement for immigrant students. In fact, these concerns are of importance for all culturally diverse environments, especially in the urban industrial cities of North America. Whether we focus on the assessment of minorities in the Dade County school system or on the Toronto boards of education, we must face the same challenges. For, in a multicultural society, schools must play an active role in promoting understanding and mutual respect among all ethnic groups. In practical terms, one of the major tasks facing schools during this decade has been the redefinition of those educational objectives and guidelines "which eventually determine course content, teaching methods, personnel and extra-curricular activities" (Jaenen, 1972, p. 216). The challenge of implementing multiculturalism into an effective educational policy and practice remains one of the most critical undertakings of the 1980s.

As we have outlined in greater detail in chapter 1, Canadian society has undergone considerable change over the past quarter of a

century. In responding to the challenges of a more diverse population and the political demands of Quebec and powerful ethnic minority groups, the policy of multiculturalism was introduced to replace
the former assimilationist tradition of Canadian society. It also sig-
nalled a need to reshape educational policy and practice to fit the realities of ethnic diversity in the schools. In effect, a system that once
stressed assimilation and cultural dominance (Hodgetts, 1968;
McDiarmid and Pratt, 1971) has been modified to make it more responsive to the needs of its ethnic minority populations. Multiculturalism may in fact prove to be one of the most important policy initiatives ever undertaken by the Canadian educational system.

Multicultural Education in Ontario

Although policies on multiculturalism relate to everybody, they have
special significance for immigrant minority groups. Multiculturalism
is not, of course, the first government effort to preserve and accommodate the cultural integrity and viability of minority groups in Canada: it was preceded by policies directed towards two of the country's significant minorities, French Canadians and native peoples.
The efforts to legislate bilingualism and to reform native education
represented significant advances by the federal government. However, neither addressed the interests of a third presence in Canadian
society, namely, the many individuals whose backgrounds are neither English-Canadian, French-Canadian, or native.

The pressure for recognition and cultural parity came from these
'other' groups themselves, who, through various briefs presented to
the Royal Commission on Biculturalism and Bilingualism (subsequently published in Book IV of the Commission's report), emphasized the dynamic role played by immigrant groups and communities
in Canada's development.

The present government policy of multiculturalism within a bilingual framework therefore represents an attempt to provide an um-
brella under which all ethnic groups in Canada can be united. As former prime minister Pierre Trudeau observed on the occasion of the
policy's announcement:

> It was the view of the Royal Commission, shared by the government and, I am
> sure, by all Canadians, that there cannot be one cultural policy for Canadians
> of British and French origin, another for the original peoples and yet a third
> for others. For although there are two official languages, there is no official

culture, nor does any ethnic group take precedence over any other. No citizen or group of citizens is other than Canadian, and all should be treated fairly (House of Commons, October 8, 1971).

In Ontario, the adoption of an active multicultural policy has real significance. This province has a large immigrant population, largely made up of new Canadians who have arrived within the last two decades. Between 1967 and 1976, over 50 percent of all immigrants to Canada settled in Ontario (Statistics Canada, 1977), the vast majority in urban areas where the presence of large industrial and commercial enterprises offered good employment opportunities. In 1971, it was found that 43.6 percent of the population of Toronto had been born outside of Canada. High percentages of foreign-born residents were also noted in other urban areas, such as Hamilton and Ottawa.

The effect that this rapid, large-scale development has had, and still is having, on Canadian society cannot be reflected by mere numbers. Immigration introduces variables not only of culture and language, but of colour and other physical features. Since the opening up of the Canadian immigration policy in 1967, large numbers of visible minority immigrants from the West Indies, Asia, and Africa have poured into Canada. Although no precise data exist on the destinations of immigrants categorized by ethnic or national group, there is little doubt that most of them have settled in the urban centres of Ontario.

Ontario's multicultural policy evolved as a result of the provincial government's attempt to find an effective response to the rapidly shifting cultural base of its population. As early as 1969, it announced that "Canada should be a bilingual country while maintaining the multicultural character" (Ontario's Multicultural Policy, Ministry of Culture and Recreation). The changing population also necessitated an adjustment of the traditional values and methods of the educational system. The Work Group on Multiculturalism and other organizations submitted a report to the Ontario government, urging the initiation of an educational policy and program to promote multiculturalism. Although then-premier William Davis did not officially announce Onrario's multicultural policy until May 24, 1977, a curriculum guideline containing multicultural content had earlier been issued by the Ministry of Education.

Ontario's multicultural policy has three fundamental objectives: 1) equality, 2) access and participation, and 3) cultural retention and sharing. How are these objectives reflected in the province's current

educational policy and practice? What problems exist in transforming the policy into reality? What considerations are being taken into
account regarding assessment and placement of students? We will
look at the results of a study that may help to provide some answers to these questions.

Of the various procedures that school children undergo, perhaps
the most critical in terms of their future are assessment and placement. It is not difficult to see why. Placement decisions are made on
the basis of judgements about a student's level of achievement and
projections of future performance. Although in theory schools favour
the idea of flexible placement based on the constant monitoring of
progress, in practice placements are likely to be permanent, because
streaming and grouping students into homogeneous classes are
convenient for delivering teaching services. Such grouping goes
hand-in-hand with a reliance on standardized tests as a means of
predicting academic performance over relatively long periods of time,
often three years or more (Samuda, 1975). Decisions made when a
child is six or seven may determine not only the quality of that child's
education for the next ten years, but also his or her future prospects
as a working adult (Mercer, 1971). Similarly, placement decisions
made when students are being programmed into either vocational or
academically-oriented programs at the secondary school level have
far-reaching consequences in terms of their future educational prospects and, perhaps, socioeconomic level.

The significance of assessment and placement methods should
be considered not only from the child's perspective, but in relation to
the major functions that the school serves in society. One of these
functions is to act as a socializing agent. As Pratt (1975) observes,
the school is "the agency through which society makes its most deliberate attempt to structure socialization." Other educators would
readily agree. Hodgetts (1978), for example, suggests that schools
"reflect the society's compulsions and imperatives more sensitively
than any other social agency" and should be "tuned to the realities
of national and global trends and consciously designed to prepare
successive generations of young men and women for more rational
and compassionate leadership."

Assessment and placement are themselves processes of socialization because they are based upon culturally determined perceptions, beliefs, and values. We might ask, for example, how our
society defines intelligence. What types of accomplishments are to
be valued by the school as significant achievements? What qualities

constitute leadership and, to use Hodgetts' terms, what 'compulsions and imperatives' in society should the school respond to? These are questions that reveal the submerged content and biases in our assessment and placement practices (Mercer, 1978).

The most important roles that a school undertakes — those of dispenser of knowledge and skills, developer of human resources, and certifier of academic and technical competence — require it to make complex decisions about who gets what and who goes where. These functions, in turn, serve to highlight the critical importance of how a school that serves different ethnocultural groups approaches student assessment and placement.

The Problems of Assessment and Placement

In a survey of Ontario schools conducted by myself and others (Samuda *et al.*, 1979), principals and board officials were asked what they thought was the most difficult aspect of student placement. Their most common response was that of assessing students appropriately, particularly in the age group of 11 to 15 years. Some concerns expressed were: What is the best way to determine the students' level of functioning? Should we pay more attention to students' social development or to their academic development? How do we distinguish between a language problem and a learning problem? How do we know if a particular assessment is accurate?

For respondents who worked in schools with high ethnic concentrations, the process of assessment was further complicated by the lack of suitable academic records in the case of many immigrant students. It is not easy to bridge the gap between the expectations of Canadian schools and the experience of these students. In order to find solutions to this problem, it may be helpful to break it down into several areas of difficulty:

1. Diagnostic assessment;
2. The background of immigrant students;
3. The students' home language
4. The students' learning style and adjustment in school.

With regard to the first area of difficulty, diagnostic assessment, significant differences between the immigrant students and the population on which standardized test norms are based render such tests invalid (Mercer, 1971; Samuda, 1975). As a result, alternative methods for assessing the ability of students from non-mainstream backgrounds must be found. When neither adequate research facilities nor resource people familiar with the problems of cross-cultural testing are available on a school board, assessment and placement are likely to become contentious issues between the immigrant communities and the local schools. The situation is further complicated when students have incomplete or no academic records, for Canadian schools rely heavily on such records to make assessments. The training of teachers also often leaves them ill-equipped to operate effectively in a cross-cultural context, even when language is not a barrier. Thus, few teachers can draw from their students the pertinent information upon which an accurate assessment can be based. This, then, constitutes the second area of concern.

The third problem area, language, is perhaps the most critical. For example, it puts an obvious constraint on the use of standardized tests with students whose first language is not English, as well as presenting a serious barrier to communication between student and teacher. The fourth and final area of difficulty, learning style and personal adjustment, is very much rooted in the student's home culture and the quality of his or her initial interaction with peers and society at large. As Berry (1974, 1976) amply demonstrates, culture can have an enormous impact upon an individual's cognitive style. Learning styles that be appropriate in the home culture may prove to be inapplicable in the new school environment (Das, 1973). Thus, qualitative differences between a student's learning style and the mode of instruction in the school can heighten his or her feelings of disorientation and consequently impair academic performance.

The range of subtle behavioural contaminants increasing the difficulty of making a fair assessment becomes clear when one considers the scope of the changes that the immigrant student faces within the classroom. Danziger (1971) observed that among the Italian immigrant students he studied, there was a significant correlation between low motivation to achieve academically and low levels of self-esteem. Similarly, Beserve (1973) and Anderson and Grant (1975) found connections between the adjustment problems experienced by West Indian students and their problems with school work. All these problems suggest that Canadian schools face a serious challenge, and must make substantial adjustments in their assessment and placement procedures if they are to accommodate the exceptional circumstances presented by students from diverse cultures.

Our survey (Samuda *et al.*, 1979) was one of the first attempts to discover how schools across Ontario were responding to this challenge. This study was conducted in 34 school jurisdictions, including 245 elementary and secondary schools in both separate and public systems. Forty-eight percent of these schools were situated in Metropolitan Toronto. The sample was chosen in such a way as to include schools with significant populations of immigrant students belonging to the most recent immigrant groups to Ontario, namely, East Indians and Pakistanis, Portuguese, and West Indians. What follows is a point-by-point summary of the study's main findings. Despite the fact that the survey was conducted eight years ago, our informal conversations with teachers and board officials lead us to believe that the conditions have not changed all that much. The findings provide the basis for an overview of some significant trends and implications for the future.

Assessment Practice

1. Our survey showed that, in general, tests were used to a relatively limited extent as part of the initial placement process: only 29 percent of all the boards surveyed reported using them. Boards with a small ethnic population used tests far more frequently than those with medium or large ethnic populations. Boards in the areas of highest ethnic concentration indicated that they were not in favour of intelligence testing for students who had been in Canada for less than two years.
2. Assessment of a new student involved an evaluation of his or her academic records, an interview with the student's parents, and acquiring basic personal and demographic information, such as age, country of origin, etc.
3. When sufficient documentary evidence was not available, the tendency was to rely heavily on data gathered through the interview, and supplemented to some extent by standardized or teacher-made tests in mathematics and English. This was generally only necessary when the students were immigrants, since Canadian-born students usually have detailed records from their previous schools. The children would then be placed in a class and their progress monitored by the classroom teacher. The large boards in Metropolitan Toronto often have professional personnel such as social workers, community liai-

son officers, and psychologists to help with assessment and placement decisions.

4. Low academic achievement and difficulty with English were reported as the main criteria for deciding whether or not a student's initial placement should be reviewed. We were not able to gather data on how frequently initial placements were actually changed.

5. Tests appeared to be used much more frequently during the review process than during the initial placement. Teacher-made tests were among the most frequently used.

6. The majority of school boards (80 percent) reported modifying tests for immigrant students. Much lower levels of modification were reported by individual schools. Most modifications were minor rather than major: they consisted of time extensions, item deletion, and word substitutions. In general, there seemed to be a preference for leaving standardized tests intact, but allowing for freer interpretations of the results.

Placement Practice

1. Typically, most students would be placed in their appropriate grade level according to age.

2. Where it was considered inappropriate to place the student according to age, special placement would be made. Almost all respondents reported having special programs for alternative placement.

3. Three kinds of special placements were judged to be most relevant to immigrant minorities. They were: English-as-a-Second-Language or Dialect programs, academic upgrading, and remedial programs. These types of placements were also reported to be the most frequent special placements in schools.

4. The highest priority appeared to be given to ESL/D programs, which were reported as the most needed, and many respondents indicated that such programs were being developed. There was also a high demand for new orientation programs.

5. There was a greater demand for new special programs in schools outside of Metropolitan Toronto than inside it.

Certain general impressions that were gained from the study merit some elaboration at this point. First, it was apparent that few school boards had well-articulated policies with respect to the reception, assessment, and placement of ethnic minority students. Those that did were confined to jurisdictions in Metropolitan Toronto: responses to ten interview questions suggested that the school boards serving the areas with the highest ethnic concentration in Ontario — namely, those in Toronto — were responding in greater measure to the problems of new Canadian students. Second, there seemed to be little recognition of the need for special education programs for minority group students, except ESL/D programs. Third, ESL/D programs were often lumped together with other special education programs, such as services for the learning-handicapped, with which they are not compatible. Fourth, the level of ethnic concentration appeared to be the most critical factor in effecting change in individual school systems.

A fifth trend worth noting was the major role that the classroom teacher played in the assessment process, particularly in terms of interviewing and orienting new students, monitoring their progress after initial placement, identifying them for referral, and preparing and administering tests. These responsibilities raise the important question of whether teachers have the experiential background and training necessary to carry out these tasks competently.

Yet another significant finding was the little importance and attention given by school administrators to counselling. In 128 interviews on this subject, only one respondent made a specific reference to the involvement of guidance and counselling in assessment, and no procedural protocol seemed to exist for guidance teachers and counsellors to participate directly. Only a few Metropolitan Toronto schools with heavy ethnic concentrations required guidance personnel to be involved in assessment and placement processes. Moreover, there were sometimes marked discrepancies between the responses on this issue given by board officials and those given by school principals, indicating a gap between board policy and school practice. These discrepancies were more evident in large city school systems. We concluded that the guidance function was underused in most schools and would have to be given more attention as a means of helping minority students adapt to Canadian schools.

There is, of course, an inevitable time lag between the announcement of a given policy and its implementation in the locus of change. With regard to multiculturalism and education, a further explanation for the time lag might be found in the manner in which innovations generally have been initiated within Toronto school boards; that is, from the top — the 'top' being the board of trustees that is the ultimate policy maker (Murray, 1977). The politicians who often sit on such boards appear to be more sensitive to the concerns (with their possible political consequences) of their ethnic minority constituents. Teachers, on the other hand, are less prepared to initiate and promote change in the educational system, which may partially be due to their training and professional experiences, and to being overwhelmed by the rapidity of the changes occurring. The closer correlation between board and school responses in non-Toronto areas suggests that where few significant innovations were being initiated, there is likely to be a far greater congruence between policy and practice.

Future Outlook

Looking ahead, there seems little reason to expect substantial change or modification in the approach to student assessment and placement in areas outside of Metropolitan Toronto. Change in these jurisdictions is likely to be limited to the implementation of ESL programs and to some increases in personnel resources for remedial instruction and special education. In addition, since survey respondents expressed a relatively high concern for orientation programs, and frequently suggested community liaison and staff sensitization as ways to accommodate ethnic minority students, it is reasonable to anticipate some positive action in these areas.

In ideological terms, the assimilationist attitude still reigns high among teachers and school administrators. Even respondents in Toronto schools used expressions such as 'provide a holding centre', 'culturalize the students', 'provide a crash course in Canadian customs', and 'give students one year to adjust to Ontario culture', etc. when discussing how to accommodate new immigrants

Such attitudes, even among relatively enlightened educators, seem to indicate that multicultural policy will likely encounter a substantial degree of resistance from schools for some time to come. This prediction is supported by Murray's (1977) findings on the attitudes of professionals in the Toronto school system. He found that while there apparently was a good deal of support for the multicultural policy from board members, individual respondents indicated that certain segments of the school system and community were against or did not favour multicultural considerations in assessment and programming.

Central to the spirit of multiculturalism is the principle of *equality*. The concept of equality in education is not easy to understand and still less easy to put into practice. Among the misconceptions that exist is the assumption that equality of educational opportunities means that the same treatment should be given to all students. The phrase 'We treat them all alike' is often used as a defence against possible accusations of discrimination. There appears to be little appreciation among educators of important aspects of differential psychology that relate to education in cross-cultural contexts.

The question that now arises is whether Canadian schools will continue to maintain the social and economic interests of one particular group, as they have done in the past (Porter, 1965), or whether they can help generate changes in accordance with the realities of a new population. At present, immigrant students are being assessed and placed in accordance with procedures and standards established for average students from the mainstream of society. The outcome of this treatment is that their adjustment to their new country is often negatively affected, which can blight both their educational and career opportunities. If the problems of assessment and placement earlier discussed are to be satisfactorily resolved, schools must move from merely a reactionary stance on multiculturalism to a position of positive commitment.

Before this can occur, teachers and administrators must receive the kind of preparation and training that will enable them to become effective agents for change. First of all, they both need to have a clearer understanding of the basic goals of the government's multicultural policy. They will also need to know what this policy means in terms of educational goals and practice. While there are some published statements on educational policy and curriculum guidelines, it seems that much more discussion and exploration of this issue are needed. Second, present efforts in in-service education need to be expanded.

Fortunately, there is increasing recognition of the need for system sensitization. The nature of this sensitization has already been given serious thought by a number of educators. It should be stressed, however, that teacher involvement should be universal rather than selective. "To argue that teachers who have certain specializations, or who intend to teach in certain areas, will never interact with children from a variety of cultural backgrounds, is to miss the point; teachers need to prepare themselves and their students for life in a multiethnic, multiracial society" (Mallea and Young, 1978).

It was very clear in our survey that many principals hold the view that to openly recognize the ethnic mix in a school is tantamount to discrimination. Yet how can a school begin to attend to the special or different needs of its pupils if cultural differences are not acknowledged? The paradox of educational equality is that in a multicultural school population, it is sometimes necessary to treat students differently in order to ensure equal opportunity. To attain this goal might well mean, for example, that an unequal allocation of physical and personnel resources must be provided to minority students in order to accommodate for their greater needs.

What, exactly, constitutes multicultural education in Ontario? Our review of the literature provided a useful framework for discussions on this somewhat complex issue. There appear to be four different approaches, each of which has different objectives and implications for practice. These are: 1) education of the culturally different; 2) education about cultural differences; 3) education for cultural pluralism; and 4) bicultural education. We believe that all of these approaches interact to make up the character of our education. However, care must always be exercised to avoid perpetuating the status quo at the expense of alleviating deeply rooted problems. For example, most of the recent measures taken to improve assessment and placement procedures are aimed at compensating for cultural differences, rather than at altering existing conditions. These present conditions are based on the assumption that immigrants to Canada desire (or should desire) to assimilate into the mainstream socioeconomic structure. The improvements are intended to provide equality of opportunity to compete in a middle-class-oriented culture.

In addition to properly assessing students and placing them in appropriate levels for transition, we need to foster a healthy learning environment by educating people about cultural differences. By focusing on the diverse riches of a multicultural society, teachers can guide all students to appreciate one another's backgrounds. If an atmosphere of acceptance and respect can be generated this would help to prevent potential feelings of alienation and anxiety among minority students, and to encourage their development of a positive self-concept and a confidence to learn.

It has been argued (Baum, 1978) that education about cultural differences might lead to greater, instead of lesser, social fragmentation, possibly resulting in negative political implications for Canada. However, such a risk, if it exists, is more related to the issues of heritage language instruction and improved social studies content than to the provision of equal opportunities by fair student assessment and placement. On the positive side, if equal educational opportunity becomes a reality, then most Canadian children will grow up capable of integrating the diverse cultural elements in the milieu. This is what multiculturalism strives for.

Many immigrants likely experience a state of mind described as 'anomie', a lack of certainty about norms and values, and a feeling that the rules that formerly guided conduct have lost their force and legitimacy. Differences in cultural background, family lifestyles, and language make it difficult for school officials concerned about the welfare of immigrant students to establish contact with the parents to inform them of community resources, including education services for themselves as well as their children. Elliston (1984) sees a vital need to encourage the involvement of individuals and groups of parents in opportunities to engage in their own informal education and in gaining a better understanding of the education process of their children. Successful adaptation to the demands of their changed conditions of life demands new learning activities.

What this requires is the creation of a community of shared experiences, referred to by Bloom (1971) as "cooperative and enabling modes of intervention." The community as a whole must be encouraged to welcome newcomers and to recognize their presence as a positive contribution to its well-being. This is possible only when cultural differences are perceived in a positive way and when there is an attitude of accommodation (Scarborough Board of Education, 1977).

Community awareness and parental involvement in programs for newcomers can be extremely important in promoting reciprocal learning and in paving the way for adaptation and change. To foster a relationship between the school and the community, it is necessary both to take education into the community, and to bring the community into the school. This scheme could aid both parties in their task of socialization when cultural discontinuity and/or disrupted educational experience are the intervening variables (Elliston, 1976).

Maintaining a democracy requires much effort and sensitivity by all its citizens. The fulfillment of multiculturalism requires people to exercise compassion, fairness, and vision in order to build a society marked by diversity and unity. Jaenen's (1973) comments provide a clear guide to all educators who feel a responsibility to initiate and promote positive changes in this direction:

> Democracy involves choices; selection requires reasonable alternatives. Therefore, when uniformity is demanded in the guise of unity the democratic structure is endangered because uniformity tends to destroy the self-renewing principles of alternatives, of free choice, of the right to change one's mind.

Chapter 9

Innovative Approaches in Assessment

John Lewis

Psychologists who deliver services in a multicultural society face the problem of deciding which aspects of a particular problem are unique to a specific group, and which cut across cultural differences and are common to all individuals. The same problem faces educators when assessing the intelligence of students of varied backgrounds.

Traditionally, the assessment of cognitive ability began with the assumption that such ability is static and unchanged by teaching and learning. (See chapter 4 for further discussion.) Although the concept of mental ability as innate has helped us to understand some aspects of human intelligence, it does not adequately explain what intelligence is, nor how it functions. In fact, static appraisal techniques have been found to be inadequate under special circumstances, such as when they are applied to the assessment of the mentally retarded (Haywood *et al.*, 1975) and culturally different minority groups (Budoff, 1973; Feuerstein, 1979). The discovery of these inadequacies has prompted assessment experts to suggest alternative approaches to assessment when dealing with culturally different children (Samuda, 1975; Mercer, 1979).

The concept of intelligence has been the subject of intense examination. While some psychologists believe that intelligence can be represented by a single number or factor, others (Sternberg, 1977; Detterman and Sternberg, 1982; Carroll, 1983) contend that tests based on a single factor or even multiple factors cannot account for all the variance of mental ability between individuals. Factor analytic studies of intelligence have been useful in identifying the number of specific abilities that make up an overall mental ability, but they fall short in explaining how a specific ability or cluster of abilities develops. Mental tests would be far more useful if, in addition to measuring intelligence as a product, they also could identify the *process* by which intelligence changes and/or accumulates as an individual acquires new experiences. Cattell's theory of fluid and crystallized intelligence, described below, seems to address some of these concerns.

Cattell's Theory of Intelligence

According to Cattell, *fluid intelligence* refers to a basic capacity to adapt to new situations. It is also an inherent capacity for learning and problem-solving that is independent of both education and cultural influences. In order to adapt to novel situations, fluid intelligence must encompass flexible inductive skills. *Crystallized intelligence* emerges from a person's use of fluid intelligence to interact with society. It is, therefore, a product of formal education. The way crystallized intelligence organizes knowledge and concepts reflects how the members of a given society process information and solve problems. *Because these abilities are already developed* they can be quantified and assembled to make up tests for general mental ability. The outcome of such measures is necessarily static in nature.

Intelligence in Cattell's conception, then, emerges from an active mind that is malleable and responsive to instruction. Intelligence not only processes information, but also anticipates new situations and plans effective solutions. It follows that any adequate assessment of intelligence as described by Cattell must address both these fluid and crystallized characteristics.

Sternberg's Componential Theory

Sternberg (1977, 1981) divides intelligence into five components that function together to help people handle problems. A 'component' is a basic elementary process that operates upon an internal representation of objects and symbols. These five are metacomponents, performance components, acquisition components, retention components and transfer components.

Metacomponents are mental mechanisms people use to select and coordinate the problem solution. Like a switchboard, they match strategies with tasks. Sternberg's research shows that planning is an important part in the performance of any task: good test-takers, for example, spend more time studying questions before working them out than their less able counterparts. In essence, metacomponents may be compared to Cattell's fluid intelligence, Brown and Campione's (1982) executive functions, and Flavell's (1977) meta cognitive processes. In each case, the ability in question is the ability to monitor the full range of memory, comprehension and other cognitive functions.

Performance components of intelligence are responsible for encoding information relevant to the solving of problems. In so doing, they rely on metacomponents that first determine the degree of similarity and dissimilarity between two or more stimuli, infer the relationship between them, and decide what needs to be done as an appropriate response. *Acquisition* components help people learn new information, while *detention* components store it. Finally, *transfer* components are responsible for transferring the acquired information to appropriate problem situations. All five components of intelligence interrelate to function as a whole, although it is possible to identify different sequences in which they function as an individual responds to a particular problem or situation.

Sternberg has identified two ways in which people process information ('do analysis', as he puts it) when they solve problems in mental ability tests. He called these the *cognitive correlates* approach and the *cognitive component* approach. Each of these approaches handles a range of tasks commonly found in mental ability tests. Sternberg hopes that by understanding how people solve various types of problems, we can design mental tests that reflect a wider range of abilities as well as show how specific abilities function. He believes that intelligent people not only solve new problems quickly, but also train themselves to solve familiar problems by rote so that the same mental process does not have to be enacted every time they are confronted with a particular task.

In the cognitive correlates approach, the testee approaches a test item or task by identifying its encoding and perceptual characteristics, and then solves it by matching it with appropriate information that is available.

In the cognitive components approach, one breaks the task down into smaller components to facilitate understanding. By doing so, one can plan a working strategy for a solution that will involve specific step-by-step operations. The cognitive component approach is most effective for tasks that involve inductive reasoning, such as analogies, matrix perception, and scenes completion.

Induction is a skill whereby one induces a rule governing the functioning of a set of elements of a phenomenon. For example, in working out a problem in figural analogies, one must identify the common components, make comparisons between patterns, and find out the rule for figural transformations. The level of sophistication in reasoning depends first on the level of task complexity, and then on the extent to which the individual has ready strategies to identify the various transformation in the analogy. A person who knows the components modes of an analogy, for example, can infer the rule that changes A to B without too much difficulty.

Verbal analogies provide excellent opportunities for observing how different individuals approach various problem situations, reflecting the flexibility or plasticity of cognitive structures. Flexibility of cognitive structure means the ease with which one can shift procedures whenever one finds the strategy that one is using is no longer feasible. Unlike figural analogies, which follow the linear transformation pattern of A : B : C, verbal analogies often follow alternate transformation patterns such as A : B, C : D etc. To deal with such patterns, it is necessary to acquire and memorize a good number of transformational models in order to make procedural shifts. Observing how low performers and high performers approach verbal analogies makes it possible to determine their relative knowledge bases, as well as the procedural flexibility with which they solve problems.

The data gathered from such observation provide insights into new dimensions of human intelligence. Some of the evidence suggest that components are involved in the function of intelligence, each of which deals with a specific task. These components are: encoding, inference, rule generation, memory, discrimination, procedural knowledge, comparative skills, executive processes, and conceptual knowledge. Working as a whole, these components generate a dynamic capacity capable of solving problems that human beings encounter.

With this view of intelligence in mind, psychologists have set out to devise new approaches to intellectual assessment that take into account not only static knowledge but also cognitive processes. While these approaches still depend on the use of tests and test scores as a measure of mental ability, they also incorporate teaching and clinical observation to determine the individual cognitive style and possible learning deficits of any one student. Such assessment, therefore, is an ongoing process in which the teacher monitors and reinforces academic progress and cognitive development. Many studies have advocated the need to shift from conventional methods of assessing minority students to these new approaches (Salvia and Ysseldyke, 1978; Garcia, 1981; Reschly, 1981; Scarr, 1981; MacIntyre, 1985). We will now present two of the most vital approaches for discussion: *comprehensive individual assessment*, and *dynamic assessment*.

Comprehensive Assessment

The goal of comprehensive assessment is to produce an accurate appraisal of a student's current level and mode of intellectual functioning within the context of his or her cultural background and experience. Specific learning needs are diagnosed and assets are identified to help the teacher formulate a personalized remedial program. In practice, such an assessment process involves a team consisting of a counsellor or psychometrician, a teacher, and a school administrator in the process of gathering data through testing, observation, consultation, and diagnosis. Often parents are invited to participate. The assessment follows these guidelines:

1. Diagnostic decisions, placement, and program changes in any counselling situation should be based on a wide range of information about the student.
2. Assessment results from a team deliberation on such information as how the student's performance is influenced by acculturation, language skills, behaviour mode, socioeconomic background and ethnocultural identity.
3. The appraisal of the student's needs, strengths, weaknesses and level of present cognitive functioning is made with reference to the background data outlined in point 2.

4. The main assessment objective is to define and design a teaching or remedial program that would best help the student to profit from the school system.
5. The remedial program should be carried out and monitored regularly by the assessment team.

The information generated by a process following these guidelines is called a comprehensive profile. In contrast to a single score, as obtained from a conventional IQ test, the comprehensive profile is made up of information from a wide range of data sources:

1. Observational data
2. School records and other available documents
3. Language dominance
4. Educational assessment
5. Sensorimotor and/or developmental data
6. Adaptive behaviour data
7. Medical records
8. Personality assessment (including self-report)
9. Intellectual assessment

The team approach, coupled with the wide range of information collected, allows a comprehensive profile about the individual who is being assessed to be constructed. The intellectual assessment should be performed last, so that its results can be interpreted in the context of all the other information gathered. The works of Sattler (1974), Salvia and Ysseldyke (1978), and Chodzinski and Samuda (1983) provide many valuable suggestions on how to collect, validate, and interpret many tests and background information for cross-cultural assessment.

Comprehensive assessment is a continuous process. As individuals develop, their intellectual and achievement profiles change. Identifying a student's information processing modes and other relevant factors for each subject area would help teachers design appropriate learning materials and procedures to meet that individual's needs. The emphasis should be on helping students maximize competencies and opportunities, particularly in the case of minorities (Reschly, 1980). With this in mind, Harold Dent (1976) has suggested that assessment procedures should follow four directives. First, the assessment must provide an accurate appraisal of a student's current level and mode of functioning within the context of his or her cultural background and experience. Second, it must identify specific educational needs rather than focus on perceived or inferred intellectual deficits. Third, it must focus on learning assets and strengths as the basis for the development of new learning skills. Finally, it must be a dynamic, ongoing process.

Dynamic Assessment

In contrast to the psychometric tradition, which treats intelligence as a static product, Vygotsky (1978) perceives intelligence as a dynamic process that changes with development and learning. As a learner interacts with other people, his or her learning stimulates cognitive development. As cognitive development proceeds, a 'zone of proximal development' can be delineated to reflect the gap between the learner's actual development, and developmental potential. This potential enables the psychologist or teacher to help improve the learner's mental ability. In this sense, assessment is dynamic and helpful.

Vygotsky (1978) defines the zone of proximal development as:

> The distance between the actual development level as determined by independent problem solving and the level of potential development as determined through problem solving under adult guidance or in collaboration with more capable peers.

The size of this zone is determined by using conventional IQ tests in a 'test-teach-test' format. An individual is first given a test (or part of it) to determine which items he or she can perform correctly and which present difficulty. After this initial performance, the psychologist or teacher provides help in completing the difficult items, by appropriate prompting until competence is achieved. Finally, similar test items are administered again to ascertain the degree to which learning has helped the student to perform better. The zone of proximal development is indicated by the number of prompts given in the teaching phase and their transfer effect. An individual who has received few prompts and who is able to solve many problems of a similar nature has achieved high transfer and, by implication, has a high learning potential. Clinical observations of the learning process would yield rough calibrations of a person's ability to benefit from prompting and learning, speed in learning new materials, and transfer capabilities. However, it should be recognized that much of this learning also depends on the nature and quality of the prompts given. The prompts are only appropriate and effective when the teacher or psychologist involved knows the componential features of both initial and transfer tasks and is able to apply them effectively.

Dynamic assessment, when compared with traditional psychometric methods, seems to yield a richer understanding of human intelligence. This approach, which is further delineated from other perspectives in chapter 10, has been developed further by the methods and tests of Budoff and Feuerstein. We now present a description of both these methodologies.

The Budoff Method

Budoff's method of assessment begins with testing the individual in a series of both familiar and novel tasks. The results provide a base-line measure that can be compared to subsequent performance. This is the *diagnostic* phase.

The second phase involves a teaching and learning process, in which the tester (the teacher) explains to the testee (the student) the principles of thought and logic required to perform the above tasks. Teachers can impart either general reasoning skills or basic concepts. They then rearrange the tasks in the original test from easy to difficult and ask the testee to do them again, beginning with the easiest item and proceeding to progressively more difficult ones. This methodology enables the assessment of two dimensions of the effectiveness of the teaching: 1) whether the student's performance has improved; and 2) the degree of improvement. From these clinical observations, the data can be acquired on the learning potential of the testee, and the manner and speed with which performance is being improved. The student's preferred cognitive modality can also be identified; that is, whether auditory or kinesthetic inputs are most helpful in attaining an improved understanding.

The above method of assessment can be used for a single task or a number of tasks. In the case of several tasks, a battery of tests is employed. So far, Budoff's research has concentrated on assessment using a single-task approach. He also believes in the use of non-verbal tests such as the Kohs Block Designs Test (1932) and the Ravens Coloured Progressive Matrices (1956) for assessing and improving children's reasoning abilities. Because both the test items and the training exercises are free of cultural bias, children of diverse backgrounds can gain true cognitive experience unhampered by negative situational factors such as the effects of failure in school, cultural block, and language deficiencies. This approach has been proven effective in improving children's cognitive ability scores (Budoff, 1974; Budoff and Hamilton, 1976).

A parallel approach to Budoff's assessment method is found in the Soviet Union. Wozniak (1975) described an approach in which the child being asssessed is required to perform a task independently. The examiner then tutors him or her on the performing aspects of the task that were failed. Finally, the child is asked to perform the same task alone. However, the Soviet approach uses no normative evaluation procedures, nor does it specify the need for a non-verbal orientation.

The Feuerstein Method

Feuerstein's major concern has been to assess the untapped cognitive potential of individuals, particularly the culturally deprived, and to remedy any deficiencies through an active intervention process that helps the individual build a new and effective cognitive structure. He believes that the acquisition of such a structure enables a person of low mental ability to become more adaptable, flexible, and therefore generally more capable of comprehending, planning, and solving problems.

A clear distinction is made between cultural *deprivation* and cultural *difference* in Feuerstein's scheme of thinking. The culturally different individual is simply one who is a member of a minority group within a society dominated by a mainstream culture that is different. Because of this background, the individual may suffer from not being tuned into what is going on in society and/or from a lack of economic opportunities. But such deficiencies may change as the individual acquires the essential skills of achieving success witthin the social structure. In any case, a strong affiliation with his or her own minority culture can often provide the culturally different individual with a sound psychological foundation to deal effectively with the requirements and expectations of the dominant culture.

A culturally deprived individual, on the other hand, is a person who is deprived of his or her own background culture — one who has, in effect, become alienated from any cultural affiliation. This alienation may be caused by any number of single or interactive factors: social class, physical factors, religion, psychological factors, and learning. Whatever the cause, cultural deprivation often leads to poor cognitive ability, which reduces the individual's chances of keeping up with peers and the school's expectations. Even manifestations such as a lack of motivation and the ability to learn and change in therapeutic and remedial situations can signal cultural deprivation. It is not difficult to realize that, under these circumstances, the use of conventional IQ tests for assessment would only compound an already unfavourable situation if it indicates that an individual has a low IQ score. A different approach of assessment is needed if change is intended to be a logical follow-up of that assessment.

In their investigation into the problems confronting the culturally deprived, Feuerstein and Hoffman (1982) concluded that such individuals suffer from "a disruption of intergenerational transmission and mediational process." Not only are they deprived of the learning experiences mediated by parents that normally should occur during childhood, but they also are prevented from developing a sense of order about the environment and from formulating effective cognitive schemes with which to handle daily life problems.

In a normal childhood, interactions between child and parents are typically replete with examples of mediated learning. In this process, the parents selectively accept or reject certain stimuli to present to the child: in effect, they filter, frame, schedule, and sequence events, and mediate relationships of time, space, causality, and affection. Through these experiences, children gradually construct their cognitive structures and link themselves with their cultural past and social reality.

It may be said that every culture provides a structure within which the organization, interpretation, and understanding of events and relationships can occur through exposure and experience. It is this organization of experience that links individuals with their society. It also enables them to be flexible, adaptable, and creative in rooting themselves with the past, handling the present, and anticipating the future in the context of their cultural milieus. Language plays an important part in this process, as do other forms of communication and sharing. Feuerstein suggests that a mediated learning experience (M.L.E.), such as occurs between children and parents in the normal process of development, is necessary to initiate every member of a society into the universal cognitive structure of that society. For those who have been deprived of this initiation, Feuerstein believes that the introduction of a mediating learning experience intended to fill in the gaps left by deprivation is helpful.

If we assume that a culturally deprived person, whether a child or adult, has a much higher potential than he or she has been able to demonstrate in conventional IQ tests, then a teacher, acting as a mediator, can help improve this person's cognitive ability by providing alternative perceptions and interpretations of the world. In order to do so, the teacher must first gain an understanding of both the individual's intelligence and cognitive potential. Feuerstein uses a dynamic assessment approach that he calls the Learning Potential Assessment Device (L.P.A.D.).

The L.P.A.D. begins with a clear delineation of psychometric goals, as follows:

1. To assess students' cognitive modifiability by observing them function in situations designed to produce a change.
2. To assess the extent of modifiability in terms of cognitive functioning, and how significant a student's attained functioning is in the hierarchy of universal cognitive operations ranging from perception to abstract thinking.
3. To determine the transfer value of what is learned in one area to other areas of operations.
4. To identify the student's preferred modalities for learning and the problem-solving strategies that work best.

The assessment process engages both the student and the assessor or counsellor in active modificational operations. As the client performs the given tasks, the counsellor intervenes whenever necessary to present alternative ways of perceiving, interpreting, and problem-solving. Any change is noted, as well as the amount of intervention required to produce the change. On the basis of these observations, the counsellor then predicts the level of change potential.

To facilitate this dynamic assessment process, conventional testing procedures have been modified to accommodate new goals. The following four characteristics make up the essence of the new approach.

1. The tester acts as a responsive, concerned, and individualized counsellor rather than a standard neutral questioner.
2. The test question or task items must be clear and well-sequenced. They should permit ready assessment of the individual's present level of cognitive functioning and the way in which his or her problem-solving skills and relational thinking may be changed.
3. The assessment must focus on the process of intelligence rather than on its product. Emphasis is placed on the change in cognitive skill.
4. The responses that reflect both the process and product of cognitive operations are viewed as salient indicators of potential.

The L.P.A.D. thus helps to tap an individual's acquisition components and performance components of intelligence, and identifies where deficits lie. Contained within are detailed lists of the impairments that may be found among culturally deprived persons in three levels of cognitive functioning: input, elaboration, and output. These are presented below:

Input Level

1. Blurred and sweeping perception.
2. Unplanned, impulsive, and unsystematic exploratory behaviour.
3. Lack of or impaired receptive verbal tools that affect discrimination (e.g., objects, events, relationships, etc., are not given appropriate labels).
4. Lack of or impaired spatial orientation — the absence of stable systems of reference impairs the establishment of topological and Euclidean organizations of space.
5. Lack of or impaired temporal concepts.
6. Lack of or impaired conservation of constancies (size, shape, quantity, orientation) across variation in these factors.
7. Lack of or deficient need for precision and accuracy in data gathering.
8. Lack of capacity for considering two or more sources of information at once; this is reflected in dealing with data in a piecemeal fashion rather than as units or organized facts.

Elaboration Level

1. Inadequacy in the perception of the existence and definition of a problem.
2. Inability to select relevant versus non-relevant cues in defining a problem.
3. Lack of spontaneous comparative behaviour or a limitation of its application by a restricted need system.
4. Narrowness of the psychic field.
5. Episodic grasp of reality.
6. Lack of or impaired need for pursuing logical evidence.
7. Lack of or impaired interiorization.
8. Lack of or impaired inferential-hypothetical ("if...then") thinking.
9. Lack of or impaired strategies for hypothesis testing.
10. Lack of or impaired ability to define the framework necessary for problem-solving behaviour.
11. Lack of or impaired planning behaviour.
12. Non-elaboration of certain cognitive categories because the verbal concepts are not part of the individual's verbal inventory (on a receptive level) or because they are not mobilized at the expressive level.

Output Level

1. Egocentric communicational modalities.
2. Difficulties in projecting virtual relationships.
3. Blocking.
4. Trial-and-error responses.
5. Lack of or impaired verbal tools for communicating adequately elaborated responses.
6. Lack of or impaired need for precision and accuracy in communicating responses.
7. Deficiency of visual transport.
8. Impulsive acting-out behaviour.

Deficits in the three levels of operation are fluidly interactive and must be considered as a whole. In terms of the need for mediation, the research of Narrol (1978) showed that an individual is amenable to remedial help if he or she exhibits deficits at either the input or output phase. In contrast, elaboration deficits may reflect a limited ceiling in cognitive capacity, which would mean that there is not a great deal of room for cognitive re-construction.

Even though the L.P.A.D. is concerned with an understanding of cognitive processes as a basis for remedial work, there are some weaknesses in the instruments employed. For one thing, the beginning and the end of the test-teach-test process tend to measure cognitive ability in terms of standardized units. In addition, because this kind of clinical assessment requires each assessor to approach the interpretation of results as well as the mediation in his or her own way, the outcomes of the assessments do not lend themselves easily to comparison. Finally, the basic assumption that everyone is modifiable is an overgeneralization.

Nevertheless, when viewed as a special assessment method aimed at facilitating therapeutic measures, the L.P.A.D. serves to meet the needs of people who are culturally deprived. Used properly, tests using this dynamic approach can yield the following information about the testee:

1. Capacity to grasp an underlying principle.
2. Amount of work required to teach a principle.
3. Capacity to transfer what is learned to solve new problems.
4. Modality preference in cognitive operations.
5. The effects of mediation strategies on changing cognitive structures.

According to the study of cross-cultural assessment by Sundberg and Gonzales (1981), the Feuerstein L.P.A.D. approach contributes significantly towards clarifying the special needs of minority individuals and groups. The following examples of L.P.A.D. instruments show the characteristics of this dynamic assessment approach. Any reader who is interested in more comprehensive information about these tests should seek out the original tests for reference.

A. *Organization of Dots*

This test requires the testee to project shapes onto an amorphous cloud of dots. The operation involves the application of the full range of encoding and projective skills. It taps planning behaviour, search strategies, impulsive behaviour, and segregation skills, as well as such executive functions as checking and monitoring. It arouses interest easily and is simple to administer.

B. The Representational Stencil Design

This test permits the counsellor to study how testees develop their problem-solving behaviour. The testee is first supplied with a series of stencils, and is then presented with a model figure and asked to mentally construct that figure by superimposing one or all of the stencils upon each other in the correct sequence. By observation, the counsellor can gain information about the degree of reflective thought used, executive processing of monitoring, impulsive behaviour, and trial-and-error approaches.

C. Complex Figure

The testee is first required to copy a complex figure and the tester notes both the details of the drawing produced and the sequence of copying. The next task is to reproduce the figure from memory. Mediation consists of teaching the sequence of copying the figure, after which the test is given again.

D. The Plateaux

This test, developed by Rey (1934), consists of four boards, each approximately 8 inches square and containing nine buttons symmetrically positioned on it. One of these buttons is permanently fixed. The task requires the testee to discover and subsequently recall the location of the permanently fixed button on each board.

E. Functional Associative Recall

The testee is presented with a number of object drawings, each having a series of transfigurations of reduced clues. He or she is first required to identify the objects and their associated simplified drawings. When the cues are removed, the next task is to recall the objects. By observing this performance, the counsellor can determine the testee's real and potential mnemonic strategies, and stable recognition of an object form as it changes through a gradual reduction of associative cues.

F. Raven's Matrices and Set Variations

The testee is trained to apply Raven's coloured progressive matrices, followed by the L.P.A.D. Set Variations. The tasks involve a series of progressively more difficult completion exercises requiring Gestalt perception. By observing the testee's learning progress, the counsellor can detect abilities of analogy, logical operations, transfer, and generalization.

The Kaufman Method

Kaufman is concerned with the assessment of fluid intelligence and achievement. The Kaufman Assessment Battery for Children, also called the K-ABC, measures intellectual functioning in two broad categories: Mental Composite Processing and Achievement. Mental Composite Processing and Simultaneous Processing are assessed through close observation, as the tests are administered individually.

The K-ABC is made up of 16 subtests designed to measure different elements of children's intellectual capacity. Ten of these are used to assess intellectual functioning, while the remaining six assess achievement. The battery is standardized on a nationwide sample of normal and exceptional students between 2.5 and 12.5 years of age. The tests are administered individually, and involve only rudimentary verbal skills. In fact, a non-verbal scale is included to test children with language differences or language disorders. Norms have been established to reflect sociocultural factors, which makes the tests useful for assessing those from ethnic minority backgrounds.

The number of subtests used for assessment varies depending on the age of the child. The guideline is: seven subtests for age 2.5, nine for age three, 11 for ages four and five, 12 for age six, and 13 for ages seven to twelve. No child is given more than 13 tests. The testing time ranges from 35 to 85 minutes, depending on the age and speed of the subject.

When administering these tests, the teacher first makes sure that the testee understands the tasks involved before performing them. The scores are then interpreted with flexibility and care in order to decide what post-test intervention strategies should be taken. Interpretation of test scores follows five empirical steps. The tester first transforms the obtained scores into percentile ranks and classifications. Next, the scores on the sequential processing scale are compared to those on the simultaneous processing scale. Third, the mental processing standard scores are compared with the achievement standard scores. Fourth, the mental processing scores are scrutinized to determine strengths and weaknesses among the subtests used. Finally, assessment is made on the basis of strengths and weaknesses on the achievement scale.

What follows is a brief description of scales and subtests used in the K-ABC battery.

A. Sequential Processing Scale

Subtest 1. Hand Movements (2.5 to 12.5 years)
This scale measures the testee's ability to perform a series of hand movements in exactly the same sequence as demonstrated by the tester.

Subtest 2. Number Recall (2.5 to 12.5 years)
The testee is required to repeat a digit sequence in the same order as the tester presents it.

Subtest 3. Word Order (4 to 12.5 years)
A series of silhouettes is verbally described to the testee who is required to identify and touch each silhouette in the same sequence as they are described. An interference task is incorporated into the presentation of the complex items.

B. Simultaneous Processing Scale

Subtest 1. Magic Window (2.5 to 11 years)
The tester partially shows a picture behind a narrow window on a screen. The testee is required to name the picture while it is partially exposed.

Subtest 2. Face Recognition (2.5 to 12 years)
The testee is briefly shown a photograph of one or two faces. He is then required to pick out the face(s) from memory from a group photograph.

Subtest 3. Gestalt Closure (2.5 to 12.5 years)
The testee is required to name an object or a scene from a partially complete inkblot drawing.

Subtest 4. Matrix Analogies (5 to 12.5 years)
The testee is required to complete a visual analogy by using the most suitable graphic or geometric form of his or her choice.

Subtest 5.

Subtest 6. Spatial Memory (5 to 12.5 years)
The testee is shown a page of pictures arranged in a specific order. He is then required to recall the spatial order of the pictures correctly.

Subtest 7. Photo Series (6 to 12.5 years)
The testee is required to arrange photographs of an event in chronological order.

C. Achievement Scale

Subtest 1. Expressive Vocabulary (2.5 to 12 years)
The testee is required to identify the object in a photograph.

Subtest 2. Faces and Places
The testee is shown the picture of a well-known person or place (real or fictitious) and is required to make an identification.

Subtest 3. Arithmetic (3 to 12.5 years)
A knowledge of arithmetic is tested by requiring the testee to count, compute, and do other mathematical operations.

Subtest 4. Riddles (3 to 12.5 years)
The testee is given a list of characteristics of a concrete or abstract concept, and is required to make inferences and name the concept.

Subtest 5. Reading/Decoding (5 to 12.5 years)
The testee is asked to identify letters and read words.

Subtest 6. Reading/Understanding (7 to 12.5 years)
The testee responds to written commands.

In appraising the appropriateness of the K-ABC battery for the assessment of the intellectual ability of minority students, one may refer to the theoretical basis on which the tests are constructed. The concept that sequential and simultaneous processing is distinctly different from mental processes has its origin in the neurophysiological concepts of Luria (1966), who felt that the left and right hemispheres of the human brain perform different functions. While sequential processing handles tasks such as the habitualization of skills, rote memory, and narration, simultaneous processing deals with spatial organization, linguistic expressions, and comparison and contrast tasks. A number of empirical studies that support a distinction between mental composite processing and achievement are cited in the K-ABC interpretation manual.

The fact that the K-ABC battery separates the mental processing scores from the achievement scores may explain why it is more useful in assessing the intellectual ability of minority children than are conventional tests such as the WISC-R and the SOMPA. Various cultural groups have different cognitive processing styles, as well as different relationships between simultaneous processing and sequential processing. Kaufman and Kaufman (1982) have studied the effect of the K-ABC on Hispanic children, and have found the assessment to be more accurate than results obtained from the WISC: whereas the K-ABC Achievement Scale uses a predominantly visual approach, the WISC-R Verbal Scale places unfair emphasis on language skills. The flexibility in interpretation of the K-ABC also helps the tester derive richer information with which to design effective post-test intervention strategies. In fact, the tester can clearly determine the characteristics of the testee's cognitive performance and verbal achievement.

Discussion

It seems, on the basis of the preliminary research results, that both the L.P.A.D. and the K-ABC are more appropriate assessment devices for testing minority children than the WISC-R and SOMPA. In certain ways, Feuerstein's method might be considered more dynamic than Kaufman's, but both share similar areas of emphasis and styles. Both methods de-emphasize factual information and general learned content, and instead concentrate on problem-solving tasks of a non-verbal and culture-fair nature. Both incorporate a training component to help the testee who doesn't understand the tasks involved. The Feuerstein approach trains the testee in order to measure learning potential, while the Kaufman method does the same thing so that more reliable scores can be obtained.

As a whole, the innovative approaches to mental ability assessment have shifted the focus away from quantitative product scores to qualitative observations and interpretations of the process of mental ability functioning. Dynamic assessment is based on the assumption that intelligence is a multifaceted, multidimensional, and fluid construct that continually undergoes change. This approach attempts to determine not only the characteristics of the various components of intelligence, but also how they function. One way of doing this is to use the verbalizations of testees as a vehicle to tap their underlying cognitive processes as they work through various problems.

Chapter 10

Mental Capacity Testing as a Form of Intellectual-Developmental Assessment

Juan Pascual-Leone and Helene Ijaz

Introduction

As we have demonstrated in previous chapters, the intellectual assessment of students in the North American school system is increasingly being perceived as an area that fails to achieve its objective of identifying the students' mental capacity and learning potential, and often causes their inappropriate placement in educational programs. We reiterate the significant fact that this is particularly so with culturally and linguistically different minority students. Traditional methods of assessment are being challenged by some ethnic groups as an example of large-scale institutional discrimination and racism against students who are of non-Anglo-Saxon and non-middle class background.

An increasing number of parents and educators are raising questions about the overrepresentation of such students in low aca-

---

This chapter was written with the collaboration and assistance of Dr. Helene Ijaz who summarized and paraphrased the original work of Professor Juan Pascual-Leone.

demic streams such as special education, vocational, and basic level programs. It is argued that the tests of intellectual assessment traditionally used in the educational system are culturally and linguistically biased in favour of respondents of middle-class white background, and that they are of limited validity with those who are socioculturally different.

The present chapter will explore the kinds of tests used, their underlying rationales, and their effectiveness and limitations. It will introduce the concept of *capacity assessment* as opposed to *knowledge-based testing*, and will provide examples of mental capacity tests as culturally fair alternatives to the traditional knowledge-based IQ tests.

IQ Tests as Knowledge-based Tests of Intellectual Assessment

Tests of intellectual assessment are used in the educational system with two major objectives: (1) to determine whether students are performing up to their expected learning potential; and (2) to identify, in cases of doubt, what that potential is. In many school boards, group intelligence tests such as Otis-Lennon, the California Test of Mental Maturity, the Kuhlmann-Anderson Test, the Henmon-Nelson Tests of Mental Ability, and the Lorge-Thorndike Intelligence Tests are administered to students at various grade levels to identify those whose scores are above or below average. This assessment is used to select educational programs and services suited to intellectual needs. In some cases, a student may be referred by her teacher to a psychologist or psychoeducational consultant for individual testing if her achievement level is not in keeping with the teacher's expectations. The most commonly used test for this purpose is the WISC-R. The underlying assumption in administering all these tests is that the concept of intelligence that they measure reflects learning potential.

Most of the IQ tests traditionally used are carefully constructed. They measure particular abilities, skills,[1] and/or knowledge, generally against a norm established on the basis of a large sample of subjects taken from the population to which the individuals belong. They consist of a variety of subtests often spanning different content domains and levels of abstraction in sensorial/perceptual and intellective/intellectual processes. They tend to combine in various assortments the different dimensions or aspects of knowledge. For instance, the WISC-R contains 'verbal' and 'performance' items. 'Verbal' items measure the knowledge that individuals have acquired through linguistic interaction (e.g., vocabulary/concept knowledge; information about the world). 'Performance' items measure visual discrimination, the perception of part-whole relationships, and the use of language. However, although the performance scale of the WISC-R is intended to measure non-verbal skills, language use is still involved. Indeed, performance is presumed to be higher if the testee is able to verbalize her analyses and syntheses. Finally, general intelligence is defined as the overall mental ability score, i.e., one's average across the various domains of the tests relative to a representative sample of 'typical' individuals from a corresponding age level. This mental ability score is expressed as the 'intelligence quotient' (IQ).

This operational definition of intelligence is based on three assumptions: (1) that the skills and abilities sampled by the test represent an optimal reflection of the factors and processes underlying intelligence, (2) that a 'population' of individuals can be selected who can set the standard for general intelligence, and (3) that this can be done without explicitly defining in advance what intelligence is, and without having a substantive theory-based criterion for selection of the normative sample (cf. Cummins, 1980; Samuda, 1986a,b,c,d). These assumptions are unwarranted, because they tacitly presume that the nature of intelligence is intuitively known. However, no causal theory of the nature of intelligence is found within the classic psychometric tradition that produced the tests.[2]

Moreover, the claims to validity of these omnibus tests of intelligence have not stood up well in empirical use, particularly in the case of children coming from non-Anglo-Saxon, non-middle-class backgrounds, such as those now making up much of the immigrant population of Canada and the United States. Lacking a cogent causal theory of general intelligence based on the study of mental processes, IQ tests tacitly construe intelligence as being a performance level. From this perspective, when one examines process-analytically their test items (and also the sociocultural origin of the subjects making normative samples) it becomes apparent that these tests essentially measure familiarity with the knowledge and intellectual skills of a middle-class white population. They constitute valid and effective measures of developmental capacity with students from backgrounds that are rich in the informational content and the experiences of this population; however, with students from a cultural, linguistic, or sociocultural background lacking these experiences and skills, their validity disappears. With these children, IQ tests largely measure the extent to which test-related experiences *were lacking* in the environment. This point has been well illustrated by a number of educational psychologists (e.g., Cummins, 1980, 1986; Feuerstein, Rand, and Hoffman, 1979; Samuda, 1985, 1986a,b,c) and neo-Piagetian researchers (e.g., Case, 1975; DeAvila, Havassy, and Pascual-Leone, 1976; Garcia, Aragon, Owne, Sachse, 1976; Globerson, 1983; Lautrey, 1980; M.S. Miller, 1975, 1980; etc.). Because of the tests' strong emphasis on previously acquired knowledge and skills *from within a given cultural environment*, they are biased. For children from other cultural backgrounds, they do not provide an objective index of *innate* capacities and learning potential.

Mental Capacity as an Index of Learning Potential

According to neo-Piagetian theory,[3] there are, in addition to skills and abilities, developmentally determined *capacities* that constitute *general-purpose* brain resources. In contrast to context-bound knowledge (e.g., skills and abilities), capacities are largely content-free. They reflect general-purpose organismic *resources*, i.e., characteristics of the brain's 'architecture' that affect an individual's information processing capabilities and executive (planning) processes.

Capacities have implications for learning potential in that they determine important structural characteristics (limits of processing complexity, amount of redundancy needed, etc.) of the information that a person is able to handle. An individual's *mental capacity* (there are other capacities, e.g., that of logical/structural learning) is defined by the maximum number of things or aspects that he/she is able to attend to simultaneously.

In human cognition, capacities derive their significance from their role in information processing. Human informational processes are described in terms of functional units — packages of processes that can produce definite psychological results or jobs. The simpler functional units are called *schemes*, and the functional units that coordinate several or many different schemes are called *structures*. Different types of cognitive structures exist, such as experiential, conceptual, and linguistic structures.

Experiential structures are the mental processes that serve to code and present spatio-temporal, causal events of everyday experience. Without these structures, there would be no psychological experience and thus no knowledge acquisition. *Conceptual structures* are generic knowledge; they represent kinds or types of experience. They are like commentaries on objects, situations, procedures, etc. They classify experiences and relate them to each other. *Linguistic structures* are founded on and shaped by experiential and conceptual structures. Thus, experiential structures are the ground where the truth of verbal structures is ultimately verified.

When a child reacts to a teacher with fear, insecurity, and shyness, he may be transferring to the teacher experiential structures that he developed in contact with other people in different circumstances. On the other hand, he may have truly generic expectations about teachers that justify his fear; these expectations constitute conceptual structures since they apply to teachers but not to other individuals. Over time, if the child experiences a number of teachers who are kind and warm-hearted (experiential structures), at some point he may generalize and tacitly conclude that this is what teachers are like. This generalization is called a *proposition*. A proposition represents a relation that is established between two or more classes (or generic types) of experiences, in this case the class of 'teachers' and that of 'kind and warm-hearted persons'. These are conceptual structures. Later, if the child's positive relations with teachers persist, he might rationalize his feelings and say to himself: "Teachers are kind and warm-hearted." At this stage, the child formulates with his linguistic structures the proposition that he had reached preverbally before. The new insight has become fully conscious and can now begin to control his behaviour fully.

While the three types of structures closely interact, they are also distinct from each other. For example, Johnson (1986) has shown that, in a task involving metaphor understanding in English, 7- to 12-year-old Hispanic-Canadian children with limited English proficiency (as measured with a standardized test) demonstrate a conceptual ability equal to that of Anglo-Canadian children. The children's performance on the English-language metaphor task was found to have a higher correlation with their mental capacity and with their Spanish proficiency than with their English proficiency.

Lack of development of linguistic structures can hamper information processing despite well-developed experiential and conceptual structures. This may occur in the case of cultural and linguistic minority children who have not had sufficient conceptual/linguistic learning experiences in their host environment and in their second language. For this reason they are not able to coordinate effectively the conceptual/linguistic structures in the host culture with experiential structures based on their native culture. As a result, such children may appear confused and slow at learning, although their mental capacities and motivation are good. These children's needs are new cultural experiences conveyed through language and through learning situations comprehensible to them. To be comprehensible, a learning situation must not overtax their mental processing capacity, i.e., it must not require them to attend to more things or aspects than they are capable of, in the intricate interplay of experiential, conceptual, and linguistic structures.

Knowledge and ideas are the products of an active, creative transformation of the raw materials of experience. They develop by applying operative knowledge to experience. In turn, operative knowledge is the result of applying to experience certain mental attentional capacities. Figure 1 illustrates different steps or 'moments' of information processing during learning, i.e., acquisition of knowledge. First, the raw materials of experience impact on the individual's *perceptions and images* and, coded by them, proceed to the mental storehouse of *knowledge*. These relevant schemes and structures are activated. Among the activated schemes there are executive schemes. *Executive schemes* are the organism's way of storing, for later activation and use, both plans of action (i.e., strategies) and regulatory controls (i.e., procedures for mobilization and use of the organismic capacities). These executive schemes, in turn, mobilize the individual's *capacities*.

Of particular importance for us is *mental (attentional) capacity*, also called 'mental energy', which is applied to relevant schemes and structures to boost their activation. As a result of this application of 'mental energy' the schemes and structures become hyperactivated and often drawn to the level of consciousness. Hyperactivated schemes and structures undergo a temporary functional change in state, which is often referred to as changing from 'long-term memory' to 'working memory'. The mental operative strategies employed during these changes are influenced by the power of the individual's mental capacity and/or by the goals of his/her affective system, i.e., current state of motivation. These affects, in turn, cue the executive schemes, which become activated and therefore determine the direction of the subjects plans, operations, or actions, influencing in this manner his or her performance. Learning potential is greatly affected by the subject's working memory and by the interactions between her mental capacities and her affective system.

Figure 1

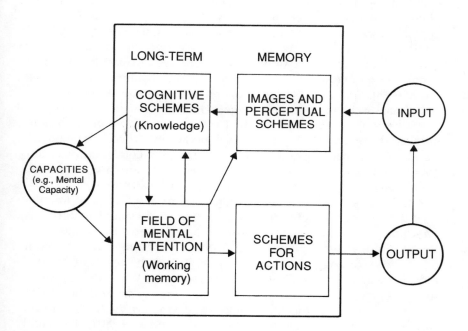

Schematic outline of the functional relations between Long-term Memory and Cognitive Capacities in Humans. The squares inside the large square symbolize activated schemes and structures within long-term memory, i.e., the subject's current 'field or activation'. The square labeled 'field of mental attention' or 'working memory' represents the collection of more highly activated (hyperactivated) schemes within the 'field of activation'. The mental attention/working memory box basically corresponds to the subject's conscious processes. The arrows pointing from mental attention/working memory to the other boxes symbolize the allocation of mental capacity (mental energy) to the corresponding schemes (i.e., the 'placement of this information in working memory'). The circles indicate functional entities that are not in long-term memory and are not schemes or structures, and are not informational processes. The arrow from the capacities circles (the cognitive resources of the brain), to the mental attention/working memory box symbolizes the mobilization or activation of mental capacity before it has been allocated to specific schemes and structures. Other arrows represent activation of schemes/structures by other schemes/structures.

Developmental Growth of Cognition

Learning potential is related to the child's growth in cognition. This cognitive growth has been described by developmental psychologists (e.g., Piaget) in terms of stages dealing with strategies in problem solving, exploring, and reacting. From age 3 to 6 years, the child is at the stage of *preoperations*, which is characterized by perceptual processes that focus on the here and now. The stage of preoperations is followed by that of *concrete operations* (age 7 to 10 years). Here, the child's intellective processes develop beyond perceptual experiences of the present to a grasp of future and past concrete events and experiences. Concrete operational growth reaches its climax at 11 to 12 years of age, when the transition to the next stage takes place. From age 11 to 15, the stage of *formal operations* unfolds. Now the child's intellectual processes proceed beyond the future and the past into the *formal possible*, the collection of future events and experiences that *might* occur under certain circumstances, although they have never been encountered before.

According to Piaget (and Vygotsky using a different terminology), the difference between any two stages of mental maturity is *qualitative*, i.e., it lies in the *kinds* of operative processes accessible to the child. Piaget believes that, rather than being based only on acquired knowledge, developmental stages are the result of internal reorganizations in mental operative functioning. When the transition to a new stage has occurred, these organizations provoke a growth in the subject's ability to utilize and transform *creatively* the knowledge previously acquired (see also Pascual-Leone, 1980).[4] The child can produce novel *creative/dynamic synthesis* that help him/her to adapt to the circumstances at hand; and the scope and power of these syntheses increase with every transition to a new stage.

Piaget's assumption also takes into consideration that children may have different cultural, sociocultural, and linguistic experiences which may influence their knowledge, skills, and ideas. These experiences are stored in memory by means of experiential structures (i.e., real life schemes or structures — Piaget referred to them by the odd name of 'infralogical') that are different from the conceptual 'logical' and linguistic schemes, or structures of the child. In spite of this variety of schemes and structures, cognitive functioning can be compared to the functioning of a very, very active (parallel processing) computer, even though computers do not have the adaptive plasticity in learning, development, perception, and problem solving that our brains do. The brain's experiential, conceptual, and linguistic structures analogically correspond to the information stored on a disk, whereas its innate capacities function somewhat like the hardware. Piaget (1985) was clearly aware of the role of mental capacities in determining the emergence of operational structures and executive schemes — he referred to them as 'regulations'. He had little understanding, however, of the exact nature of regulations.

The Development of Mental Capacity and the Executive/Cognitive Styles Controlling its Manifestation

The present author has studied the concept of mental capacities for the past two decades and has refined their definition, focusing in particular on mental attentional capacity. This capacity is the main (but not the only!) cause of our *'working memory'*, i.e., a set of hyperactivated schemes and structures (subjectively experienced as a limited field of focal consciousness or 'mental space'), which in turn are the main (but not the only!) determinants of our mental processing. It has been suggested (Pascual-Leone, 1970, 1980; Pascual-Leone and Goodman, 1979) that mental attentional capacity (the true core of developmental intelligence) corresponds to the innate component of intelligence identified in factor-analytical studies as 'g-factor' or 'fluid' intelligence. We have quantitatively measured mental capacity (*M-capacity*) using a theory-guided measure called *M-power*, which is defined in terms of the maximum number of units of knowledge (schemes, structures) that an individual can simultaneously boost into hyperactivation.

One test we have used to measure M-capacity is the *Figural Intersections Task (FIT)*. Figures 2 to 5 show sample items from the children's version of this test.

This test consists of two sub-tasks: (1) For every test item, the respondent is asked to place a dot inside each figure that is found on the right-hand side of the page. (In Figure 2 the first item shows a square; in Figure 3 it shows a square and a triangle.) (2) On the left-hand side of each item she must place a dot that is simultaneously inside all the figures that were also found on the right-hand side. The number of relevant figures changes from item to item.

Figure 2

Rac fit
8303

Dr. J. Pascual-Leone

Department of Psychology

York University

Date: _____

Name: _____

Birth date: _____

Age: ___ Years: ___ Months: _____

Class: _____

School: _____

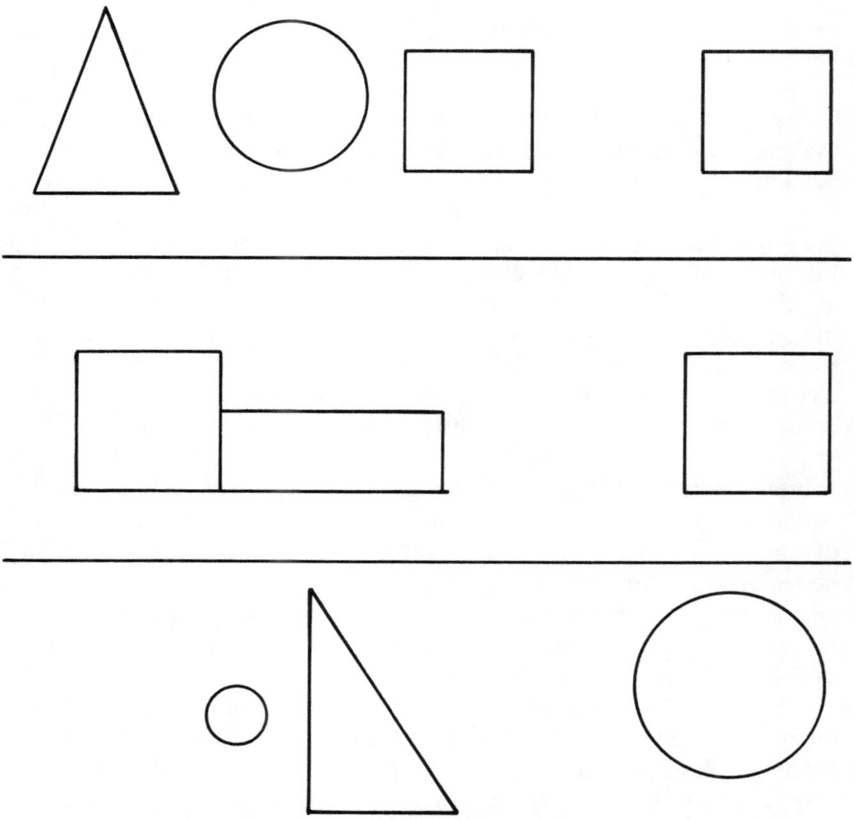

Some introductory items of the Figural Intersections Test (FIT). These items serve to teach the child all the basic information (i.e., the basic schemes) he/she needs in order to respond.

Figure 3

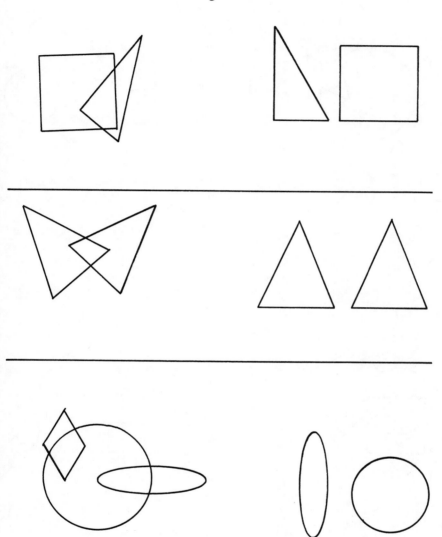

Some introductory items of the Figural Intersections Test (FIT). These items serve to teach the child all the basic information (i.e., the basic schemes) he/she needs in order to respond.

Figure 4

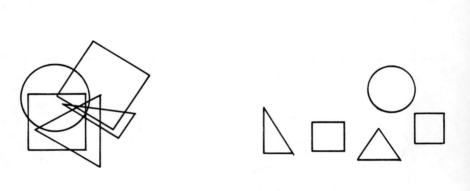

Some testing items of the Figural Intersection Test (FIT). The items are randomly ordered in terms of complexity. The subject is asked to place a dot inside each of the figures found on the right side of the page, and then has to place a single dot on the compound figure of the left side; this dot must be so placed that it is simultaneously inside all the relevant figures — the figures relevant in each item are those found in this item on the right side of the page.

Figure 5

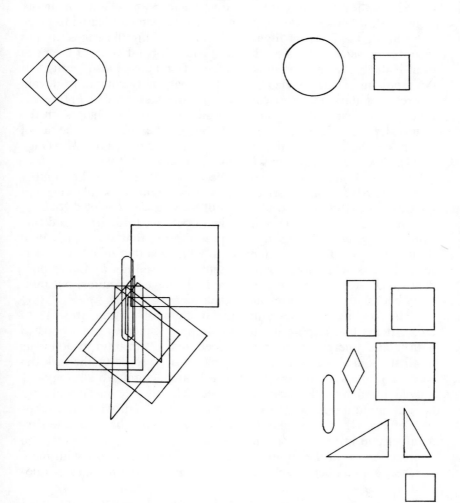

Some testing items of the Figural Intersection Test (FIT). The items are randomly ordered in terms of complexity. The subject is asked to place a dot inside each of the figures found on the right side of the page, and then has to place a single dot on the compound figure of the left side; this dot must be so placed that it is simultaneously inside all the relevant figures — the figures relevant in each item are those found in this item on the right side of the page.

Prior to taking the test, respondents are trained in all the operative skills they will require. Figures 2 and 3 show training items from the test booklet. During training, the respondent learns to place a dot inside the relevant figures (without touching the edges) and to identify the same figures on the right and left-hand sides of the page even if their sizes and orientations are different. She also learns that the grouping on the left-hand side of the page may contain irrelevant figures that have to be discarded (e.g., the last item in Figure 3). Finally, she learns to put one dot inside each of the figures on the right-hand side of the page, but only one on the left-hand side, a dot that has to be inside all the relevant figures at the same time (Figure 4). Practice is provided with both types of test items.

Figures 4 and 5 show two of the actual test pages. The number of figures is randomly varied from two to eight, thus allowing the construction of items that, although of varying degrees of difficulty, require both *the same procedure* (i.e., operative structures) and *the same executive skills* as the simpler figures that were presented during training. This procedure usually ensures that inability to perform the task with more complex items is caused not by the respondent's lack of operative or executive knowledge structures, but rather by her relative lack of mental capacity.

The key ideas underlying this method of testing are: (1) to create items that require progressively more schemes to be boosted with mental energy in order to succeed, and (2) to train respondents in all the knowledge schemes they might need to solve the task before they are actually tested. The essential cognitive strategy involved in solving the task is twofold. The testee must separately keep in mind the relevant figural patterns involved, with the exception of one figure that she uses as background. She must then remember and utilize the operative scheme that serves to identify the intersection of all the figures. In essence, she must boost with mental energy a number of schemes that is equal to the number of relevant figures in a test item.

We have shown that in normal children M-capacity increases developmentally in power up to age 15, and that it follows the stages in cognitive development proposed by Piaget. This developmental pattern is shown in Table 1.

M-power is symbolized by the sum $e + k$. Here e stands for a constant that represents the child's mental capacity at the end of age two; this capacity serves to boost into hyperactivation the executive schemes that carry the task's general instruction; and, therefore, provide the basis for cognitive functioning at subsequent stages of development.[5] The k component grows by increments of one unit every other year from three years of age until adolescence. That is, mental capacity increases developmentally at the growth rate of one more unit of capacity (with which to boost an additional scheme or knowledge structure) approximately every two years until the age of 15.

Table 1

Predicted maximum M = power values as a function of age, and their correspondence to the Piagetian substage sequence.

$M = power (e + k)$	*Piagetian substage*	normative chronological age (*years*)
e + 1	low preoperations	3, 4
e + 2	high preoperations	5, 6
e + 3	low concrete operations	7, 8
e + 4	high concrete operations	9, 10
e + 5	substage introductory to formal operations	11, 12
e + 6	low formal operations	13, 14
e + 7	high formal operations	15-adults

This surprising growth pattern has been verified by different investigators using a variety of tasks based on the theory of M-capacity (e.g., Bereiter and Scardamalia, 1979; Burtis, 1982; Case and Serlin, 1979; Fabian, 1982; Goodman, 1979; Johnson, 1982, 1986; Parkinson, 1975; Pascual-Leone, 1970, 1978; Pascual-Leone and Hameluck, 1986; Todor, 1977, 1979). M-capacity measures have been developed by Pascual-Leone and his associates as well as by other neo-Piagetians in domains as different as visual information processing (M.S. Miller, 1980; Parkinson, 1975; Pascual-Leone, 1970, 1978, 1981); language (understanding of metaphors: Johnson, 1982, 1986); understanding or construction of sentences using linguistic connectives or possessive verbs (Benson, 1982;

Fabian, 1982; Johnson, Fabian, and Pascual-Leone, 1987); motor performance (Pascual-Leone and Hameluck, 1986; Todor, 1977, 1979), short-term memory (Benson, 1982; Burtis, 1982; Case, 1972, 1974, 1985), figural transformations (DeAvila, 1974; Logan, 1974; Pulos, 1979), and Piagetian problem-solving tasks (Case, 1985; de Ribaupierre and Pascual-Leone, 1979; Parkinson, 1975; Pascual-Leone, 1969; Scardamalia, 1977; Toussaint, 1976). Across domains, the age-group estimates of mental capacity obtained with M-capacity tests have been found to be essentially the same, provided there has been adequate training of respondents in the skill and knowledge structures required for the test.

The reliability and validity of M-capacity measures have been supported in many experiments (see the above references). In the case of one task (FIT), the tests have included thousands of subjects from culturally and socioeconomically diverse populations in Canada, the United States, Spain, Italy, England, Venezuela, Switzerland, and South Africa. Added support for the M-capacity construct has also come from a visual information-processing task, the CSVI (Compound Stimuli Visual Information) task (e.g., M.S. Miller, 1980; Parkinson, 1975; Pascual-Leone, 1970, 1978, 1981). A study by Globerson (1983) in Israel illustrates well the uncommon qualities of the CSVI task. In her study, conducted with Hebrew-speaking children from all over Israel, a variety of tests of intelligence and cognitive processing were administered. In addition to Pascual-Leone's CSVI task and a related Serial Stimuli Visual Information (SSVI) task, tests used included Raven Matrices, WISC verbal and performance scales, Cases's tests of M-capacity, and an Embedded Figures Test (testing field dependence). The subjects belonged to either a low SES (socioeconomic status) a middle SES, or a high SES group. As expected, the WISC verbal scale strongly distinguished among groups, as did the WISC performance scale and the other standard tests including the Raven. Showing less of an SES difference were Case's tests of M-capacity, and showing no SES differences at all were the CSVI and the SSVI. These findings illustrate well results obtained in other, albeit less dramatic, social-class studies.

The measures of M-capacity, when properly developed and administered, are remarkably insensitive to sociocultural differences. In another recent study, R. Miller and his associates (Miller, Pascual-Leone, Campbell & Juckes, 1986) administered two M-capacity measures, the FIT and the CSVI, to children between the ages of 7 and 12 years living in black townships in South Africa, under most inadequate schooling conditions. The results obtained from both tests showed that these children have the same M-capacity observed in middle-class Canadian children studied by Goodman (1979), although their initial knowledge base was inferior.[6]

The South African children were tested four times with parallel forms of the Figural Intersection Task to enable them to acquire the relevant operational structures. Essentially, the results obtained for all ages were in keeping with the predictions made on the basis of chronological age. Furthermore, the actual percentage of correct responses for the different item types was found to be related to the *M-demand* of the items.[7] If the M-demand of the given items was equal to or smaller than the M-capacity of the age-group samples, as predicted by the subjects' chronological age and by their performance on the CSVI task, the percentage of correct responses obtained for the different items in the second testing was above 60 percent. In the *first* testing trial, however, on item types with an M-demand equal to or smaller than the subjects' predicted M-power, performance was below that of the Canadians tested by Goodman. The second testing of the South African children yielded group M-capacity estimates that were virtually identical to those of Canadian children of corresponding age, and on the item types with an M-demand greater than the subjects' predicted M-power, the South Africans *outperformed* the Canadians.

The better performance of the South Africans over that of the Canadians does not, of course, mean that their mental capacity was greater. It simply means that they had acquired better knowledge structures, because they had been tested twice whereas the Canadians had been tested only once. This difference became apparent as soon as the M-demand of the test items became greater than the respondents' M-power. This finding is interesting in that it illustrates the situation in which children from culturally different environments often find themselves when being tested with norm-referenced tests such as IQ tests or achievement tests. Since due to lack of prior experience they have not developed adequate experiential structures for coping with the task at hand, they underperform compared to more experienced subjects when the task becomes too difficult.

Capacity Testing as a Form of Dynamic Assessment

Unlike IQ tests, capacity tests do not properly measure performance based on previously acquired informational processes, i.e., knowledge (skills and abilities), but rather measure the *processing mechanisms* themselves: the developmentally growing capacities and executive controls needed to generate *truly* novel, non-automatized performances (Pascual-Leone, 1980, 1984). These processing mechanisms (as opposed to the *informational processes* — i.e., knowledge, skills — on which the mechanisms act to produce performances) are the core determinants of developmental intelligence. The determinants of developmental intelligence are what Piaget (1985) called 'regulations' but did not study; and what Spearman (1927) called the 'mental energy' of general ('g' factor) intelligence, and what teachers at times call the source of a child's mental mobility and mental span. The capacity of the processing mechanisms themselves can be assessed by dynamically comparing in a theory-guided manner the child's intellectual performance across suitably chosen types of tasks. The suitability of these tasks is decided using Developmental Theory: knowledge about cognitive development attained through observational, correlational, clinical, and experimental investigations of children. Developmental theory offers rational, theory-guided methods of task analysis that yield detailed hypotheses about the processes and the processing mechanisms involved in a task. These hypotheses can be empirically verified and/or corrected by using the developmental method: for instance, presenting the task to age-group samples of suitably chosen (e.g., average) children and then examining how children's performance in the task evolves as a function of age; how different kinds of children differ in their performance; and how different kinds of tasks differ in their developmental traces. This procedure of simultaneously comparing types of tasks and types of children of various ages complements the traditional methods of correlations and experimentation, by adding the systematic experimental study of processing mechanisms themselves. These processing mechanisms are known to evolve naturally from the baby to the adult.

Because of the use of developmental theory and method, the creation and standardization of capacity tests do not always utilize (although they could) a norm-referenced method that postulates an ideal 'population'. Instead, experimental-developmental procedures are used to verify whether the theoretical task analyses of types of tasks (in terms of the capacities required to perform) serve to predict the tasks' relative developmental difficulty — as well as the individual differences that might be found in it (cf. Pascual-Leone and Sparkman, 1980; de Ribaupierre and Pascual-Leone, 1983). This developmental method is the one basically used by Piaget and his followers and, with less organismic emphasis, by the Vygotsky school and to some extent by its Western followers (e.g., Wertsch, 1985). It is also the method used by Feuerstein (Feuerstein, Rand and Hoffman, 1979; Feuerstein *et al*, 1980), Budoff (1974), Brown and her associates (e.g., Campione, Brown and Ferrara, 1982), and other learning-oriented researchers on 'metacognition'. It is also used by neo-Piagetian psychologists and educators (e.g., Case, 1985; de Ribaupierre and Pascual-Leone, 1983; Fischer and Lamborn, in press; Fischer and Silvern, 1985; Pascual-Leone, 1978, 1980; Scardamalia and Bereiter, 1984).

In this approach, a *dynamic assessment* of individual characteristics is attempted, with the form of questioning and amount of knowledge provided during or prior to testing adjusted to the subject's knowledge-based skills and abilities. The content of testing itself might still be the same as that of static, knowledge-based tests; but now the focus has radically changed from largely content-based (quantitative-qualitative) results, to *process-based* qualitative-structural or quantitative-structural results interpreted by developmental theory. Although a norm-based standardization is not essential for dynamic assessment, capacity-based tasks, after having been fully investigated developmentally, can be standardized. In fact, they can be standardized with more ease than knowledge-based tests, since the underlying process theory provides adequate criterion and construct validity. These criteria can serve to select subjects for the normative sample who are good representatives of the 'ideal population' against which the tasks in question *should* be standardized. In contrast, knowledge-based tests are usually not supported by a process theory, even when used to measure *general* (i.e., developmental) intelligence or learning potential. Consequently, developers of such tests are at a loss when trying to define criteria to select individuals who should represent the 'ideal population'. It is no wonder that the most common characteristic of well-schooled and school-successful children, that of being members of the white middle-class, has proved to be a dominant characteristic that IQ tests measure, even though theoretically it is not a characteristic intended by the test developers. For the same reason, IQ tests are good measures of intellectual capacity for high middle-class children, although not for other children. With M-capacity tests, this restriction of validity to individuals of a certain cultural and socio-cultural background does not apply (e.g., Case, 1974, 1975; DeAvila, Havassy, and Pascual-Leone, 1976; Globerson, 1983; M.S. Miller, 1975, 1980).

Methods of Capacity Assessment

Capacity assessment, as a form of intellectual assessment, is not new. There are five major approaches to capacity assessment: (1) classic 'culture-free' tests; (2) the train-test-train procedure; (3) dynamic assessment via on-line human mediation; (4) qualitative stage assessment; and (5) M-measurement.

Classic 'culture-free' tests represent the most traditional method of capacity assessment. Unlike the other approaches to capacity assessment, they are not dynamic and are less adaptable to individual differences in repertoire of knowledge and skills. They are designed to tap content domains that are familiar to people in every culture and, for this reason, are presumed to be *culture-fair*, i.e., to minimize (without eliminating altogether) performance differences that are due to cultural unfamiliarity with the content domain or the type of test in question. Often the content domain chosen is visual experiential structures, e.g., visual patterns, that have to be analyzed. (Raven's Progressive Matrices is the best known example of this type of test.) Their limitation comes from the fact that as a rule they are not culture-free, since the analytical mental procedures needed in them are unevenly used across cultures and social classes. This problem can be reduced, but only in part, by testing twice (or three times) with the same measure (or better, with a *parallel form* of the measure). In this way the initial testing is used as training to foster the respondent's familiarity with the task; only the results of the second testing are then taken as valid. Conducted in this manner, such tests can often yield acceptable estimates of M-capacity (cf. Bereiter and Scardamalia, 1979), at least with children from a socio-cultural background that is close enough to that of the original test standardization.

Train-test-train procedure: In this second method of capacity assessment, learning is used as a control. Tasks are organized in learning loops (Pascual-Leone, 1976), i.e., each type of item is preceded by an introductory section in which simple versions of the item type are dynamically (i.e., interactively with a teacher) taught to the examinee in a respond-correct-practice-respond-correct manner. Only when the respondent has mastered the procedure required to respond to the item type in question are more complex versions of the task items introduced. The train-test-train approach has been used informally by Montessori, Piaget, Rey, Feuerstein, and others. Aspects of this method have been more formally discussed by Budoff (1974), DeAvila and Havassy (1975), Feuerstein *et al.* (1979), Pascual-Leone (Pascual-Leone, 1976; DeAvila, Havassy, and Pascual-Leone, 1976), Case (1985), Case and Bereiter (1984), Brown and her associates (Brown, Bransford, Ferrara and Campione, 1983; Brown and Ferrara, 1982; Campione, Brown and Ferrara, 1982), Scardamalia and Bereiter (1984), Scardamalia, Bereiter and Steinbach (1984), and others. When used in the context of conceptual and problem-solving tasks that are well-structured in terms of developmental complexity (as is the case with Piagetian and neo-Piagetian tasks), the test-train-test procedure can become an effective paradigm for the dynamic assessment of intellectual capacity.

Dynamic assessment via human mediation: This procedure involves testing an individual twice, first providing no help and then giving on-line mediation (i.e., tutorial guidance). Performance in the first testing indicates what the examinee can accomplish by herself, without help. It reflects both her innate capacity level (i.e., level of processing mechanisms or purely organismic resources) and the sophistication of her repertoire (knowledge, skills, abilities). During the second testing, the examiner intervenes when needed to assist the testee with difficulties arising from oversights or misunderstandings, and to monitor her attention with suitable emphasizers and probes. Prior to this second testing, the examiner determines the testee's learning style and proceeds to present the testing material in a suitable manner. This strategy ensures that failure on the part of the respondent to perform does not arise from lack of knowledge, but rather from limitations of her degree of mental capacity and learning potential.

Dynamic assessment via human mediation originates with Vygotsky's theory of the Zone of Proximal Development (Vygotsky, 1978). Related approaches to measuring intellectual potential are the Learning Potential methods of Budoff, the Dynamic methods of Feuerstein, the Metacognitive methods of Brown, Campione,

Bransford, and others, and the Intentional-Cognition or Executive-Development methods of Ontario's neo-Piagetians (e.g., the schools of Bereiter, Case, Olson, Pascual-Leone, Scardamalia, etc.).

Of the methods of dynamic assessment mentioned above, the best known in Canada might be Feuerstein's *Learning Potential Assessment Device* (LPAD). The LPAD was originally developed in Israel for use with immigrant children who came from culturally different backgrounds; but the method has been used with other student populations. Feuerstein *et al.* (1979; 1980) define intelligence as "the capacity of an individual to use previously acquired experience to adjust to new situations." Central to this definition is the "capacity of the individual to be modified by learning." The purpose of the LPAD is to assess an individual's potential for 'modifiability' through learning. Like other dynamic assessment procedures, the LPAD uses an active process of teaching the information, procedures, attending strategies, etc., that are needed prior to the actual administration of the test. Principles and special skills are introduced during this dynamic pretraining, which facilitate the solution of progressively more complex task items — provided that the subject has the requisite mental (developmental) capacity. The LPAD emphasizes the existence in examinees of mental-analytical habits, as well as the importance of mediation during testing to facilitate creative dynamic synthesis in the testee.

Feuerstein *et al.* (1979) present some impressibe data to demonstrate the effectiveness of the LPAD in identifying particular aspects of modifiability in youngsters, including immigrants, previously diagnosed as mentally retarded by traditional psychometric assessment procedures. The innovative methods of LPAD are an advance over knowledge-based testing procedures. However, they have three limitations: (1) test administration is extremely time-consuming and therefore costly; (2) it represents a very specialized form of interpersonal assessment and thus requires highly trained testers; and (3) it fails to yield a quantitative estimate of a student's mental capacity/learning potential relative to that of other testees, which prevents the construction of norms against which the instrument can be better validated.

Qualitative Stage Assessment: We basically owe this method to Piaget and his school, but at present there are a number of different theories (the neo-Piagetian theories) which could be exploited for the purpose of assessment (e.g., Case, 1985; Fischer, 1980; Fischer and Silvern, 1985; Fischer and Lamborn, in press; Halford, 1982). The (often implicit) method of assessment is essentially the same in all these theories, although the tasks and content domains utilized might differ from one to the other. It consists of the evaluation of the subject's *natural-developmental stage*, i.e., his/her ordinal — or metric ordinal — position in the natural ladder of the developmental, qualitative, levels of performance. (These levels are found across developmentally critical tasks from within a suitable content domain, and also across domains.)

The method consists of assessing the developmental intelligence of the subject by way of determining his/her current natural-developmental stage. This method is theory-guided, in the sense that it necessitates, perhaps more than previous assessment methods, the acceptance and use of strong theoretical assumptions about development. These assumptions give power to the task-analytical methods on which the procedure is based. Notice that failure to make these assumptions changes the procedure into another instance of knowledge-based intellectual assessment which, as in any knowledge-based assessment, cannot escape the problems of traditional psychometrics.

These theoretical assumptions, too involved for detailed explanation here, are the central tenets (postulates) of Piagetian and/or neo-Piagetian developmental psychology. In essence they consist of the following four claims:

(1) The psychological organism develops and learns by way of progressive approximations that are achieved by means of *differentiation* (adaptation and correction) and *coordination* of previously existent schemes and structures. The result of these differentiations and coordinations is the emergence of newly adapted, differentiated processes, i.e., schemes or structures, that are being progressively incorporated into (and coordinated with) the previous ones.

(2) Adaptive differentiation and coordination of structures is dependent upon the *stage* of growth of mental capacity (Piaget thought of this mental capacity as a functional level of 'regulations'). This growth occurs as a function of maturation and of general (i.e., non-specific) experiences.

(3) The stage of growth of mental capacity is *truly general* in the strong sense that the functional capabilities it provides, in terms of ability to differentiate/coordinate schemes and structures, can be applied equally well across content domains (for as long as the subject has had sufficient experience in the domain).

(4) The current developmental power of a subject's mental capacity (or level of 'regulations') can best be assessed when content-specific learning is not confounded with age-bound development. For this reason it can be best assessed in situations of the type called 'problem solving', where the performance to be produced is not automatized but is *truly new* to the subject; and where he/she must *creatively synthesize* the response by using his/her power of mental capacity (i.e., current level of 'regulations').

An important neo-Piagetian implication of these four developmental assumptions, rarely appreciated in its significance for assessment, is as follows: Provided that the assessment tasks are suitable, as indicated in (4), and that the assessment of power of mental capacity is properly done, *any content-domain can be used to assess the power of mental capacity.* Furthermore, *this assessed power of mental capacity can be assumed to be the same available for use in any content domain.* This theoretical conclusion, which Pascual-Leone is extracting from Piagetian and neo-Piagetian theories under the assumption of a unitary, general-purpose mental capacity, is most important: it should enable us to make the diagnosis of the subject's power of mental capacity using any content domain; and therefore using the domain where the subject has greater familiarity and skill. The highest qualitative stage level within truly novel problem-solving situations attained by the subject, in *any* of the content domains where he/she was tested, should, according to this conclusion, reflect mental capacity. By allowing the diagnosis of mental capacity (i.e., of developmental intelligence) in *any* of the content domains available for testing, it becomes possible to assess the subject under conditions that might be most culturally fair — assuming, of course, that the subject has been properly tested in all relevant content domains that could possibly be optimal in this regard. This procedure should generate a powerful method of assessment. It has not been used in any large scale for two reasons: (1) psychologists and educators have not appreciated this implication of the Piagetian and neo-Piagetian theories (many, infatuated with data showing the role of a learning factory, refuse to believe in the existence of a general-purpose, unitary mental capacity); and (2) the assessment of developmental intelligence using this method becomes very time-consuming. It is time-consuming because subjects must be tested with a large battery of Piagetian or neo-Piagetian tasks, tapping different content domains that might be potentially relevant for evaluation.

Pascual-Leone's approach differs from that of Piaget and other neo-Piagetians in that it explicitly offers a *causal theory* for the Piagetian and neo-Piagetian structuralist/descriptive theories (see Pascual-Leone, 1980, 1984, 1987a, 1987b). This theory contains a method of task analysis and technical notation for conducting these analyses, which are not meant to replace but to generalize, supplement, and quantify the other qualitative-structuralist methods. This neo-Piagetian quantitative method is called *M*-measurement.

M-measurement: Like the other methods of dynamic assessment, *M*-measurement uses learning mediated by a psychologist/teacher as a control variable. In this manner testees are led to acquire, prior to the main task, all the knowledge and skill components they need in order to perform. But the integration of necessary components into the total performance is never practiced; this is left to the subject's spontaneous power of creative mental synthesis ('putting the task together'). The scope and complexity of these creative mental syntheses serve to measure the mental (M) capacity of the subject (Pascual-Leone, 1976, 1980, 1987). Unlike other forms of dynamic or stage assessment, M-measurement formalizes mediated learning, and thus permits a quantitative evaluation of the respondent's mental capacity/learning potential in a manner that is relatively insensitive to his or her previous knowledge base. M-measurement exhibits many features of dynamic assessment and has overcome a shortcoming of Feuerstein's method, i.e., its lack of a proper scale of measurement. For this reason it is able to *predict* the age-normed performance in Feuerstein's tasks (Bachor, 1976); something that Feuerstein's own methods cannot do. This new method yields quantitative estimates of children's mental capacity that can be used for standardization or comparison purposes. It provides estimates of the testee's *functional M-capacity*, i.e., the capacity he or she normally uses, as well as the *M-reserve* or structural M-capacity, the latent capacity that could potentially be used. Unlike Feuerstein's LPAD, M-measurement is administered easily, and its administration is considerably less time-consuming and costly than is the case with Feuerstein's or the Qualitative-Stage assessment.

M-measurement can be used as a group test as well as individually. Administered individually, it might provide more information because in this case the introductory training and the continuous mediation of the experimenter makes the test better adapted to the examinee's individual characteristics and weak points.

When the executive and skill components of an M-measure task are properly taught to the subject in advance of testing, while still not training in the synthesis of the performance, the task should be valid with children of any cultural, social, and linguistic background. Suitable M-measures could be administered to children as young as two or three years of age, thus providing the ground for early assessment of mental capacity and learning potential.

These measures also make relatively few linguistic demands; their instructions can therefore be easily translated into other languages. For this reason, they particularly lend themselves for use with respondents from different cultural backgrounds. In the case of linguistically based M-measures, test performance has been found to be more closely related to the sophistication of the concepts mastered with the help of the mother tongue than to the subject's proficiency in the language of testing (Johnson, 1986). Limited proficiency in the language used in testing does not necessarily affect the M-level score; or at least not as much as in the case of conventional IQ measures.

Although formal use of this method for actual school assessment needs experimentation, its use in psychological research suggests that M-measurement can be developed into a general methodology for intellectual assessment. In addition to already existing measures in the areas of visual information processing, short-term memory, language, metaphor processing, motor performance, and problem-solving of the Piagetian variety, M-measures can be developed in virtually any domain to tap different content-related aspects of learning capacity. This use of multiple M-measures tasks tapping different relevant content domains would be advantageous in that it would permit direct quantitative comparison of performance levels across content domains.

A number of M-measures have been shown to be good predictors of children's (or adult's) learning potential (e.g., Bachor, 1976; de Ribaupierre and Pascual-Leone, 1979; Johnstone and El-Banna, 1986; Niaz and Lawson, 1985). Their ability to predict learning potential has been evidenced in tasks involving Piaget's Concrete or Formal Operations, as well as in tasks involving more academically standard mental operations such as those intervening in perceptual readiness, writing, or science education.

The tasks used most extensively to date for M-measurement are two visual information processing tasks, the Figural Intersections Task (FIT), described earlier, and the Compound Stimuli Visual Information (CSVI) Task (Globerson, 1983; Pascual-Leone, 1970, 1978). These tests have high reliability and construct validity. They yield estimates of the respondents' M-capacity that in regression analyses have been found to predict performance on other cognitive tasks. In the research settings where M-measurement research has been conducted up to now, diverse M-tasks have been found to yield for the same subject similar quantitative estimates of M-capacity. Furthermore, *averaging* these different M-estimates from the various tasks usually yields a better predictor of performance, even when predicting dependent variables that belong to a different content domain. Thus, a number of indicators suggest that the various M-tasks are assessing the same basic process (i.e., M-capacity); and that this process is being measured by means of interval scales that are relatively content-free.

It is a recognized principle of psychological testing that negative or poor results on a test might not reflect the optimal performance of the subject, but could be caused by irrelevant contingencies experienced at the time of testing (e.g., anxiety, fatigue, bad rapport with the assessor, lack of experience regarding the content domain tested, etc.). Similar problems might occur with M-measures, although the introductory training period should serve as a good warm-up for the testee. Therefore, when the results obtained do not seem to represent a true picture of child's learning potential, repeated testing with a parallel form is recommended. This parallel-form reassessment is easy to do with M-measures that tap the same or different domains. Since M-scores generated by these measures can be directly averaged to increase the reliability and validity of the M-estimate, the problem of validity of a negative result can always be empirically resolved — something at times difficult to do with other types of measure.

Capacity Testing as a Culture-Fair Assessment

In summary, two modes of cognitive assessment have been discussed: (1) the assessment of knowledge-based strategies, skills, and abilities, as exemplified by traditional IQ tests, and (2) the assessment of general-purpose, 'content-free' capacities found in capacity tests. IQ tests were said to be based on knowledge that is culture-dependent, and this makes them biased in favour of respondents with suitable previous cultural experiences.

Capacity tests were said to measure innate mental capacities and executive controls, and this characteristic makes them relatively independent of socio-cultural experiences and schooling. Mental capacity was defined in terms of the maximum number of schemes and structures that a subject can *simultaneously* boost to high activation. It was said to grow developmentally, following the stages of cognitive development identified by Piaget and neo-Piagetian theories. M-measurement seems to yield scales that assess in a fundamental way (by means of interval scales) mental capacity, i.e., what educators and psychologists often call developmental intelligence.

Five types of capacity tests have been described: classic 'culture-free' tests, the train-test-train procedure, dynamic assessment via on-line mediation, qualitative-stage assessment, and M-measurement. Capacity tests were conceptualized as assessing the process of *creative/dynamic syntheses* in cognitive functioning (i.e., the processing mechanisms themselves) rather than the possession of strategies, knowledge, and skills.

The capacity measures discussed differed in two respects: (a) in the degree of formality of the dynamic assessment involved, and (b) in the degree to which they assess, along with capacity, task-specific strategies and acquired knowledge. The cross-cultural and cross-lingual validity and applicability of M-tasks is inversely related to the degree to which they also assess culture-dependent knowledge.

We have reached the conclusion that of the types of test reviewed, M-measures hold the greatest promise of becoming truly culture-fair methods for assessing *developmental intelligence*; (i.e., mental capacity and learning potential). They can be applied to children across different age levels, languages, and socio-cultural backgrounds. They yield M-levels that make clear predictions, via task analysis, about the qualitative patterns of performance to be expected from children; and yet they can be standardized and administered as classic quantitative psychometric tests are. Finally, their results can be easily interpreted within the framework of any of the Piagetian or neo-Piagetian theories of cognitive development.

Much more research directed to assessment with these new methods is required before final conclusions can be drawn regarding their use in the school system. But from the available experimental data it seems that M-measurement deserves to be carefully investigated. As an applied technology it promises to yield more equitable procedures for assessing intellectual potential (particularly with culturally and linguistically diverse children) than has been achieved with traditional psychometric tests.

FOOTNOTES

1. The term 'ability' used here refers to the minimum amount of concrete know-how needed to perform specific (behavioural or mental) actions or discriminations. By contrast, 'skills' represent complex organizations of abilities that are required to perform certain tasks defined as important by a culture. for example, reading and writing represent 'skills' that involve 'abilities' such as visual discrimination, motor coordination, etc.
2. There are theories of intelligence in the Piagetian/neo-Piagetian and the Vygotskian traditions, as well as in recent psychometric/information-processing work (e.g., Sternberg, 1984).
3. Pascual-Leone (1969; Pascual-Leone and Smith, 1969) introduced the term 'neo-Piagetian' into the psychology literature and initiated the neo-Piagetian approach. There are now various neo-Piagetian theories that differ in a number of fine points. From the practical perspective of this chapter, however, the differences are irrelevant. Here we call neo-Piagetian not only those psychologists who accept this label, but also those who, like Bruner, Feuerstein, and others, follow or creatively elaborate upon the Swiss developmental school (e.g., Piaget, Rey) and/or the Russian school (e.g., Vygotsky, Luria).
4. Piaget refers to mental operative functioning as 'operativity' and distinguishes the levels of Preoperations, Concrete Operations, and Formal Operations.
5. The mental capacity developed throughout the first two years of life (Alp, 1987; Holloway, Blake, and Pascual-Leone, 1987) is used, Pascual-Leone believes, to boost into *high activation*, and thus make dominant, the executive plans that govern the subject's task strategy.
6. 'Knowledge base' refers to knowledge, experiences, and executive skills relevant to the completion of a test.
7. 'Item type' or 'Item class' was defined by the number of relevant figures intersecting. The 'M-demand' of items is equal to the number of those figures.

Chapter 11

Towards Nondiscriminatory Assessment: Principles and Application

Ronald J. Samuda

The theme permeating the issues, problems, practices, and innovations discussed in the previous chapters can be summed up in a single sentence: namely, evaluation procedures applied to minority students should be valid for the purposes for which they are being used. That might seem like a kind of truism; yet, it has been necessary for us to present the evidence and the arguments to show that the assessment and placement of minorities as constituted in most school jurisdictions represent the most potent factors in retarding the scholastic progress of large numbers of students in the schools of Canada and the U.S. We have demonstrated the consequences of such practices as leading to an overrepresentation of minority group students in special education classes and in vocationally oriented programs while systematically excluding them from the academic programs that can lead to professional and socioeconomic mobility. In short, much of the assessment and placement paraphernalia tend to discriminate against minorities while favouring the middle class mainstream.

Our concerns have been backed up by the conclusive demonstrations of disparity in the proportionate distribution of students in program categories in Canada and the United States. Moreover, we reiterate references to the various reviews in the area of non-discriminatory assessment that have presented analyses, guidelines and recommendations for changing the system by improving the assessment and placement processes, thereby leading to a reasonable degree of educational equity (DeAvila, 1976; Dent, 1976; Deutsch, 1967; Mercer, 1973; Samuda, 1975, 1980; Sattler, 1982; Ysseldyke, 1978). The research results have been bolstered by the public outcry for a fairer system leading to certain changes in the policies of education (e.g. Public Law 94-142 in the U.S.), which now require that tests and evaluation materials must be provided and administered in the student's own language, that tests be validated for the purpose for which they are used, be administered by trained personnel preferably familiar with the cultural and linguistic backgrounds of the students upon whom the tests are being used, and be tailored to areas of specific educational need.

More briefly stated, the policies require that assessment instruments and procedures should not only be valid for the purpose for which they are used, but, of equal importance, that program placement should also be tailored to the needs of the student. Unfortunately, such policies have not been universally implemented and many fail to recognize that the problem of bias is multifaceted (Jones, 1985; Reschly, 1980). In the Canadian context, there has been a mounting demand to make changes that will guarantee a more equitable system. Pressure from a number of community groups in the metropolitan Toronto area, especially, and from the Ontario Human Rights Commission, led to the formation of a Cabinet Committee on Race Relations and the resolve of the provincial government to assume a leadership role. On several occasions, the liberal premier, David Peterson, singled out the issues of the assessment and streaming of minority students as being of central concern. On March 21, 1986, at the Provincial Race and Ethnocultural Relations Conference in Toronto, the Education Minister, Sean Conway, pledged to develop a provincial race relations policy that would serve as a prototype for Ontario school boards, and the essential focus of that policy was student assessment and program placement.

This chapter represents the culmination of a series of meetings by a consultative committee comprising representatives from school boards, universities, various agencies, and officers of the education ministry, to address the issues and problems of assessment and placement. The report of the committee was based on a literature review as well as input received from three of the authors (Samuda, Cummins, and Pascual-Leone). The essential conclusion of the consultants was that change in the area of nonbiased assessment will depend not only on the knowledge of education policy makers and school personnel but also upon their awareness and sensitivity in such crucial factors as current research, cultural and linguistic bases inherent in currently available ability tests, different learning styles requiring a variety of teaching modes, curriculum that is relevant and reflective of diverse racial and cultural realities and which recognizes the contributions of minority groups, opportunities within classrooms for students to express and share their experiences in a variety of modes (verbal, written, and artistic), assessment conducted on a regular and continuous basis, incorporating both formal and informal assessment procedures, and alternate assessment methods based on developmental theory (e.g., dynamic and capacity assessment) in addition to conventional standardized tests.

The consultative committee (see appendix for list of participants) directed its efforts towards three basic goals: 1) to prepare a list of answers to questions posed; 2) to enunciate a list of guiding principles that address the needs and problems identified in the terms of reference; and 3) to develop a list of recommendations to effect change and improvement with regard to the validity of the assessment and placement of minority students. The latter task was organized and directed to decision makers at four different levels, namely, provincial/state (policy) level, universities, school boards, and schools. The principles promulgated in the report were culled from the research literature in the United States and Canada where the concern for better methods of minority student education are almost identical, for the issues are universal and the objectives are similar whether we consider the plight of Haitians in the Miami Dade school system or whether we contend with the assessment and placement of Portuguese children from the Azores in the schools of metropolitan Toronto. The same problems exist in Vancouver, and San Francisco, Edmonton and New York. We believe that the conclusions and recommendations of the consultative committee are not specific to Ontario alone but can serve as a model for all systems of education seeking to establish an equitable system of nondiscriminatory assessment and placement for *all* students. The recommendations and principles go beyond the mere choice and application of testing techniques. Rather, the thrust is towards levels of responsibility and accountability in implementing change. We have also summarized the changes actually taking place in one school board that has taken to heart the gist of the committee's recommendations.

A. *Identify the strengths and weaknesses of assessment materials used in Ontario, in other provinces, and in other countries at the present.*

B. *Identify the mechanisms which are used in Ontario to informally and formally assess, place, and program recent immigrant and visible minority students.*

1. In order to reasonably address these two questions it was necessary to reference current research and literature dealing with assessment and placement programs for minority students: e.g., Samuda and Crawford, 1980; Cummins, 1984, 1986; MacIntyre, 1985; Toronto Board of Education, 1975; Pascual-Leone, 1987.

2. While tests presently being used give a sense of a pupil's current level of functioning in terms of selected skills and abilities related to the culture on which the tests are based, there is often misinterpretation of what has been assessed and failure to assess other and potentially more important competencies.

3. Effective assessment models should: a) reflect the concept of equality and equality of education for a just society taking into account pupils' learning styles, motivation patterns, linguistic variations, cultural variations, and diverse capacities; b) put assessment into a broader and more appropriate educational context to include how assessment relates to and reflects instruction, how parental involvement interacts with the assessment process, and taking into account what the knowledge base, mind set, role definition, and relationships are of the people in the process, namely, pupils, parents, psychometric resource staff, classroom teachers, and administrators.

4. Current weaknesses in assessment (and program placement) practices include: a) lack of explicit direction in legislation with regard to special education/IPRC processes as these pertain to (recent) immigrants, culturally and/or racially diverse or visible minority students and their parents; b) misconceptions on the part of some test givers and test result users that intellectual capacity has been assessed when what has really been measured is acquired knowledge as defined by mainstream middle-class test developers; c) failure to realize test limitations and that the current practice of relying on standardized testing procedures is inadequate. The fact is that no test, whether formal or informal, will be sufficient in and of itself, for it is a fallacy to think that more and better of the same thing will lead to assessment equity.

C. Identify the barriers that adversely affect the assessment and program opportunities of children because of their race, culture, ethnicity, and language.

1. Monolingual/ethnocentric tests and testers.

2. Inadequate and inaccurate knowledge of tests, testing and minority students.

3. Lack of a well defined policy regarding assessment and program placement of minority students and/or discrepancies between policy and practice.

4. The tendency to maintain the status quo because of the implications of change (e.g., too expensive to change test instruments and materials and the difficulty of changing the personal beliefs and behaviours of teachers).

5. Underutilization of the student's home language, culture and background in the school curriculum.

6. Insufficient knowledge and awareness on the part of teachers concerning the unique and different individual and cultural learning styles.

7. Inadequate training and sensitivity to the problems and needs of minority students on the part of school based staff, especially those in guidance and counselling positions.

8. Lack of understanding on the part of educators of behaviours representative of diverse cultural backgrounds.

9. Unconscious stereotyping and prejudice on the part of educators that reflect patterns of interaction and expectation within the broader community.

10. Inadequate communication with parents and significant others who know the student.

11. Faulty notions of what tests really measure, and misconceptions of the information that tests do actually yield.

12. Insufficient information and knowledge on the part of policy makers concerning the state of the art in testing.

13. Inconsistent assessment practices.

14. Lack of ongoing assessment, and lack of open-ended program placement.

15. Erroneous and unfair practices of labelling students based on one test result or limited assessment data.

16. A mind set that achievement difficulties in students are unalterable.

17. Interpretation of psychological tests as indicators of expectations for student performance rather than as indicators of necessary program intervention.

18. Policies and practices that are contradicted by research (e.g., testing immigrants with standardized tests within two years of arrival).

19. Lack of ministry/state and board level policies and resources regarding assessment and placement of minority students.

20. The prevalence of static homogenous groupings in classrooms and schools.

21. Lack of booster or transitional programs to encourage and help students move to different levels and experience different program options.

22. The prevalence of transmission-oriented learning environments.

23. Inflexibility with respect to modes of acquiring and expressing understanding and knowledge, i.e., the primacy of printed words.

24. Insufficient information given to parents and students concerning program choices and the implications of these choices at critical transition points.

25. The technology of assessment itself (i.e., test instruments, computer hardware and software) may intimidate or distract the minority student. A certain amount of orientation to the technology is necessary for some minority group students.

26. Inadequate identification and utilization of resource personnel in schools.

D. Identify causes of overrepresentation of some minority groups in lower academic streams.

1. Low teacher expectations.

2. Low student expectations.

3. Curriculum that does not include the multicultural back-grounds or contributions of nonwhites to the society as a whole.

4. General rigidity of the system and the curriculum that does not utilize or take advantage of cultural diversity as positive teaching resources.

5. Negative impressions of ESL and/or heritage language, often perceived as hindrances rather than advantages.

6. Indications of systematic racism in society and in schools as supported by current research.

7. Pedagogy that is primarily based on a passive model of teaching and learning as opposed to interactive teaching-learning models.

8. Non-recognition and/or non-acceptance on the part of some mainstream educators of different values, behaviours, and learning styles of various minority student groups.

9. The penchant for homogenous classroom groupings.

10. The tendency to group ESL students in basic level or special education programs (e.g., ESL viewed as a disability/learning handicap).

11. Lack of guidance personnel at both the elementary and secondary school levels with adequate training in antiracist education, including non-biased assessment.

12. Insufficient interaction and interface between elementary and secondary school personnel (teachers, counsellors, and principals).

13. Lack of parental involvement in student assessment, and in program placement decisions.

14. In some cases inappropriate assessment; in others, no assessment at all when in fact assessment should have occurred.

E. Identify strategies that support the appropriate placement and educational progress of children with diverse racial, cultural, ethnic, and linguistic roots.

1. Involve the parents in the student's education.
2. Promote strong home-school communication links.
3. Promote a positive view of bilingualism, heritage languages, and multiculturalism.

4. Promote the initiation of professional training for school psychologists and selected teachers in non-biased testing (e.g., dynamic assessment and capacity testing).

5. Create and offer training courses for teachers in the area of formal and informal assessment.

6. Use multiple assessment instruments and involve more than one approach to assessment.

7. Promote heterogenous groupings in classrooms.

8. Promote strategies for cooperation rather than competition within the curriculum (e.g., role playing, simulating advocacy positions).

9. Promote interactive small groups in planning classroom instructional strategies.

10. Offer a curriculum that is accurate and interactive in representing minorities, and guard against a hidden curriculum that may contribute to racism.

11. Promote representation of minorities in the teaching force.

F. Identify ways and means of ensuring a multi-faceted approach to student assessment in a broad based education context.

1. Employ both formal and informal methods of assessing students as articulated in Principle 7 to follow in the next section.

2. Promote opportunities for students to interact and develop skills and competencies such as leadership and social skills through co-curriculum activities (social, sports, cultural, art groups) that would enable staff to observe the students in non-classroom non-academic settings and situations.

3. Develop training courses for education staff in both formal and informal assessment procedures and require professional staff to become skilled in the various assessment modes.

4. Develop policies and practices that link assessment to program response/modification rather than assigning students to a particular existing level or 'status quo' program.

5. Develop a policy and procedures that require teachers and other relevant education staff to assume a collaborative approach using a variety of assessment data in making decisions about program placements for students.

6. Focus on the classroom teacher as a key person in assessing the student and promote the need for various ongoing assessment procedures in the context of daily classroom activities.

In the following section we provide the guiding principles enunciated by the committee as they relate to attitudes, organizational, and pedagogical concerns, as well as the actual issues of assessment itself for minority groups.

Guiding principles of assessment and placement of minority students for educational equity

A. Attitudinal:

1. Available empirical evidence indicates that mental capacity and learning potential are equally distributed across all races, ethnic groups, and social classes. Accordingly, equality of educational opportunity should result in equality of educational outcome. There are, therefore, no empirical grounds to support over-representation of some minorities in special education, vocational or basic level programs, or under-representation of minority students in gifted/ enrichment programs.

2. Knowledge of the learning history, cultural background,and life experience of children is essential for the appropriate assessment and placement of students within the school system. For this reason, it is essential to involve parents in the process of assessment of their children, and to clearly apprise parents of the implications of various decision options regarding program choices.

B. Organizational and Pedagogical:

1. The learning environment is a significant factor in the student's cognitive growth, academic progress, and social development. Informed assessment of students is more likely to occur in classrooms characterized by an *interactive* teaching-learning environment, that is, a setting where students have an opportunity to participate actively in the learning process and to show their progress and learning styles by expressing and sharing their experiences in a variety of modes.

2. Program placement must be open-ended to allow students access to a variety of program options. Empirical evidence does not substantiate academic advantages of streaming students except for the very gifted.

C. Assessment:

1. Assessment should be used for purposes of intervention, mediation, and programming, and not just for assigning students to a particular level or program.

2. Assessment by education staff must be informed with respect to the test being used and to the students being tested. It is essential of a student, whether this potential is manifested or not in the student's actual performance. A comprehensive assessment practice

3. Assessment of mental-capacity and general intelligence is intended to recognize the latent mental capacity and learning potential of a student, whether this potential is manifested or not in the student's actual performance. A comprehensive assessment practice should therefore encompass the following four methods of assessment:

Formal (standardized) models including a) conventional psychometric tests (knowledge based) such as achievement, intelligence, and socialization; b) tests based on developmental theory (e.g. dynamic assessment mental capacity assessment, learning potential).

Informal (interpersonal) models including a) group assessment, that is, assessment of the student in the context of the total school/classroom program (e.g., class tests, academic progress, personal development etc.); b) individual assessment derived from interviews, personal behaviour, socialization, observation (directed and casual).

4. Educators should use the best data available from a variety of assessment models in order to make program and placement decisions in favour of the student. Positive data, whether based on formal (standardized) testing or informal (interactive ongoing) procedures, should be used to override any negative assessment data.

5. To make informed program and placement decisions with respect to the student, it is necessary to assess his or her capacity to learn and grow, not just his/her current knowledge and/or socialization base. Therefore, evaluation of a student's potential depends upon the collaborative judgment of a number of professionals interpreting a variety of assessment data pertaining to the student.

Recommendations and Strategies for Change and Improvement Leading Towards Non-biased Assessment

The Consultative Committee's report was addressed to four different levels of responsibility at the state or provincial level, university, school board, and school level. The report also emphasized that anti-racist education should encompass knowledge of and sensitivity to multiculturalism, race relations, bilingualism, and affirmative action as well as knowledge of non-biased assessment. The recommendations are given below:

A. *Provincial or State Policy Level Decision-makers Should:*

1. Develop and publicize a policy statement (i.e., a clear statement of direction) with regard to the assessment and program placement of students.

2. Develop a 'student assessment resource guide' that clearly addresses assessment and placement as well as the programming of minority students.

3. Communicate to education communities current research pertaining to anti-racist education and non-biased testing as well as citing positive (board level) practices for assessment and placement of minority students.

4. Fund research and development in the area of 'non-biased assessment' and support activities designed to operationalize this research and development at the school level.

5. Help to fund innovative 'assessment and placement' programs in various selected boards to help establish an experience base for other boards to reference. Develop non-biased approaches to assessment as well as conducting standardized testing (achievement, aptitude, psychological, capacity) in the student's native tongue — if and where deemed appropriate.

6. Select a team of experts in the area of capacity testing comprised of theorists and practitioners to develop and implement, on a pilot basis in selected school boards, instruments for non-biased assessment.

7. Collaborate with the Ministry of Citizenship and Culture and relevant parent groups for the purpose of enhancing public awareness and community education regarding the assessment and placement of minority students.

8. Establish a committee to a) periodically review assessment and placement policies and practices as these pertain to minority students at the school board and school levels; b) serve as an appeal board in matters pertaining to assessment and program placement of minority students; c) periodically review the hiring and selection practices as these pertain to professional staff at the ministry, university, and board levels; d) periodically review admission procedures at universities and, especially, faculties of education as these pertain to potential teacher candidates from minority groups.

B. The University Level (Faculties of Education):

It is recommended that:

1. Registration requirements for psychologists who work in educational settings include knowledge and expertise in the area of non-biased assessment (e.g., capacity testing). Certification requirements should also be tailored to, and built on, the needs of the local state or provincial school population.

2. University faculties of education should develop and make available to school board education staff, courses in the area of anti-racist education including topics such as multiculturalism, bilingualism, race relations, and non-biased assessment.

3. All professional staff involved with assessment and placement of minority children (psychologists, guidance counsellors, special education teachers) should have background knowledge in the area of anti-racist education.

4. Faculties of Education should develop and offer courses in testing and evaluation with a focus on the administration of various types of standardized testing, including capacity testing and dynamic assessment to be used in schools.

5. Professional staff involved with assessment and placement of minority students should have skills not only in administering various types of tests, but also in interpreting and communicating the test results to parents.

6. University faculties of education and school boards should collaborate for the purpose of developing and delivering programs designed to respond to teacher training needs and 'continuing professional development needs' at both the pre-service and in-service levels. *Pre-service* programs should include introductory courses in anti-racist education as well as courses in student evaluation in general and the assessment of minority students in particular. *In-service* training in the area of anti-racist education and student assessment should be made available to practising teachers. Boards and faculties should collaborate to provide Additional Qualification courses in these areas.

7. Faculties of education and other related disciplines (e.g. Psychology and Sociology) should make a concerted effort to hire professional staff with training and knowledge in the areas of anti-racist education. The various university disciplines and departments should also collaborate to develop common joint course offerings related to staff development at both pre-service and in-service levels.

C. School Boards should:

1. a) Undertake a review of current policies and practices regarding assessment and placement of minority students so as to determine their adequacy and fairness in relations to emerging Ministry of Education guidelines and current research in the area of non-biased assessment; b) conduct a survey of student populations on a regular basis to determine actual program placements of minority students; c) where data indicate a disproportionate number of minority students in special education programs, basic level or vocational courses, and/or under-representation of minority students in gifted or 'enriched' programs, develop and/or refine policy and procedures to ensure a more equitable distribution of minority students.

2. Plan for and offer in collaboration with universities and other education agencies in-service courses in the area of anti-racist education and assessment of minority students.

3. Encourage and expect administrative personnel (supervisory officers, principals, resource teachers) to assume a leadership role in the area of anti-racist education and non-biased assessment of minority students.

4. Develop policy and practices that link assessment to program response and modification, rather than merely assigning students to a particular existing level or 'status quo' program.

5. Develop a policy and procedures that require teachers and other relevant education staff to assume a collaborative approach using a variety of assessment data in making decisions about program placements for students. This collaborative approach would need to include the student's parent or guardian.

D. Schools and Classroom Teachers

It is recommended that:

1. School principals should assume a leadership role at the local school level with regard to anti-racist education and non-biased assessment of minority students.

2. The principal and teachers should evaluate current student assessment and program placement practices in the school, and collaborate on improvements as necessary. For example, they should examine ways in which non-biased assessment practices can be promoted in the school, and examine the relationship between assessment and instruction in the classrooms.

3. In each school the principal and teachers should develop a school-based 'language arts policy' (in relation to Ministry and board language guidelines) that reflect the particular nature of the local school community and that contains strategies for non-biased assessment.

4. The principal and teachers should develop a school level policy and practices for communicating with parents.

5. To the extent that the principal is responsible for the hiring of school staff, consideration should be given to bringing in staff who are knowledgeable and skilled in the area of anti-racist education and representative of the community being served from the viewpoints of language, ethnicity, race, and culture.

The North York Board of Education: A Model Case Study

We have chosen to exemplify the North York School Board's procedures because they appear to signify the ways in which the principles and recommendations given in this chapter can be realized. The North York Board also presents us with the circumstances where the school population is culturally diverse, where sizable numbers of visible minorities reside, and where the administrators, professional consultants, and teachers have sought to cope with problems of assessing and placing ethnic minority immigrants in as equitable a manner as possible. It seems to us that the North York Board has gone a far way in making adjustments to the systems of assessment and program delivery and therefore provides us with a kind of model. We were indeed fortunate in having as a participant on the consultative committee, the head of the board's psychological services, Dr. Ruth Baumel, who supplied the data for what follows.

Nondiscriminatory Assessment and Psychological Services:

The North York Board of Education has, for several years, sought to find nondiscriminatory ways of assessing students so as to meet the needs of their culturally diverse school population. The input from a task force on testing and streaming completed in June 1984 was later augmented and elaborated upon by a subcommittee on assessment and psychological services in June 1985. The policies and practices now in place at North York represent a kind of prototype of the process by which a school board might tackle the onerous challenge of minority student assessment and placement in a very mixed area.

It is significant to note that board policy requires the involvement of a multicultural consultant when dealing with the cases of minority students who have been in the country for less than one year. Even for those ethnic minorities who are not very recent arrivals, but who are experiencing academic difficulties, such consultants are frequently called in for their advice in arriving at a program of modification. Special education procedures also affect the timing of assessment that is conducted after the classroom modification has been attempted. The psychoeducational consultant is often involved in observing the student prior to planning for a modification program. When assessment is undertaken, it is done in as broad a context as possible, using the techniques of observation as well as employing both formal and informal methods. In its efforts to cope with the diverse and atypical student population, the board has sought to use a wide variety of new approaches to nondiscriminatory assessment.

The North York board does not depend on a single score or set of scores; instead, students are considered for reassessment every three years in addition to the observation procedures as minority students become more familiar with the language and culture of the school. Moreover, in accordance with the recommendations made above, such assessments are conducted only with the written permission of parents and include a meeting with parents to discuss the results.

To increase the sensitivity of its staff to the pitfalls of assessment, all professional workers are required to take part in a 'racism' conference. In its search for answers to the assessment of minorities, the board has initiated training and research in the use of several innovative techniques mentioned in the previous chapters.

In the area of intelligence tests, for example, the board has undertaken training in the use of the Kaufman-ABC. Some users have complained about the bulkiness of the test and the difficulty of seeing the processing of thought as the student works. They report also the lack of verbal input in the administration of the test.

Jane Mercer's SOMPA (system of multi-phasic assessment) was also employed. However, the norms are based (as Ralph Agard has emphasized) on California data, and the black students in Toronto do not compare with their U.S. counterparts to the extent that the SOMPA's 'estimated learning potential' may not be appropriate.

The Naglieri Matrix Analogies Test is a new instrument originating in the United States with some similarities to the Raven Progressive Matrices. The board has administered three thousand of these tests for the screening of gifted students, including students in the 'special needs' schools. The fact that the test also has a short form makes it quick, convenient and easy to administer.

The Extended Similarities Test has also been used and provides additional exemplars for a similarities task. It has been used in some inner-city schools as a predictor of readiness to switch to the Basic Level from the Vocational Secondary or from the Basic Level to the General. Other new tests employed in the board include the Stanford-Binet (new version) but the results are as yet inconclusive.

Other innovations taking place at North York include the use of the Vineland Adaptive Behaviour test to complement the results of intelligence tests; the renorming of the WRAT-R to obtain North York norms; the adoption of newer and better-normed versions of many academic tests and the use of the Test of Early Reading Ability in several studies.

The board is in the process of exploring measures of language such as the Woodcock-Johnson Language Proficiency test, revised versions of the Peabody Picture Vocabulary test, and the Roberts Apperception test as a projective technique. It is refreshing to note that the psychologists and teachers do not particularly espouse any one test but have specifically stated that although many of the instruments have proven useful, no one instrument has provided a 'magic bullet'. Rather, careful assessment (including observation and interpretation) that looks at students in as broad a context as possible seems the best current approach. No doubt, the one approach that showed the greatest promise was the methodology espoused by Reuven Feuerstein (already summarized in previous chapters) whereby a program of instrumental enrichment is linked to the Learning Potential of Assessment Development. A series of studies (Luther, Murdock, and Stokes, 1985) was conducted in special needs schools at the elementary, junior high, and secondary levels to evaluate the efficacy of instrumental enrichment. The general conclusion was that the results appear to support the hypothesis that the Feuerstein method is beneficial to the cognitive and learning function of many kinds of students. This is the kind of enterprise that augurs well for the changes we have advocated throughout.

In the determination of its policies and procedures for assessing students from various cultural, racial, and ethnic backgrounds, the North York board is functioning at the cutting edge in the employment and training of staff, the use of various kinds of tests, and, more importantly, in its endeavour to match program modifications with the needs of the culturally diverse student population.

REFERENCES

Alp, I. E. (1987). *M-centration and Mental capacity in one to three year olds*. Unpublished doctoral dissertation, York University, North York, Ontario.

Anastasi, Anne (1958). *Differential psychology* (2nd ed.). New York: The Macmillan Company.

Anastasi, Anne (1968a). *Psychological testing* (3rd ed.). New York: The Macmillan Company.

Anderson, W., & Grant, R. (1975). *The new newcomers: Problems of adjustment of West Indian children in metropolitan Toronto schools*. Toronto: York University.

Angoff, W., & Ford, S. (1973). Item-race interaction on a test of scholastic aptitude. *Journal of Educational Measurement, 10*, 95-105.

Asher, E. J. (1935). The inadequacy of current intelligence tests for testing Kentucky mountain children. *Journal of Genetic Psychology, 46*, 480-486.

Ausubel, D. P. (1963). Negativism as a phase of ego development. *American Journal of Orthopsychiatry, 20* (1950), 796-805. In J. M. Seidman (Ed.), *The Child* (pp. 475-485). New York: Holt, Rinehart & Winston.

Bachor, D. (1976). *Information processing capacity and teachability of low achieving students*. Unpublished doctoral dissertation, University of Toronto, Toronto, Ontario.

Baratz, S. S., & Baratz, J. C. (1970). Early childhood intervention: The social science base of institutional racism. *Harvard Educational Review, 40*, 29-50.

Baum, G. (1978). Perspectives on multiculturalism. *The Grad Post*.

Benbow, C., & Stanley, J. (1980). Sex differences in mathematics ability: Facts or artifacts? *Science, 210*, 1262-1264.

Benson, N. J. (1982). *Comprehension and production of possession verbs in children: A process-analytical developmental study*. Unpublished M.A. thesis, York University, North York, Ontario.

Bentler, P., & McClain, J. A. (1976). Multitrait - multimethod analysis of reflection-impulsivity. *Child Dev., 47,* 218-226.

Bereiter, C., & Scardamalia, M. (1979). Pascual-Leone's *M* construct as a link between cognitive-developmental and psychometric concepts of intelligence. *Intelligence, 3,* 41-63.

Bernstein, B. (1960). Language and social class. *British Journal of Sociology, 11,* 271-276.

Berry, J. (1976). *Human ecology and cognitive style: Comparative studies in cultural and psychological adaptation.* Beverley Hills: Sage Publications.

Berry, J., & Lonner, W. (Eds.). (1974). *Applied cross-cultural psyschology.* Selected papers for the Second International Conference of the International Association for Cross-Cultural psychology. Amsterdam: International Association for Cross-cultural Psychology.

Berry, J., Kalin, R., & Taylor, D. (1977). *Multiculturalism and ethnic attitudes in Canada.* Ottawa: Minister of State for Multiculturalism.

Beserve, C. (1973). *West Indian immigrant children: A study of adjustment.* M.A. thesis, University of Toronto.

Binet, A., & Simon, T. (1916). *The development of intelligence in children.* Tr. Elizabeth S. Kite. Baltimore: The Williams and Wilkins Company.

Bloom, B. (1964). *Stability and change in human characteristics.* New York: John Wiley and Sons.

Bloom, B. S. (1976). *Human characteristics and school learning.* New York: McGraw-Hill.

Bloom, L. (1971). *The social psychology of race relations.* London: Allen and Unwin.

Bociukiw, B. (1978). The federal policy of multiculturalism and the Ukrainian-Canadian community. In M. Lupul (Ed.), *Ukrainians, Canadians, multiculturalism, and separation: An assessment* (pp. 98-128). Edmonton, Alberta: The University of Alberta Press for the Canadian Institute of Ukrainian Studies.

Bodmer, W. F. (1972). Race and IQ: The genetic background. In K. Richardson, & D. Spears (Eds.), *Race and intelligence* (pp. 83-113). Baltimore: Penguin Books.

Bouvier, L. F., & Lee, E. S. (1974). Black America. *Population Profiles, 10*, 1-8.

Boyd, W. (1950). *Genetics and the races of man.* Boston: Little, Brown.

Bransford, J. D., & Stein, B. (1984). *The ideal problem solver.* New York: Freeman.

Breton, R., Reitz J., & Valentine, V. (1980). *Cultural boundaries and the cohesion of Canada.* Montreal: The Institute for Research of Public Policy.

Brigham, C. C. (1923). *A study of American intelligence.* Princeton, N.J.: Princeton Univ. Press.

Brown, A., & Copione, J. (1982). Modifying intelligence in modifying cognitive skills: More than a semantic quibble. In D. Detterman, & R. Sternberg (Eds.), *How & how much can intelligence be increased.* Norwood, New Jersey: Ablex Publishing.

Brown, A. L., & Campione, J. C. (1985). Modifying intelligence versus modifying cognitive skills: more than a semantic quibble. In D. K. Detterman, & R. J. Sternberg (Eds.), *How and how much can intelligence be increased?* Norwood, N.J.: Ablex.

Brown, A. L., & Ferrara, R. A. (1982). Diagnosing zones of proximal development. In J.V. Wertsch (Ed.), *Culture, communication and cognition: Vygotskyan perspectives.* New York, N.Y.: Academic Press.

Brown, A. L., Bransford, J. D., Ferrara, R. A., & Campione, J. C. (1983). Learning, remembering, and understanding. In P. H. Mussen, J. H. Flavell, & E. M. Markman (Eds.), *Handbook of child psychology* (pp. 77-166). New York: John Wiley & Sons.

Budoff, M. (1973). *Learning potential and educability among the educable mentally retarded.* Progress report grant No. OE6-0-8-08056-4597. National Institute of Education H.E.W. Cambridge Mass.: Research Institute for Educational Problems.

Budoff, M. (1974). *Learning potential and educability among the educable mentally retarded* (Rep. No. 312312). Cambridge, Mass.: Research Institute for Educational Problems, Cambridge Mental Health Association.

Budoff, & Hamilton (1976). Optimizing test performance of moderately and severely mentally retarded adolescents and adults. *American Journal of Mental Deficiency, 81*, 49-57.

Burks, B. S. (1928). The relative influence of nature and nurture upon mental development: A comparative study of foster parent-foster child resemblance and true parent-true child resemblance. *Yearbook Natural Social Studies Education, 27*, 219-316.

Burnet, J. (1984). Myths and multiculturalism. In R. Samuda, J. Berry, & M. Laferreire (Eds.), *Multiculturalism in Canada: Social and educational implications*. Boston: Allyn and Bacon.

Burt, C. (1958). The inheritance of mental ability. *American Psychologist, 13*, 1-15.

Burt, C. (1968). Mental capacity and its critics. *Bulletin of the British Psychological Society, 21*, 11-18.

Burtis, P. J. (1982). Capacity increase and chunking in the development short term memory. *Journal of Experimental Child Psychology, 34*(3), 387-413.

Campbell, C. M. (1985). *Learning and development: An investigation of a neo-Piagetian theory of cognitive growth*. Unpublished master's thesis, University of Natal, Durban, South Africa.

Campione, J. C., Brown, A. L., & Ferrara, R. A. (1982). Mental retardation and intelligence. In R. J. Sternberg (Ed.), *Handbook of intelligence*. Cambridge: Cambridge University Press.

Canady, H. G. (1971). The problem of equating the environment of Negro-white groups for intelligence testing in comparative studies. *The Journal of Social Psychology, 17*, (1943), 3-15. In R. C. Wilcox (Ed.), *The psychological consequences of being a black American* (pp. 89-101). New York: John Wiley & Sons.

Carroll, J. (1983). Studying individual differences in cognitive abilities: Through and beyond factor analysis. In R. Dillion & R. Schmeck (Eds.), *Individual differences in cognition VI*. New York: Academic Press.

Case, R. (1972). Learning and development: A neo-Piagetian capacity construct. *Human Development, 15*, 339-358.

Case, R. (1974). Mental strategies, mental capacity and instruction: A neo-Piagetian investigation. *Journal of Experimental Child Psychology, 18*, 382-397.

Case, R. (1975). Social class differences in intellectual development: A neo-Piagetian investigation. *Canadian Journal of Behavioural Science, 7*(3), 244-261.

Case, R. (1985). *Intellectual development: Birth to adulthood.* New York: Academic Press.

Case, R., & Serlin, R. (1979). A new processing model for predicting performance on Pascual-Leone's test of M-space. *Cognitive Psychology, 11*, 308-326.

Case, R., & Bereiter, C. (1984). From behaviourism to cognitive development: Steps in the evolution of instructional design. *Instructional Science, 13*, 141-158.

Cattell, J. McK. (1890). Mental tests and measurements. *Mind, 15*, 373-381.

Cattell, R. B. (1963). Theory of fluid and crystallized intelligence: A critical experiment. *Journal of Educational Psychology, 18*, 165-244.

Cattell, R. B. (1971). *Abilities: Their structure growth and action.* Boston: Houghton Mifflin.

Chodzinksi, R., & Samuda, R. (1985). A training model for implementing non-biased assessment procedures, In R. Samuda & A. Wolfgang (Eds.), *Intercultural counselling & assessment.* Toronto: C. J. Hogrefe Inc.

Clark, K. B. (1963b). Educational stimulation of racially disadvantaged children. In A. H. Passow (Ed.), *Education in depressed areas* (pp. 142-162). New York: Teachers College Press, Columbia University.

Clark, K. B., & Plotkin, L. (1972). A review of the issues and literature of cultural deprivation theory. In K.B. Clark *et al.* (Ed.), *The educationally deprived* (pp. 47-73). New York: Metropolitan Applied Research Center.

Claydon, I. (1980). *Refugee letters: Some aspects of Australia's changed institutional response.* Victoria: La Trobe University.

Cloward, R. A., & Jones, J. A. (1963). Social class: Educational attitudes and participation. In A. H. Passow (Ed.), *Education in depressed areas* (pp. 190-216). New York: Teachers College Press, Columbia Univ.

Coleman, J. S., Campbell, E. Q., Hobson, C. J., McPartland, J., Mood, A. M., Weinfeld, F. D., & York, R. L. (1966). *Equality of educational opportunity.* Washington, D.C., Department of Health, Education and Welfare, Office of Education.

Collins, J. E. (1928). Relation of parental occupation to intelligence of children. *Journal of Educational Research, 17,* 157-169.

Coon, C. S., Garn, S. M., & Birdsell, J. B. (1950). *Races.* Springfield, Ill.: C. C. Thomas.

Cooper, R., & Zubek, J. (1958). Effects of enriched and restricted early environments on the learning ability of bright and dull rats. *Canadian Journal of Psychology, 12,* 159-164.

Covington, M. V., & Beery, R. G. (1976). *Self-worth and school learning.* New York: Holt, Rinehart and Winston.

Cummins, J. (1980). Psychological assessment of immigrant children: Logic or intuition? *Journal of Multilingual and Multicultural Development, 1* (2), 97-107.

Cummins, J. (1984). *Bilingualism and special education: Issues in assessment and pedagogy.* San Diego: College-Hill Press.

Cummins, J. (1986). Empowering minority students: A framework for intervention. *Harvard Educational Review, 56*(1), 18-36.

Danziger, K. (1971). *The socialization of immigrant children.* Toronto: York University, Institute of Behavioural Research, Ethnic Research Program.

Das, J. (1973). Cultural deprivation and cognitive competence. In N. Ellis (Ed.), *International review of research in mental retardation.* New York: Academic Press.

Davis, A., Gardner, B. B., & Gardner, M. R. (1941). *Deep South.* Chicago: Univ. of Chicago Press.

Davis, A., & Havighurst, R. J. (1946). Social class and color differences in child-rearing. *American Sociological Review, 11*, 698-710.

de Ribaupierre, A. (1983). Un modele neo-Piagetian du developpement: La theorie des operateurs constuctifs de Pascual-Leone. *Cahiers de Psychologie Cognitive, 3*, 327-356.

de Ribaupierre, A., & Pascual-Leone, J. (1979). Formal operations and *M* power: A neo-Piagetian investigation. *New Directions for Child Development, 5*, 1-43.

de Ribaupierre, A., & Pascual-Leone, J. (1980). Formal operations and *M* power: A neo-Piagetian investigation. In D. Kuhn (Ed.), *Intellectual development beyond childhood* (pp. 1-43) (Source books on New Directions in Child Development). San Francisco: Jossey-Bass.

DeAvila, E. A. (1974). *Children's transformation of visual information according to non-verbal syntactical rules.* Unpublished doctoral dissertation, York University, North York, Ontario.

DeAvila, E., & Havassy, B. (1975). A Piagetian alternative to IQ: Mexican-American study. In Nicolas Hobbs (Ed.), *Issues in classification of children: A handbook on categories, labels and their consequences.* San Francisco: Jossey-Bass.

DeAvila, E. A., Havassy, B., & Pascual-Leone, J. (1976). *Mexican-American schoolchildren: A neo-Piagetian approach.* Washington, D.C.: Georgetown University Press.

Dent, H. (1976). Assessing black children for mainstream placement. In R. Jones (Ed.), *Mainstreaming & the minority child.* Minneapolis: CEC Publications.

Detterman, & Sternberg (1982). *How and how much can intelligence be increased.* Norword, NY: Abley Publishing.

Deutsch, C. P. (1968). Environment and perception. In M. Deutsch, I. Katz, & A. Jensen (Eds.), *Social class, race and psychological development* (pp. 58-85). New York: Holt, Rinehart and Winston.

Deutsch, M. (1967). Minority groups and class status as related to social and personality factors in scholastic achievement. In M.

Deutsch *et al.* (Ed.), *The disadvantaged child* (pp. 89-131). New York: Basic Books.

Dew, N. (1984). The exceptional bilingual child: Demography. In P. C. Chinn (Ed.), *Education of culturally and linguistically different exceptional children*. Reston, Va.: Council for Exceptional Children.

Diana vs. California State Board of Education (1970) (No. C-7037). Rfp, U.S. District Court of Northern California.

Dobzhansky, T. (1962). *Mankind evolving*. New Haven, Conn.: Yale Univ. Press.

Dockrell, W. B. (Ed.). (1970). *On intelligence*. Toronto: The Ontario Institute for Studies in Education.

Doebler, L., & Eicke, F. (1979). Effects of teacher awareness of the educational implications of field-dependent/field-independent cognitive style on selected classroom variables. *J. Educ. Psych., 71*, 226-232.

Drake, St. C. (1966). The social and economic status of the Negro in the United States. In T. Parsons, & K. B. Clark (Eds.), *The Negro American* (pp. 3-46). Boston: Beacon Press.

Dunn, L. C., & Dobzhansky, T. (1952). *Heredity, race and society* (rev. ed.). New York: New American Library.

Ebel, R. L. (1961). Must all tests be valid? *American Psychologist, 16*, 640-647.

Ebel, R. L. (1963). The social consequences of educational testing. *Proceedings of the 1963 Invitational Conference on testing problems* (pp. 130-143). Princeton, N.J.: Educational Testing Service.

Ebel, R. L. (1968). The measurement responsibilities of teachers. In V. H. Noll, & R. P. Noll (Eds.), *Readings in educational psychology* (2nd ed.) (pp. 383-391). New York: The Macmillan Company.

Eells, K., et al. (1951). *Intelligence and cultural differences*. Chicago: Univ. of Chicago Press.

Erlenmeyer-Kimling, L., & Jarvik, L. F. (1963). Genetics and intelligence: A review. *Science, 142*, 1477-1479.

Fabian, V. (1982). *Language development after 5: A neo-Piagetian investigation of subordinate conjunctions.* Unpublished doctoral dissertation, University of California, Berkeley.

Fabinyi, A. (1971). More promising more dangerous. In C. Turnbull (Ed.), *Hammond Innes introduces Australia.* London: Andre Deutsch.

Fein, R. (1966). An economic and social profile of the Negro American. In T. Parsons & K. B. Clark (Eds.), *The Negro American* (pp. 101-133). Boston: Beacon Press.

Fennema, E., & Sherman, J. (1977). Sex-related differences in mathematics achievement, spatial visualization and affective factors. *Am. Educ. Res. J., 14*, 51-72.

Feuerstein, R. (1979). *The dynamic assessment of retarded performers.* Baltimore: University Park Press.

Feuerstein, R., Rand, Y., & Hoffman, M.B. (1979). *The dynamic assessment of retarded performers.* Baltimore: University Park Press.

Feuerstein, R., Rand, Y., Hoffman, M. B., & Miller, R. (1980). *Instrumental enrichment.* Baltimore: University Park Press.

Feuerstein, R., & Hoffman (1982). *Intergenerational conflict of rights: Cultural imposition and self realization.* Unpublished manuscript.

Fischer, K., & Lamborn, S. D. (in press). Sources of variation in developmental levels: Cognitive and emotional transitions during adolescence. In A. de Ribaupierre, K. Scherer, & P. Mounoud (Eds.), *Transition mechanisms in cognitive-emotional development: The longitudinal approach.* Paris: European Science Foundation.

Fischer, K. W., & Silvern, L. (1985). Stages and individual differences in cognitive development. *Annual Review of Psychology, 36*, 613-48.

Fishman, J. A., et al. (1964). Guidelines for testing minority group children. *Journal of Social Issues Supplement, 20*, 129-145.

Flavell, J. H. (1963). *The developmental theory of Jean Piaget.* New York: Van Nostrand.

Freeman, F. N., Holzinger, K. J., & Mitchell, B.C. (1928). The influence of environment on the intelligence, school achievement and conduct of foster children. *27th Yearbook, National Society of Social Science Education* (Part I), 103-217.

French, J. W., & Michael, W. B. (1968). The nature and meaning of validity and reliability. In N. E. Gronlund (Ed.), *Readings in measurement and evaluation* (pp. 165-172). New York: Macmillan Company.

Frye, N. (Ed.). (1962). *Design for learning*. Toronto: University of Toronto Press.

Frye, N. (Ed.). (1970). Hierarchical theories of mental ability. In B. Dockrell (Ed.), *On intelligence*. Toronto: Ontario Institute for Studies in Education.

Frye, N. (Ed.). (1973). *Educability and group differences*. New York: Harper and Row.

Galton, F. (1962). *Hereditary genius: An inquiry into its laws and consequences*. London: Macmillan, 1869. Cleveland, Ohio: The World Publishing Company.

Galton, F. (1883). *Inquiries into human faculty and its development*. London: Macmillan.

Garcia, F. L., Aragon, A. R., Owne, T. R., & Sachse, T.P. (1976). *A report on the multilingual assessment project: An investigation of the large scale use of three neo-Piagetian instruments*. Northwest Regional Educational Laboratory, 710 S.W. Second Avenue, Portland, Oregon.

Garcia, J. (1981). The logic & limits of mental aptitude testing. *American Psychologist, 36*, 1172-1180.

Garcia, S. B., & Yates, J. R. (1986). Policy issues associated with serving bilingual exceptional children. In A. C. Willig, & H. F. Greenberg (Eds.), *Bilingualism and learning disabilities: Policy and practice for teachers and administrators*. New York: American Library Publishing Co.

Gardner, J. W. (1961). *Excellence*. New York: Harper.

Garn, R. M. (1961). *Human races*. Springfield, Ill.: C. C. Thomas.

Gilchrist, J., & Murray, W. (Eds.). (1968). *Eyewitness: Selected documents from Australia's past.* Adelaide: Rigby Ltd.

Glass, B., & Li, C. C. (1953). The dynamics of racial intermixture — an analysis based on the American Negro. *American Journal of Human Genetics, 5,* 1-20.

Globerson, T. (1983). Mental capacity and cognitive functioning: Developmental and social class difference. *Developmental Psychology, 19,* 225-230.

Goldberg, M. L., *et al.* (1966). *The effect of ability grouping.* New York: Teachers College Press.

Goodlad, F. J., & Anderson, R. H. (1959). *The non-graded elementary school.* New York: Harcourt, Brace and Co.

Goodman, D. R. (1979). *Stage transitions and the developmental trace of constructive operators: An investigation of a neo-Piagetian theory of cognitive growth.* Unpublished doctoral dissertation, York University, North York, Ontario.

Gordon, E. W., & Wilkerson, D. A. (1966). *Compensatory education for the disadvantaged.* New York: CEEB.

Gordon, H. (1923). *Mental and scholastic tests among retarded children.* London: Board of Education (Educational Pamphlet No. 44).

Goslin, D. A. (1968). Standardized ability tests and testing. *Science, 159,* 851-855.

Gottesman, I. I. (1968). Biogenetics of Race and Class. In M. Deutsch, I. Katz, & A. Jensen (Eds.), *Social class, race and psychological development* (pp. 11-51). New York: Holt, Rinehart and Winston.

Government of Ontario (1977). *Notes for a statement by the premier of Ontario to a multicultural leadership luncheon.* Toronto: Government of Ontario.

Grant D. J., & Bray, D. W. (1970). Validation of employment tests for telephone company installation and repair occupations. *Journal of Applied Psychology, 54,* 7-14.

Gray, S. W., & Klaus, R. A. (1965). An experimental preschool program for culturally deprived children. *Child Development, 36*, 887-898.

Gronlund, N. E. (1971). *Measurement & evaluation in teaching* (2nd ed.). New York: The Macmillan Company.

Guilford, J. P. (1967). *The nature of human intelligence.* New York: McGraw-Hill.

Haggerty, M. E., & Nash, H. B. (1924). Mental capacity of children and parental occupation. *Journal of Educational Psychology, 5*, 559-572.

Hakuta, K. (1986). *Mirror of language.* New York: Basic Books.

Halford, G. (1982). *Development of thought.* Hillsdale, N.J.: Erlbaum.

Haskins, R., & McKinney, J. (1976). Relative effects of response tempo and accuracy on problem solving and academic achievement. *Child Dev., 47*, 690-696.

Hauser, P. M. (1966). Demographic factors in the integration of the Negro. In T. Parsons, & K. B. Clark (Eds.), *The Negro American* (pp. 71-101). Boston: Beacon Press.

Havell, J. (1977). Cognitive monitoring: A new area of cognitive development. *American Psychologist, 34*(10), 900-910.

Havighurst, J., & Breese, F. H. (1947). Relations between ability and social status in a midwestern community III. Primary mental abilities. *Journal of Educational Psychology, 38*, 241-247.

Haynes, J. R. (1981). *The complete problem solver.* Philadelphia: Franklin Institute Press.

Haywood, H., Filler, J., Shipman, M., & Chatelanat, G. (1975). Behavioural Assessment in Mental Retardation. In P. Reynolds (Ed.), *Advances in psychological assessment* (Vol. 3). San Francisco: Jossey Bass.

Herrnstein, R. (1971). IQ. *The Atlantic Monthly*, 43-64.

Hess, R. (1970). Class and ethnic influences upon socialization. In P. Mussen (Ed.), *Carmichael's manual of child psychology* (Vol. 2) (3rd ed.). New York: Wiley.

Hess, R. D., Shipman, B. C., Brophy, J. E., & Beal, R. M. (1968). *The cognitive environments of urban pre-school children.* The Graduate School of Education, Univ. of Chicago.

Hildreth, G. (1950). Individual differences. In S. W. Monroe (Ed.), *Encyclopedia of educational research.* New York: Macmillan.

Hilliard, A. (1974). Restructuring teacher education for multicultural imperatives. In W. Hunter (Ed.), *Multicultural education through competency-based teacher education.* Washington: AAC-TEE.

Hodgetts, A. (1968). *What culture? What heritage?* Toronto: Ontario Institute for Studies in Education (OISE).

Hodgetts, A., & Gallagher, P. (1978). *Teaching Canada for the '80's.* Toronto: Ontario Institute for Studies in Education (OISE).

Hollingshead, A. B. (1949). *Elmtown's Youth.* New York: John Wiley and Sons.

Holloway, R., Blake, J., Pascual-Leone, J., & Middaugh, L. (1987). *Are there common mental capacity constraints in cognitive, communicative and play abilities in infants?* Unpublished manuscript, York University, Psychology.

House of Commons (1971). Canadian culture: Announcement of implementation policy of multiculturalism within a bilingual framework. 28th Parliament, 3rd Session. October 8, 1971. *Debates, 8,* 8545-8548.

Hughes, D., & Kallen, E. (1974). *The anatomy of racism: Canadian dimensions.* Montreal: Harvest House.

Hunt, J. McV. (1961). *Intelligence and experience.* New York: The Ronald Press.

Hunt, J. McV. (1967). The psychological basis for using pre-school enrichment as an antidote for cultural deprivation. In A. H. Passow, M. Goldberg, & A. J. Tannenbaum (Eds.), *Education of the disadvantaged* (pp. 174-213). New York: Holt, Rinehart and Winston.

Hunt, J. McV., & Kirk, G. E. (1971). Social aspects of intelligence: Evidence and issues. In R. Cancro (Ed.), *Intelligence* (pp. 262-306). New York: Grune and Stratton.

Jackson, J. (1977). The functions of language in Canada: On the political economy of language. In W. Coombs, D. Taylor, & M. Tremblay (Eds.), *The individual, language and society in Canada* (pp. 61-76). Ottawa: Canada Council.

Jaenen, C. (1973). Cultural diversity and education. In N. Bryne, & J. Quarter (Eds.), *Must schools fail?* Toronto: McClelland and Stewart.

Jencks, C. (1972). *Inequality*. New York: Basic Books.

Jenkins, M. D. (1971). Problems incident to racial integration and some suggested approaches to these problems — a critical summary. In R. C. Wilcox (Ed.), *The psychological consequences of being a black American* (pp. 45-56). New York: John Wiley and Sons.

Jenkins, M. D. (1971). The upper limit of ability among American Negroes (1948). In R. C. Wilcox (Ed.), *The psychological consequences of being a black American* (pp. 102-106). New York: John Wiley and Sons.

Jensen, A. R. (1969). How much can we boost IQ and scholastic achievement? *Harvard Educational Review, 39*, 1-123.

Jensen, A., & Figuera, R. (1975). Forward and backward digit span inter-action with race and IQ: Prediction from Jensen's theory. *J. of Educ. Psych., 67*, 882-893.

Johnson, D. (1976). Cross-cultural perspectives on sex differences in reading. *The Reading Teacher, 29*, 747-752.

Johnson, J. M. (1982). *The development of metaphor comprehension: Its mental-demand measurement and its process-analytical models*. Unpublished doctoral dissertation, York University, North York, Ontario.

Johnson, J. M. (1986). *The developmental growth of metaphor comprehension in children's first and second language*. Report submitted to the Development of Bilingual Proficiency Project, Modern Language Centre, Ontario Institute for Studies in Education, University of Toronto.

Johnson, J. M., Fabian, V., & Pascual-Leone, J. (1987). Quantitative hardware-stages that constrain language development. *Human development* (in press).

Johnstone, A. H., & El-Banna, H. (1986). Capacities, demands and processes - a predictive model for science education. *Education in Chemistry* (May), 80-85.

Jones, R. (Ed.). (1985). *Nondiscriminatory (high validity) assessment of minority group children: A casebook.* Berkeley: University of California.

Juckes, T. (1985). *An investigation of the M-operator of the neo-Piagetian theory of constructive operators in Zulu-speaking children.* Unpublished honours thesis, University of Natal, Durban, S. Africa.

Kagan, J., & Kogan, N. (1970). Individual variation in cognitive-processes. In P. Mussen (Ed.), *Carmichael's manual of child psychology* (Vol. 1) (3rd ed.). New York: Wiley.

Kalbach, W. (1979). Immigration and population change. *In TESL Talk: Immigration and Multiculturalism: A Decade to Review,* *10*, 16-31.

Kamin, I. (1976). Heredity, intelligence, politics and psychology: II. In N. Block, & G. Dworkin (Eds.), *The IQ Controversy* (pp. 374-382). New York: Random House.

Keely, C., & Elwell, P. (1981). International migration: Canada and the United States. In M. Kritz, C. Keely, & S. Tomasi (Eds.), *Global trends in migration: Theory and research on international population movements* (pp. 181-207). New York: Centre for Migration Studies.

Keller, S. (1963). The social world of the urban slum child: Some early findings. *American Journal of Orthopsychiatry, 33*, 813-822.

Ketcham, W. A., & Fitzgerald, N. M. (1963). The mathematics achievement of high school students. *University of Michigan School of Education Bulletin, 34.*

Kinsbourne, M. (1974). Direction of gaze and distribution of cerebral thought processes. *Neuropsychologia, 12*, 279-281.

Kleinfeld, J. (1975). Effective teachers of Indian and Eskimo students. *School Dev., 83*, 301-344.

Klineberg, O. (1931). A study of psychological differences between racial and national groups in Europe. *Archives of Psychology, 13.*

Klineberg, O. (1935a). *Negro intelligence and selective migration*. New York: Columbia Univ. Press.

Klineberg, O. (1935b). *Race differences*. New York: Harper.

Klineberg, O. (Ed.). (1944). *Characteristics of the American Negro*. New York: Harper & Row.

Kritz, M. (1981). International migration patterns in the Caribbean: An overview. In M. Krist, C. Keely, & S. Tomasi (Eds.), *Global trends in migration: Theory and research on international population movements* (pp. 208-233). New York: Center for Migration Studies.

Laosa, L. (1978). Maternal teaching strategies in Chicano families of varied educational and socioeconomic levels. *Child Dev., 49*, 1129-1135.

Lautrey, J. (1980). *Classe sociale, milieu familial, intelligence.* (Social Class, family environment, and intelligence). Paris: Presses Universitaires de France.

Leahy, A. M. (1935). Nature-nurture and intelligence. *General Psychological Monographs, 17*, 235-308.

Lee, E. S. (1951). Negro intelligence and selective migration: A Philadelphia test of the Klineberg hypothesis. *American Sociological Review, 16*, 227-233.

Linden, K. W., & Linden, J. D. (1968a). *Modern mental measurement: A historical perspective. Guidance mongograph series, III: Testing*. Boston: Houghton-Mifflin.

Logan, R. (1974). *A quantification of the development of processing capacity*. Unpublished M.A. thesis, York University, North York, Ontario.

Luria, A. R. (1966). *Human brain and psychological processes*. New York: Harper and Row.

Luther, M., Murdock, J., & Stokes, N. (1985). *A study of Feuerstein's thinking skills method with children, adolescents, and adults in North York special needs schools*. Paper presented at the Ontario Educational Research Council Conference, Toronto.

Lynd, R. S., & Lynd, H. M. (1929). *Middletown: A study in American culture*. New York: Harcourt, Brace and World.

Lynd, R. S., & Lynd, H. M. (1937). *Middletown in transit.* New York: Harcourt, Brace and World.

Lysenko, V. (1947). *Men in sheepskin coats: A study of Ukrainian assimilation.* Toronto: Ryerson.

Maccoby, E., & Jacklin, C. (1974). *The psychology of sex differences.* Stanford: Stanford University Press.

Mackler, B., & Giddings, M. G. (1965). Cultural deprivation: A study in mythology. *Teachers College Record, 66,* 608-613.

Maldonado-Colon, E. (1986). Assessment: Considerations upon interpreting data of linguistically/culturally different students referred for disabilities or disorders. In A. C. Willig, & H. F. Greenberg (Eds.), *Bilingualism and learning disabilities: Policy and practice for teachers and administrators.* New York: American Library Publishing Co.

Mallea, J., & Young, J. (1978). *Teacher education for a multicultural society.* Paper presented at a Symposium on International Education and Community Development. Toronto: Faculty of Education, University of Toronto.

Manpower and Immigration (1974). *Three years in Canada.* Ottawa: Information Canada.

Marr, W. (1976). *Labour market and other implications of immigration policy for Ontario.* Toronto: Ontario Economic Council.

Maslow, A. H. (1944). What intelligence tests mean. *Journal of General Psychology, 31,* 85-93.

Mayer, K. B. (1959). *Class and society* (rev. ed.). Studies in Sociology. New York: Random House.

McCall, R., Applebaum, M., & Hogarty, P. (1973). *Developmental Changes in Mental Performance.* Monographs of the Society for Research in Child Development, Series 150(3), *38.*

McDiarmid, G., & Pratt, D. (1971). *Teaching prejudice.* Toronto: Ontario Institute for Studies in Education (OISE).

McIntyre, R. (1985). Techniques for identifying learning impaired minority students, In Samuda & Wolfgang (Eds.), *Intercultural counselling & assessment.* Toronto: C. J. Hogrefe Inc..

McIntyre R., Keaton A., & Agard, R. (1980). *Identification of learning disabilities in Ontario: A validity study.* Toronto: Ministry of Education.

Meichenbaum, D., & Goodman, J. (1971). Training impulsive children to talk to themselves: A means of developing self-control. *J. Abn. Psych., 77*, 115-126.

Mercer, J. (1971). Institutionalized anglocentrism: Labelling mental retardates in the public schools. In P. Orleans, & W. Russell (Eds.), *Race, change and urban society.* Los Angeles: Sage Publications.

Mercer, J. R. (1973). *Labelling the mentally retarded.* Los Angeles: University of California Press.

Mercer, J. (1978/79). Test "validity", "bias" and "fairness": An analysis from the perspective of the sociology of knowledge. *Interchange, 9*(1).

Mercer, J. (1979). *Sompa technical manual.* New York: Psychological Corporation.

Miller, M. S. (1975). *Associative and conceptual learning: Towards a neo-Piagetian evaluation of Jensen's intelligence theory.* Unpublished M.A. thesis, York University, Ontario.

Miller, M. S. (1980). *Executive schemes versus mental capacity in predicting intellectual underperformance among lower socioeconomic status groups.* Unpublished doctoral dissertation, York University, North York, Ontario.

Miller, R., Pascual-Leone, J., Campbell, C., & Juckes, T. (1987). *Learning and development: A neo-Piagetian cross-cultural analysis.* Manuscript submitted for publication, 1986.

Milner, E. (1951). A study of the relationship between reading readiness in grade one school children and patterns of parent-child interaction. *Child Development, 22*, 95-112.

Minsel, W., & Herff, W. (1985). Intercultural counselling: West German perspectives. In R. Samuda & A. Wolfgang (Eds.), *Intercultural counselling: Global perspectives.* Toronto: C. J. Hogrefe.

Montagu, A. M. F. (Ed.). (1974). *Frontiers of anthropology.* New York: G. P. Putnam's Sons.

Morrish, I. (1971). *The background of immigrant children.* London: Allen and Unwin.

Moynihan, D. P. (1965). Employment, income and the ordeal of the Negro family. *Daedalus*, 745-770.

Mueller, K. H., & Mueller, J. H. (1953). Class structure and academic and social success. *Educational and Psychological Measurement, 13*, 486-496

Munro, I. (1978). *Canada: Origin and options - immigration*. Toronto: Wiley Publishers.

Murray, J. (1977). *Toronto educational governance/ multiculturalism case study*. Toronto: Ontario Ministry of Education.

Narrol, H., Silverman, H., & Waksman, M. (1982). Developing cognitive potential in vocational High School students. *Journal of Educational Research*.

Newman, H. H., Freeman, F. N., & Holzinger, K. J. (1937). *Twins: A study of heredity and environment*. Chicago: Univ. of Chicago Press.

Niaz, M., & Lawson, A. (1985). Balancing chemical equations: The role of developmental level and mental capacity. *Journal of Research in Science Teaching, 22*, 41-51.

Nicholls, A. (1971). Newcomers. In E. Turnbull (Ed.), *Hammond Innes introduces Australia*. London: Andre Deutsch.

Nunn, Sir P. (1945). *Education: Its data and first principles* (3rd ed.). London: Edward Arnold and Company.

Ontario Human Rights Commission (1977). *Life together*. Toronto.

Ontario Ministry of Education (1980). *Children with learning disabilities*. Curriculum ideas for teachers series. Toronto: Ministry of Education.

Ortiz, A. A., & Yates, J. R. (1983). Incidence of exceptionality among Hispanics: Implications for manpower planning. *NABE Journal, 7*, 41-54.

Parkinson, G. M. (1975). *The limits of learning: A quantitative investigation of intelligence*. Unpublished doctoral dissertation, York University, North York, Ontario.

Pascual-Leone, J. (1969). *Cognitive development and cognitive style: A general psychological integration.* Unpublished doctoral dissertation, University of Geneva.

Pascual-Leone, J. (1970). A mathematical model for the transition rule in Piaget's developmental stages. *Acta Psychological, 32,* 301-345.

Pascual-Leone, J. (1976). On learning and development Piagetian style. I. A reply to Lefebvre-Pinard. *Canadian Psychological Review, 17,* 270-280.

Pascual-Leone, J. (1978). Compounds, confounds and models in developmental information processing: A reply to Trabasso.

Pascual-Leone, J. (1980). Constructive problems for constructive theories: The current relevance of Piaget's work and a critique of information-processing simulation psychology. In R. Kluwe & H. Spada (Eds.), *Developmental models of thinking.* New York: Academic Press.

Pascual-Leone, J. (1981). M-Capacity, the component analysis of visual patterns, and metasubjective analysis: A commentary to Mr. Minami's work. *Hiroshima Forum for Psychology, 8,* 104-106.

Pascual-Leone, J. (1984). Attention, dialectic and mental effort: Towards an organismic theory of life stages. In M. L. Commons, F. A. Richards, & G. Armon (Eds.), *Beyond formal operations: Late adolescence and adult cognitive development.* New York: Praeger.

Pascual-Leone, J. (1987a). An organismic process model of Witkin's field-dependence-independence. In T. Globerson & T. Zelniker (Eds.), *Cognitive style and cognitive development.* Norwood, N.J.: Able.

Pascual-Leone, J. (1987b). Organismic processes for neo-Piagetian theories: A dialectical causal account of cognitive development. *International Journal of Psychology, 22.*

Pascual-Leone, J. (1987). Reflections on life-span intelligence, consciousness and ego development. In C. N. Alexander, E. J. Langer, & R. M. Oetzel (Eds.), *Higher stages of development: Adult growth beyond formal operations.* New York: Oxford University Press.

Pascual-Leone, J., & Smith, J. (1969). The encoding and decoding of symbols by children: A new experimental paradigm and a neo-Piagetian model. *Journal of Experimental Child Psychology, 8,* 328-355.

Pascual-Leone, J., & Goodman, D. (1979). Intelligence and experience: A neo-Piagetian approach. *Instructional Science, 8,* 301-367.

Pascual-Leone, J., & Sparkman, E. (1980). The dialectics of empiricism and rationalism: A last methodological reply to Trabasso. *Journal of Experimental Child Psychology, 29,* 88-101.

Pascual-Leone, J., & Hameluck, D. (1986). *Mental processing constraints on motor performance and their brain lateralization.* Paper given at the University of Waterloo Conference on Child Development, Waterloo, Ontario.

Pascual-Leone, J., & Bovet, M. G. (1966). L'apprentissage de la quantification de l'inclusion et al theorie operatoire. *Acta Psychologica, 25,* 334-365.

Petras, E. (1981). The global labour market in the modern world economy. In M. Kritz, C. Keely, & S. Tomasi (Eds.), *Global trends in migration: Theory and research on international population movements* (pp. 44-63). New York: Center for Migration Studies.

Pettigrew, T. F. (1964). *A profile of the Negro American.* Princeton, N.J.: D. Van Nostrand.

Piaget, J. (1985). *Equilibration of cognitive structures.* Chicago: University of Chicago Press.

Pollitzer, W. S. (1958). The Negroes of Charleston, S.C.: A study of hemoglobin types, serology and morphology. *American Journal of Physical Anthropology, 16,* 241-263.

Porter, J. (1965). *The vertical mosaic: An analysis of social class and power in Canada.* Toronto: University of Toronto Press.

Pratt, D. The social role of textbooks in Canada. *Socialization and Values in Canadian Society.* Carleton Library Series *84,* 100-126.

Pressey, S. L., & Ralton, R. (1919). The relation of the general intelligence of school children to the occupation of their fathers. *Journal of Applied Psychology, 3,* 336-373.

Pulos, S. (1979). *Developmental cognitive constraints on structural learning.* Unpublished doctoral dissertation, York University.

Raven, J. (1965). *Guide to using the coloured matrices sets A AB B.* London: H.K. Lewis.

Reitz, J., et al. (1981). *Ethnic inequality and segregation in jobs.* Centre for Urban and Community Studies. University of Toronto.

Reschly, O. J. (1981). Psychological testing in educational classification & placement. *American Psychologist, 36,* 1094-1102.

Rex, J. (1972). Nature versus nurture: The significance of the revived debate. In K. Richardson & D. Spears (Eds.), *Race and intelligence*) (pp. 167-178). Baltimore, Md.: Penguin Books.

Rhwer, W., Jr. (1971). Learning, race and school success. *Review of Educational Research, 41,* 191-220.

Richmond, A. (1969). Immigration and pluralism in Canada. In *International Migration Review, 4,* 5-24.

Riessman, F. (1962). *The culturally deprived child.* New York: Harper & Row.

Rosenthal, R., & Jacobson, L. (1968). *Pygmalion in the classroom: Teachers' expectation and pupil's intellectual development.* New York: Holt, Rinehart, and Winston.

Rudnycki, J. (1980). Multiculturalism - A way forward. *Language and Society, 3.*

Salt, J. (1981). International labour migration in Western Europe: A geographical review. In M. Kritz, C. Keely, & S. Tomasi (Eds.), *Global trends in migration: Theory and research on international population movements.* New York: Center for Migration Studies.

Salvia, J., & Ysseldyke, R. B. (1978). *Assessment in special & remedial education.* Boston: Houghton Mifflin.

Samuda, R. J., (1975). *The psychological testing of American minorities.* New York: Harper and Row.

Samuda, R. J., & Crawford, D. (1980). *The testing, assessment, counselling and placement of ethnic minority students: Current methods in Ontario.* Toronto: Ministry of Education.

Samuda, R. J., & Woods, S. (Eds.). (1983). *Perspectives in immigrant and minority education*. Washington: University Press of America.

Samuda, R. J., Berry J., & Laferriere, M. (Eds.). (1984). *Multiculturalism in Canada: Social and educational implications*. Boston: Allyn and Bacon.

Samuda, R. J., & Wolfgang, A. (Eds.). (1985). *Intercultural counselling and assessment: Global perspectives*. Toronto: C. J. Hogrefe.

Samuda, R. J. (1985). *Racism and the assessment of minorities: Implications, consequences, alternatives*. Unpublished paper presented to the Metropolitan Separate School Board of Toronto. Kingston: Queen's University.

Samuda, R. J., & Kong, S. L. (Eds.). (1986). *Multicultural education: Programs & methods*. Kingston/Toronto: Intercultural Social Sciences Publications.

Samuda, R. J. (1986a). The role of psychometry in multicultural education: Implications and consequences. In R. J. Samuda & S. L. Kong (Eds.), *Multicultural education: Programmes and methods* (pp. 47-57). Intercultural Social Sciences Pub. Inc.

Samuda, R. J. (1986b). *Psychometric abuse in placing minority students*. Paper given at Symposium of IAAP Jerusalem Congress, Bilingual and Bicultural Education.

Samuda, R. J. (1986c). *Improving the assessment of minorities*. Paper presented at Race Relations and Education Conference, University of Windsor, Ontario.

Samuda, R. J. (1987). *The link between racism and the assessment of minorities*. Paper presented at Symposium of the IACCP Regional North American conference at Kingston, Ontario.

Sattler, J. M. (1982). *Assessment of children's intelligence & special abilities* (2nd Ed.). Boston: Allyn & Bacon Inc.

Scarborough Board of Education (1977). *Meeting the needs of Scarborough immigrant students*. A brief to the Ontario Minister of Manpower and Immigration.

Scardamalia, M. (1977). Information processing capacity and the problem of horizontal decalage: A demonstration using combinatorial reasoning tasks. *Child Development, 48*, 28-37.

Scardamalia, M., & Bereiter, C. (1984). Fostering the development of self-regulations in children's knowledge processing. In S. S. Chipman, J. W. Segal, & R. Glaser (Eds.), *Thinking and learning skills: Current research, and open questions* (Vol. 2). Hillsdale, NJ: Lawrence Erlbaum Associates.

Scardamalia, M., Bereiter, C., & Steinbach, R. (1984). Teachability of reflective processes in written composition. *Cognitive Science, 8*, 173-190.

Scarr (1981). Testing "for" children: Assessment & the many determinents of intellectual competence. *American Psychologist, 36*, 1159-66.

Seashore, H., Wesman, A., & Doppelt, J. (1950). The standardization of the Wechsler Intelligence Scale for Children. *Journal of Consulting Psychology, 14*, 99-110.

Shane, H. G. (1962). The school and individual differences. *The sixty-first yearbook of the national society for the study of education* (Part I). Chicago: University of Chicago Press.

Sherman, M., & Key, C. B. (1932). The intelligence of isolated mountain children. *Child Development, 3*, 279-290.

Shields, J. (1962). *Monozygotic twins brought up apart and brought up together*. London: Oxford Univ. Press.

Shipman, V., et al. (1976). *Stability and change in family status, situational and process variables and their relationships to children's cognitive performance* (Report PR-75-28). Princeton: Educational Testing Service.

Sigel, I., & Coop, R. (1974). Cognitive style and classroom practice. In R. Coop, & K. White (Eds.), *Psychological concepts in the classroom*. New York: Harper and Row.

Sinnott, E. W., Dunn, L. C., & Dobzhansky, T. (1958). *Principles of genetics* (5th ed.). New York: McGraw-Hill.

Skodak, M., & Skeels, H. M. (1949). A final follow-up study of one hundred adopted children. *Journal of Genetic Psychology, 75*, 85-125.

Skutnabb-Kangas, T., & Cummins, J. (in Press). *Minority education: From shame to struggle*. Clevedon, England: Multilingual Matters.

Social Planning Council of Toronto (1981). *Racial and Ethnic Discrimination in Employment.* Working Papers for Full Employments, 5.

Sokal, M. M. (1971). The unpublished autobiography of James McKeen Cattell. *American Psychologist, 26,* 626-635.

Spearman, C. E. (1927). *The abilities of man, their nature and measurement.* New York: Macmillan.

St. John, N. (1971). Thirty-six teachers: Their characteristics and outcomes for black and white pupils. *Am. Educ. Res. J., 8,* 635-648.

Standards for Development and Use of Educational and Psychological Tests (3rd Draft, Feb. 1973). *APA Monitor, 2,* I-XV.

Standiford, P. (1926). Parental occupation and intelligence. *School and Society, 23,* 117-119.

Stephenson, B. (October 1980). Education in the 1980s: Alice through the rear-view mirror. *Teacher Education, 17,* 4-12.

Sternberg, R. J. (1977). *Intelligence, information processing and analogical reasoning: The componential analysis of human abilities.* New Jersey: Lawrence Erlbaum Associates.

Sternberg, R. (1981). Testing & Cognitive Psychology. *American Psychologist, 36*(10), 1181-89.

Sternberg, R. J. (1984). Toward a triadic theory of human intelligence. *The Behavioural and Brain Sciences, 47,* 269-315.

Sternberg, R. J. (1985). Instrumental and componential approaches to the nature and training of intelligence. In S. F. Chipman, J. W. Segal, & R. Glaser (Eds.), *Thinking and learning skills (Vol. 2): Research and open questions.* Hillsdale, NJ: Lawrence Erlbaum Associates.

Stevenson, H., et al. (1978). *Schooling, environment, and cognitive development: A cross-cultural study.* Monographs of the Society for Research in Child Development, Series 175, *43*(3).

Steward, M., & Steward, D. (1974). Effects of social distance on teaching strategies of Anglo-American and Mexican-American mothers. *Dev. Psych., 10,* 797-807.

Stewig, J., & Higgs, M. (1973). Girls grow up to be mommies: Sexism in picture books. *Sch. Library J.*, *19*, 44-49.

Sundberg, N., & Gonzales, L. (1981). Cross cultural and cross ethnic assessment overview and issues. In P. McReynolds (Ed.), *Advances in Psychological Assessment* (Vol. 5.). San Francisco: Jossey Bass Inc.

Sunshine, P., & Di Vesta, F. (1976). Effects of density and format on letter discrimination by beginning readers with different learning styles. *J. Educ. Psych.*, *68*, 15-19.

Suppes, P., & Hensen, D. (1965). Accelerated program in elementary-school mathematics: The first year. *Psychology in the Schools* (Vol. 2), 195-203.

Suppes, P., & Momingston, M. (1972). *Computer-assisted instruction at Stanford, 1966-68: Data, models, and evaluation of the arithmetic programs*. New York: Academic Press.

Taft, R. (1977). Coping with unfamiliar cultures. In N. Warren (Ed.), *Studies in cross-cultural psychology*. London: Academic Press.

Taft, R. (1982). *The social and ideological context of multicultural education in immigrant countries*. Paper read at a Symposium organized by Wenner-Gren Foundation, Stockholm.

Taft, R., & Cahill, D. (1981). Education of immigrants in Australia. In J. Bhatnagar (Ed.), *Educating immigrants*. London: Croom-Helm.

Terman, L. M., & Merrill, M. A. (1937). *Measuring intelligence*. Boston: Houghton-Mifflin.

Todor, J. (1977). Cognitive development, cognitive style and motor ability. In B. Kerr (Ed.), *Human Performance and Behaviour*. Proceedings of the 9th Canadian Psycho-Motor Learning and Sports Psychology Symposium, Banff, 223-228.

Todor, J. (1979). Developmental differences in motor task integration: A test of Pascual-Leone's Theory.

Wesman, A. G. (1968). Reliability and confidence. *Test Service Bulletin, 44*. New York, The Psychological Corporation, 1952. In N. E. Gronlund (Ed.), *Readings in measurement and evaluation* (pp. 193-202). New York: The Macmillan Company.

Wesman, A. G. (1968a). Intelligent testing. *American Psychologist*, *27*, 267-274.

West, J. (1945). *Plainville, U.S.A.* New York: Columbia Univ. Press.

Wheeler, L. R. (1932). The intelligence of East Tennessee mountain children. *Journal of Educational Psychology*, *23*, 351-370.

Wickelgren, W. A. (1974). *How To Solve Problems.* New York: Freeman.

Witkin, H., Moore, C., Goodenough, D., & Cox, P. (1977). Field-dependent and field-independent cognitive styles and their educational implications. *Rev. Educ. Res.*, *47*, 1-64.

Wolf, R. (1964). The measurement of environments. *Proceedings of the 1964 invitational conference on testing problems* (pp. 93-106). Princeton, N.J.: Educational Testing Service.

Woodworth, R. S. (1941). *Heredity and environment: A critical survey of recently published materials on twins and foster children* (No. 47). New York: Social Science Research Council Bulletin.

Young, J. (1978). *Education in a multicultural society: What sort of education?* (Unpublished paper) Toronto: Ontario Institute for Studies in Education (OISE).

Ysseldyke J., & Algozinne B. (1982). *Critical issues in special and remedial education.* Boston: Houghton Mifflin.

Zubrzycki, J. (1977). Australia as a multicultural society. *Proceedings of the Australian ethnic affairs council.* Canberra: Australian Government Publishing Service.

Zubrzycki, J. (1981). International migration in Australia and the South Pacific. In M. Kritz, C. Keely, & S. Tomasi (Eds.), *Global trends in migration: Theory and research on international population movements* (pp. 158-180). New York: Center for Migration Studies.

Author Index

Subject Index

Appendix

Ontario Ministry of Education
Evaluation and Supervisory Services Branch/ Curriculum Branch

Committees for
Student Assessment and Program Placement for Equal Educational Opportunity

Listing of Participants

Consultative Committee
• Dr. Ralph Agard, North York Board of Education
• Ms. Jean Augustine, Metropolitan Separate School Board
• Dr. James Cummins, Ontario Institute for Studies in Education
• Dr. Ahmed Ijaz, Scarborough Board of Education
• Dr. Frances Henry, York University
• Mr. Guy Matte, Ontario Teachers' Federation
• Dr. Juan Pascual-Leone, York University
• Dr. Ruth Baumel, North York Board of Education
• Mr. Bill Roach, Ontario Association of Education Administrative Officials
• Ms. Ruth Rozenberg, Ontario Human Rights Commission
• Dr. Ron Samuda, Queen's University
• Dr. Suzanne Ziegler, Toronto Board of Education

Project Committee
• Frank Bobesich, Evaluation and Supervisory Services Branch
• Teresa Gonzalez, Curriculum Branch
• Joe Rapai, Curriculum Branch
• Margaret Wolchak, Centre for Primary and Junior Education

Steering Committee
• Howard Gillies, Research and Information Branch
• Mary-Jane Hardy, Curriculum Branch
• Libby Richmond, Regional Services
• Maurice Marchand, Special Education Branch/Provincial School Branch
• Fran Moscall, Centre for Primary and Junior Education
• Sandra Wolfe, Centre for Computers in Education